Leading the Common Core Initiative

Leading the Common Core Initiative

A Guide for K–5 School Librarians

Carl A. Harvey II and Linda L. Mills

Education Resource Center
University of Delaware
Newark, DE 19716-2940

LIBRARIES UNLIMITED

AN IMPRINT OF ABC-CLIO, LLC
Santa Barbara, California • Denver, Colorado • Oxford, England

Copyright © 2015 by Carl A. Harvey II and Linda L. Mills

All rights reserved. No part of this publication may be reproduced, stored in a retrieval system, or transmitted, in any form or by any means, electronic, mechanical, photocopying, recording, or otherwise, except for the inclusion of brief quotations in a review, without prior permission in writing from the publisher.

Library of Congress Cataloging-in-Publication Data

Harvey, Carl A.
  Leading the Common Core initiative : a guide for K-5 school librarians / Carl A. Harvey II and Linda L. Mills.
      pages cm
  Includes bibliographical references and index.
    ISBN 978-1-61069-491-9 (pbk.) -- ISBN 978-1-61069-492-6 (ebook)   1. Elementary school libraries—United States.   2. School librarian participation in curriculum planning.   3. Education—Standards—United States.   4. Education, Elementary—Curricula—United States.   5. Education, Primary—Curricula—United States.   I. Mills, Linda L.   II. Title.
   Z675.S3H2688 2015
   027.8'222—dc23   2014026773

ISBN: 978-1-61069-491-9
EISBN: 978-1-61069-492-6

19 18 17 16 15   1 2 3 4 5

This book is also available on the World Wide Web as an eBook.
Visit www.abc-clio.com for details.

Libraries Unlimited
An Imprint of ABC-CLIO, LLC

ABC-CLIO, LLC
130 Cremona Drive, P.O. Box 1911
Santa Barbara, California 93116-1911

This book is printed on acid-free paper ∞
Manufactured in the United States of America

Contents

Acknowledgments vii

Introduction ix

1. What Are the Common Core Standards? 1

2. What Are the Connections with School Library Standards? 9

3. How Will the Common Core Impact the Administration
   of a School Library? 15

4. How Will the Common Core Impact Instruction In/Out
   of the School Library? 29

5. Common Core, Professional Development, and Advocacy 57

6. Sample Lesson Plans—Kindergarten 69
   Farm Animals 70
   Frogs 72
   Healthy Eating/Nutrition 75
   Shapes (Math) 76
   Snowflakes 77

7. Sample Lesson Plans—First Grade 79
   Famous Americans 80
   Insects 82
   Long Ago and Today 86
   Measurement and Data 88
   Mem Fox Author Study 90

8. Sample Lesson Plans—Second Grade 95
   Writing/Animals 96
   Nutrition/April Pulley Sayre Author Study 98
   Friendship: Owen and Mzee 101

Reading: Poetry with Douglas Florian 104
Telling Time 106

9. Sample Lesson Plans—Third Grade **109**
Biomes 110
Writing/Opinions 123
Fairy Tales 126
Research: Landmarks of the United States 131
U.S. Presidents 135

10. Sample Lesson Plans—Fourth Grade **137**
Writing: Good Beginnings 138
Force/Motion 140
Nonfiction Feature Search 143
Research: Famous Scientists 148
Wander Indiana 153

11. Sample Lesson Plans—Fifth Grade **155**
United States 156
Reading: Biographies 158
Explorers 168
Jamestown 171
Primary Sources: September 11 179

Appendix A: Children's Literature Bibliography 185

Appendix B: Blank Budget Justification Sheet 199

Appendix C: Staff/Student Survey Samples 201

Appendix D: Common Core Bibliography 207

Appendix E: Research Journal 209

Appendix F: Technology on the Net 219

Index 223

Acknowledgments

As with all my adventures, I thank my family for their unwavering support. They have always been there whenever I've been off trying something new and cheering me on the whole time. I'd also like to thank the countless school librarians across this country who I've had the opportunity to learn from over the years. Whether it be at a face-to-face conference or a virtual connection, I have had the chance to learn so much that has helped make me be a better school librarian. This book is one small way I can give back for all that I have received over the years.

—C. H.

I would like to thank my husband, Steve, for his support in this project. He reassured me I could do this and never complained when I was tied up at the computer every night! I would also like to dedicate this to my mom who passed away December 26, 2013. She always believed in me and told me that I could accomplish whatever I set my mind to do.

—L. M.

We both would like to thank ABC-Clio, Libraries Unlimited, and Sharon Coatney for all of their support and assistance as we worked through putting this book together. It has been quite an endeavor, and we appreciate all of their help in getting us to the finished book!

Introduction

If there is anything constant about the field of school librarianship, it is change. Really ... think about it for a minute and can you honestly say that what you are doing now is the same thing you did when you graduated from library school (for those who just graduated ... wait ... it will happen). But, in all honesty, it is one of the best things about our field. As school librarians today, we constantly have to be ahead of the curve. We have to be looking ahead to the opportunities and taking full advantage of each one that comes our way. In this day and age, sitting back along the sidelines is a quick way to find your library job gone. Like it or not, we are constantly educating administrators and teachers and parents and anyone else we talk to about the role of the school librarian in today's school libraries!

The Common Core State Standards (CCSS), released in June 2010, are the next round of opportunities for school librarians. Whether you believe in the concept of national standards and the further implications this will have on assessment or not, the Common Core has been adopted in forty-four states and three territories of the United States according to the Common Core State Standards website (www.corestandards.org). Even if you are in a state that isn't adopting the Common Core, they will still have their own standards and assessment—many standards that you find in the Common Core. These documents are going to be guiding what is taught in our schools over the next few years. So, we have to begin to see how to leverage them to not only improve student learning, but also how to paint the picture of the twenty-first-century school library using the CCSS.

For school librarians to do this well, we must be well versed in the Common Core Standards. We cannot wait until teachers come to us. Since this will mean changes for many teachers, we can approach teachers and demonstrate how the school librarian and the school library program can assist them and their students. The Common Core Standards make good connections to what we in school library land have often held dear: inquiry, informational text, and technology integration. We are the perfect folks to help lead this charge in our buildings.

For example, taking the lead on providing books and materials to use for teaching and learning will show others (teachers, administrators, curriculum directors, parents) that we are a vital part of this new learning environment. When examining the Common Core Standards, the emphasis on nonfiction literature is very strong. Using our expertise, we can show teachers (and administrators) the excellent literature available containing rich language, not just fact after fact presented in a cut and dry manner. And, we can help them design, implement, and assess instruction using these rich resources.

In the following pages, we will share with you examples and opportunities for school librarians and school library programs to connect to the Common Core Standards. For some, these may be activities that you are already doing and need to look at through a different lens. For others, the ideas may be completely new concepts. Wherever you are on the spectrum, we hope you will find help and useful ideas that you can take and adapt for your own school library program.

Chapter 1 is the basics. What are the Common Core Standards? What do I need to know about them? Where can I find them? Chapter 2 will begin to connect those Common Core Standards with school library land and school library standards such as the AASL's *Standards for the 21st-Century Learner*. While the heavy focus of this book is on the instructional role of the school librarian, the Common Core is going to make you stop and think a bit about how you administer your library program, so that will be the focus of chapter 3.

Chapter 4 will discuss the impact the Common Core Standards are going to have on classroom and library instruction. Chapter 5 will focus on professional development and the leadership role the school librarian can play in helping this to happen in the building. We will also focus on advocacy for the school library program and the school librarian with all of the stakeholders.

Finally, chapters 6 through 11 will feature a variety of units and lessons that make direct connections to the Common Core for school librarians to use. Whether you copy these lessons verbatim and use them step-by-step or as a springboard for your own planning, the lesson plans will be rich examples of the possibilities for school library instruction. The chapters are broken down into one grade level each, with the focus on elementary age students, kindergarten through grade five. Because of our own background, we'll include lessons that work in both a fixed and/or flexible environment, so there will be ideas and possibilities for everyone.

We could spend a lot of time wallowing in the current state of school libraries in this country, or we can spend our time moving forward and working on what the future state of school libraries will become. Looking forward is always much more profitable than looking backward. The Common Core Standards are not a silver bullet, but they do provide a spark for a conversation with teachers, administrators, and the entire school community about the power of the school library program and what it can provide for students and staff.

1
What Are the Common Core Standards?

To begin discussing the Common Core Standards (http://www.corestandards.org/), one must first know what they are, why they were established, and who created them. The Common Core Standards were created by a group of educators, school administrators, businesspeople, and other experts to address the discrepancy between each of the state's educational standards and to provide a clear and consistent framework to prepare students for college and the workforce. Although each state had standards, what students were expected to learn varied widely. All of our graduates will eventually compete for jobs with students from other states or countries that might have higher standards. The reasoning for common standards was for all students to be ensured that they were receiving a high-quality education. Shared experiences and best practices would also be available so that the needs of all students would be addressed.

After much discussion, the first draft of the Common Core Standards were published by the National Governors Association (NGA) and the Council of Chief State School Officers (CCSSO) in July 2009. These standards addressed only Math and English Language Arts. The purpose was to "provide a consistent, clear understanding of what students are expected to learn, so teachers and parents know what they need to do to help them." Forty-four of the fifty states are members of this initiative with only the states of Texas, Indiana, Virginia, Alaska, Oklahoma, and Nebraska not adopting these standards at the state level. One state, Minnesota, has adopted only the Language Arts standards. Indiana, while initially adopting the standards, has pulled out as of spring 2014. Several states are in flux about their future and the Common Core as there is a concern about it being too heavy-handed from the federal government. However, many of the same standards in the Common Core can be found in the states that have opted to not participate or withdrew from using the Common Core.

The timeline for implementation of the Common Core is really quite quick. In September 2009, a twenty-five-member Validation Committee was established with the charge of examining the standards independently. In November 2009, the first draft

Figure 1.1 Reading Standards for Informational Text K–5

Kindergartners:	Grade 1 students:	Grade 2 students:
Key Ideas and Details		
1. With prompting and support, ask and answer questions about key details in a text.	1. Ask and answer questions about key details in a text.	1. Ask and answer such questions as *who, what, where, when, why,* and *how* to demonstrate understanding of key details in a text.
2. With prompting and support, identify the main topic and retell key details of a text.	2. Identify the main topic and retell key details of a text.	2. Identify the main topic of a multiparagraph text as well as the focus of specific paragraphs within the text.
3. With prompting and support, describe the connection between two individuals, events, ideas, or pieces of information in a text.	3. Describe the connection between two individuals, events, ideas, or pieces of information in a text.	3. Describe the connection between a series of historical events, scientific ideas or concepts, or steps in technical procedures in a text.

Common Core State Standards (www.corestandards.org)

of the standards was released to the states for comments. In March 2010 a public draft was released with feedback given through April 2010. Finally on June 2, 2010, the final version of the Common Core Standards was released to the public.

Public and educational debate has been conducted since that time. However, states have already begun implementing the standards starting in kindergarten and first grade, with most states aiming for full implementation by 2014–2015.

These standards were developed by looking at what students needed to know when graduating and attending college and then working backward throughout the grade levels. The standards are meant to be robust and ensure all students will have basic knowledge as a building block. The Language Arts standards in particular are meant to help students become investigators and question askers instead of rote memorizers of facts. Each grade-level skill builds upon the next grade level. The Math standards are also meant to strengthen students' numerical reasoning and mental math skills.

Each state that has adopted the Common Core agreed to adopt the entire list of standards, but could add an additional 15 percent of their own standards if they so wished. According to a survey published in *The State Education Standard*, only eleven states had announced they would publish additional standards (Alabama, Arizona, California, Colorado, Iowa, Kansas, Massachusetts, Minnesota, Montana, New Mexico, and New York). Other states have either not committed or have reserved the right to add to the standards at a later date.

The Common Core initiative is quick to point out that these are not national standards dictated by the federal government. The federal government had no input into the process or the development of the standards; it was purely a state-led process. However, many recent initiatives such as President Obama's Race to the Top grant funds were based on whether a state had adopted the Common Core Standards.

What Are the Common Core Standards Not?

The Common Core only contains Language Arts and Math standards. As part of the Language Arts standards, there are specific strategies for helping students navigate and learn how to better read and write in the content areas of Social Studies and Science. However, the Common Core does not contain specific Social Studies or Science standards.

The Common Core is not a document packed with teaching strategies. It only sets a bar for what each student should know by the end of a specific grade level. The Common Core relies heavily on the teacher to be the professional and take the lead in designing instruction that helps students meet those grade-level targets.

However, the standards do require teachers to make a shift in how they teach going forward from how they have taught in the past. This is where the role of the librarian can be crucial. Teachers will need help in redesigning courses and projects and discovering new resources to use. If the school librarian is present at the beginning of this process, think of the potential and power of the opportunity!

In their book *Pathways to the Common Core: Accelerating Achievement* (Heinemann 2012), Lucy Calkins, Mary Ehrenworth, and Christopher Lehman outline the benefits of the Common Core State Standards. Some of the points they make include the focus on higher-level comprehension skills, a balanced weight of reading and writing, and support of cross-curricular teaching. The Common Core is not always seen as completely wonderful. There are critics, such as Diane Ravitch and Steven Krashen, who argue it is all being set up to make money for the testing companies involved. They argue the funds could better be spent on adequate resources such as library materials for teachers and students to utilize in the learning process.

Language Arts Structure

As previously mentioned, the standards are set up in a progression. If one follows the progression from kindergarten all the way to twelfth grade, it is easy to see how each year builds on the previous one.

Each of the two main content areas begins with an introduction. There is also a statement introduction about how these standards are applicable to English Language Learner (ELL) students and a statement on how these standards apply to students with disabilities. At this point, the standards are broken into chunks (K–5 and 6–12) with three appendixes. Appendix A covers the research support of the standards as well as the glossary of key terms; appendix B covers text exemplars and sample performance tasks; and appendix C covers samples of student writing.

Math Structure

The math standards are structured in a similar manner. There is an introduction prior to launching into the standards. There are two main parts: Standards for Mathematical Practice, which includes the same eight standards for all grades and describes ways for students to engage with the subject matter following processes to ensure mathematical reasoning, and Standards for Mathematical Content, which include the different standards for each grade level. These standards are the ones that define what students should understand and be able to do. Each of the domains includes clusters of related standards so that mathematics is presented as connected ideas. The layout is somewhat different in that you see the standards grouped together by grade level rather than the progression from grade level to grade level as you see in the Language Arts standards. Appendix A for Math concerns designing high school courses based on the Common Core, which will not be a focus in this book since our main topic is elementary schools and the Common Core.

Other Content Areas

The Common Core Standards primarily focus on Math and Language Arts. According to the Common Core website, the CCSSO and the NGA are not leading the initiative for other content areas, but are aware of other organizations. However, other organizations are aligning their standards or revising their standards to correspond with the Common Core. Science is being led and managed by Achieve, with the help of the National Research Council, the National Science Teachers Association, and the American Association for the Advancement of Science. These standards are being referred to as the Next Generation Science Standards and were released in April 2013. You can find additional information about these standards at www.nextgenscience.org.

The American Council on the Teaching of Foreign Languages has worked to publish an alignment to correspond with the ELA Common Core Standards. The following website provides more information on this endeavor: www.actfl.org/sites/default/files/pdfs/Aligning_CCSS_Language_Standards_v6.pdf. Finally, the revision for arts education is being led by the National Coalition for Core Arts Standards. To learn more about this revision go to nationalartsstandards.org.

The National Council of Social Studies released on September 17, 2013, what they call their C3 Framework. This document, entitled *College, Career and Civic Life (C3) Framework for Social Studies State Standards: Guidance for Enhancing the Rigor of K–12 Civics, Economics, Geography and History*, was a result of three-and-a-half years of work by twenty-two states and fifteen professional organizations. This framework was designed to offer guidance for state Social Studies standards and to align academic programs to the CCSS for English Language Arts and Literacy in History/Social Studies. The document also emphasizes and enhances the rigor of the Social Studies discipline along with building critical thinking skills, problem solving, and skills to engage future citizens. All of these skills interlock nicely with the CCSS as both sets of standards are preparing students for college and career readiness along with civic life. The NCSS promotes the premise that Social Studies education should have direct and explicit connections to the Common Core State Standards for English Language Arts. To find out more about this framework, visit their website at http://www.socialstudies.org/c3.

Assessments

As it is the driving factor in today's school, the Common Core Standards are also part of the development of the next wave of assessment. The NGA and the CCSSO are not heading up the creation of national assessment. Instead, there are two major assessment consortiums that have been formed—Partnership for Assessment of Readiness for College and Careers (PARCC; http://www.parcconline.org/) and Smarter Balanced Assessment Consortium (Smarter Balanced; http://www.smarterbalanced.org/). Each consortium was formed with a federal grant (www.gpo.gov/fdsys/pkg/FR-2010-04-09/pdf/2010-8176.pdf) that comes with several guidelines including:

- Rigorous assessment of progress toward "college and career readiness"
- Common cut scores across all Consortium states
- Achievement and growth information
- Valid, reliable, and fair for all students, except those with "significant cognitive disabilities"
- Online administration
- Multiple measures used
- Operational in 2014–2015 school year

Partnership for Assessment of Readiness for College and Careers (PARCC)

The PARCC assessments (www.parcconline.org) aim to increase graduation rates. These assessments are also intended to provide data to educators throughout the year

Figure 1.2 PARCC Assessment States

Arizona
Arkansas
Colorado
District of Columbia
Florida *
Illinois
Kentucky
Louisiana
Maryland
Massachusetts
Mississippi
New Jersey
New Mexico
New York
North Dakota
Ohio *
Oklahoma
Pennsylvania *
Rhode Island
Tennessee

* Rumblings or Indications they are pulling out of the assessment. The list of states continues to change based on legislation and government leaders. The local Department of Education at each state may have the most updated information about what their states are doing.

Source: https://www.parcconline.org/parcc-states

to not only guide instruction and interventions, but to help improve the effectiveness of teachers and the school. According to their website, the PARCC assessment will contain four main components, two summative assessments, and two optional non-summative assessments.

The performance-based assessments (PBA), which will be given as close to the end of the year as possible, for the ELA will focus on writing effectively when analyzing text. The Math PBA will focus on applying skills, concepts, and understandings to solve multistep problems requiring abstract reasoning, precision, perseverance, and strategic use of tools. The end-of-year assessment (EOY) will be administered after 90 percent of the school year has been completed. The ELA/literacy EOY will focus on reading comprehension. The Math EOY will be comprised of innovative items scored by computer.

The optional non-summative assessments will include a diagnostic assessment focusing on students' knowledge and skills and a midyear assessment with an emphasis on "hard-to-measure" standards.

Smarter Balanced Consortium

Smarter Balanced (www.smarterbalanced.org) has been designed to balance summative, interim, and formative assessments. Providing accurate year-to-year indicators of a student's progress toward college and career readiness is what it hopes to do. Just as with PARCC there will be two optional interim assessments. These can be given on a timetable to be determined at the local level. The interim assessments contain both performance-based assessments (PBA) and computer adaptive assessments.

In the last twelve weeks of the school year, the two summative assessments will be administered. The PBA component may include online research, group projects, and presentations and on average will take one to two class periods to complete. The computer adaptive components will have a wide variety of question types that cover all the Common Core Standards.

Still Developing

Much of what is known about the assessments and implementation progress in the various states is a work in progress. Likely in the years ahead, there will be a clearer picture of what this will look like and the impact it will have. For now, states are doing the best they can with following an implementation guideline.

School districts and leaders must work together to implement these standards within the time period allotted. To do this several steps must be followed. First, teachers and school librarians must analyze the standards not only in grade-level groups, but across grade levels to understand how key concepts build on one another. Second, teachers and school librarians must take advantage of the vast amount of resources available. Sites such as EngageNY (http://engageny.org) offer materials for all stakeholders involved. Finally, cadres of educators must be formed within each state to lead the way in implementation. In each of these steps school librarians have the opportunity to step up to the plate and assume a leading role in helping to lead

Figure 1.3. Smarter Balanced States/Territories

Alaska
California
Connecticut
Delaware
Hawaii
Idaho
Iowa
Kansas
Maine
Michigan
Missouri
Montana
Nevada
New Hampshire
North Carolina
North Dakota
Oregon
Pennsylvania*
South Carolina
South Dakota
U.S. Virgin Islands
Vermont
Washington
West Virginia
Wisconsin
Wyoming

*Rumblings or Indications they are pulling out of the assessment. The list of states continues to change based on legislation and government leaders. The local Department of Education at each state may have the most updated information about what their states are doing.

Source: http://www.smarterbalanced.org/about/member-states/

implementation of these standards. Who better to understand what each grade level is teaching than the school librarian? The school librarian who does this well will be the person who also is thought about when it is time to collaborate within the classroom. The school administrator who witnesses this dedication by the school librarian will understand how important and essential this person is to the education of all students within a building.

Recently a few state legislators have been revisiting the adoption of the Common Core Standards as they are now not as comfortable with them. Some states are slowing down the implementation in order to further study the standards. Some wish their state standards were more rigorous. Only time will tell what will happen with the Common Core. However, school librarians need, regardless of the initiative, to be aware of what the key issues influencing curriculum and instruction are in the nation, their state, and their school.

Resources/Works Cited

Burns, Marilyn. "Go Figure: Math and the Common Core." *Educational Leadership*, December/January 2013, 42–46.

Calkins, Lucy, Mary Ehrenworth, and Christopher Lehman. *Pathways to the Common Core: Accelerating Achievement*. Portsmouth, NH: Heinemann, 2012.

Doorey, Nancy A. "Coming Soon: A New Generation of Assessment." *Educational Leadership*, December/January 2013, 29–34.

Krashen, Stephen. "The Common Core: A Disaster for Libraries, a Disaster for Language Arts, a Disaster for American Education." *Knowledge Quest* 42, no. 3 (2014): 36–45.

"Partnership for Assessment of Readiness for College and Careers/PARCC." *Partnership for Assessment of Readiness for College and Careers/PARCC*. Accessed October 27, 2013. http://parcconline.org/.

"Read the Common Core Standards." *Common Core State Standards Initiative*. Council of Chief School Officers and the National Governors Association. June 2, 2010. Accessed October 27, 2013. http://www.corestandards.org/the-standards.

"Smarter Balanced Assessment Consortium." *Smarter Balanced Assessment Consortium*. Accessed October 27, 2013. http://www.smarterbalanced.org/.

2
What Are the Connections with School Library Standards?

In 2007, the American Association of School Librarians (AASL) adopted the *Standards for the 21st-Century Learner*. These are visionary standards demonstrating what students leaving our schools and school libraries should be able to do. Next came *Standards for the 21st-Century Learner in Action*, which provided a picture of what these standards could look like at various grade levels. The last of the trilogy of standards publications was *Empowering Learners: Standards for School Library Programs*, which is designed to talk about what a school library program should look like to best help students achieve the standards found in *Standards for the 21st-Century Learner*. There are multiple other publications and articles that have been written to support implementation of the AASL Standards. You can find many of those resources at www.ala.org/aasl/learning4life/resources.

As school libraries are always seeking to further their collaboration with classroom teachers, the AASL Standards are not something that can be taught in isolation. Instead they need to be married with content curriculum in order to be successful. This marriage is what makes the standards so powerful for students.

The Crosswalk

While this was happening with the AASL Standards, the Common Core State Standards (CCSS) began to be developed. As many states signed onto the initiative, it became logical that AASL look at aligning its standards with the Common Core. A committee was formed to create a crosswalk document that showed where the two sets of standards had commonality. This was done for both Language Arts and Mathematics standards. The Crosswalk of the Common Core Standards and the Standards for the 21st-Century Learner are available on the AASL website (www.ala.org/aasl/guidelinesandstandards/commoncorecrosswalk). You can go to either the CCSS or the AASL Standards to see the connections.

Putting Them Together

It is quite likely that your teachers have not heard about the AASL Standards, but they would have to be living under a rock not to have heard about the Common Core State Standards. As school librarians, our job is to infuse the AASL Standards into the projects and activities that one does with students. Certainly, the school librarian could make it very obvious to the teacher and help them see and understand the AASL Standards, but those aren't going to be the teacher's focus. Instead Common Core will be, so if we school librarians combine our expertise and focus, an amazing learning opportunity can be designed for students.

Diving a Little Deeper

The crosswalk that AASL developed really makes the connections between the Common Core and AASL Standards very clear, but let's talk in general terms about each of the AASL Standards and how they connect to the Common Core.

Inquire

This is one of the most obvious areas. If you look at the Common Core Writing Standards—especially standards number 7, 8, and 9—you will see a heavy focus on research and inquiry. This is a perfect dovetail with the first AASL standard. What a perfect opening for school librarians looking to collaborate with teachers!

For example, in fifth grade the Common Core talks about short research projects where students get information from several sources and have the ability to refocus if the projects get offtrack. Perhaps the inquiry might be a project that talks about what is the best state in the United States in which to live (except for their current state) and why. In such a project, the Common Core Standards, several Social Studies standards, and AASL standard 1 are being covered.

Also think about the in-depth reading standards for information and literary text in the Common Core. The first standard of both Reading Standards for Literature and Reading Standards for Informational Text requires each grade level to ask questions, cite evidence in the text, and draw inferences. These skills are the same as you see in the indicators under AASL standard 1.

Create Knowledge

Much of what was written under Inquiry above, carries over to this AASL Standard as well. The major focus here is to create new knowledge. Think back to that small inquiry in fifth grade about the best state in which to live. Students could begin to generate a campaign for marketing the state and the reason or reasons people would want to live there. This connects perfectly to Common Core Writing standard 1 for writing opinion pieces.

It also makes connections under the Reading Standards for Informational Text 7 and 8. Students have to use the evidence in their research to back up their claims of why they would want to live in a particular state.

Share Knowledge

This is the platform for sharing students' work. Certainly school librarians are essential to the inquiry and organizing of the new information, but they can be just as valuable in teaching students new and different ways to share information. In addition, with all the amazing advances in technology and publishing options, making sure that students and staff understand how to share knowledge is just as important as the knowledge itself. Using knowledge ethically and responsibly is also the job of the accomplished school librarian.

These concepts are both hammered in the AASL standard 3 as well as in the Common Core Writing Standards. Students are encouraged to use technology and other formats to share what they've learned from their inquiry and experiences. The publishing offerings give students an entirely new audience for their writing and their work, and they need to know how what they choose to do could impact what they write and say.

Consider the state project again. It could be that students create an eBook about their state and why it is the best place to live. It could be they generate a public service announcement (PSA) or commercial on why people should move to this state. There are countless options, and the school librarian can play a major role in this project by suggesting and collaborating with teachers who might feel unsure about creating projects that deal with technology.

Personal Growth

Probably one of the AASL Standards that school librarians (okay, any librarian) like the most is the last one, because it focuses a lot on reading, and not just reading for inquiry or projects, but also reading for the love of reading. Reader advisory is what librarians love to do. Matching the right book with the right student is a key component.

Teachers often get bogged down in having a student choose a book on the student's reading level. It certainly is important to find books where students can be successful, but school librarians also want to match readers to subjects in which they are interested. This is a perfect role for the school librarian. School librarians know the collection better than anyone, so helping match the reader to the book is an easy task.

Beyond helping match students to the right books that they need either for research or for reading for pleasure, the school librarian is the perfect person in the school to match teachers to the right books for use in their classrooms. One example that a school librarian colleague gave was that each week they have a teacher who comes down and asks what books in the library that teacher could use as read-alouds to focus on a certain skill. His class is listening to some of the best material in the library whether they are new materials or old materials. It is exciting to witness a teacher expanding his choices in read-alouds.

Too many times, teachers are unaware of the vast sea of fantastic informational texts available to use. They get in their comfort zone with the material they've been using, but over time some of the titles become dated and lack appeal for students. In addition, the Common Core Standards ask educators to use a great deal more informational text than perhaps they had used in the past. Many publishers are labeling their materials as Common Core ready. However, just as every fiction book published is not high quality, neither are all informational textbooks. Recommending great informational texts is a job for the suave school librarian.

One of the components that the Common Core emphasizes is using "rich text." All nonfiction or informational text materials are not created equal. School librarians will discover the best authors that emphasize this type of language usage. Teachers can pick up nonfiction books and use them, but it is the school librarian who is able to find and recommend the best in nonfiction. Authors such as Simon Seymour, Steve Jenkins (*How Many Ways Can You Catch a Fly, Never Smile at a Monkey, Actual Size*), Nic Bishop (*Lizards, Frogs, Marsupials*), and Dianna Hutts Aston (*A Butterfly Is Patient, An Egg Is Quiet, A Seed Is Sleepy*) are ones that teachers might not be aware of. Rich language usage is a prime consideration in each of these author's books. See appendix A in this book for a bibliography of other good informational texts to consider.

The Common Core Standards also have literature and informational text embedded throughout the grade levels, as do the AASL Standards. Reading, viewing, and listening are key components in standard 4. Responding to literature is also important throughout both sets of standards. Library collections have moved beyond print books to eBooks, websites, and other online sources of information and reading to serve patrons completely.

Math

As you can see, the examples used all focus on connection to the English/Language Arts Common Core Standards and the AASL Standards. It is a little harder to make the leap from the Math Common Core Standards to the AASL Standards; however, there are plenty of opportunities where math skills would be a necessary part of an inquiry project. For example, with a fifth-grade project on the election, students might be asked to calculate the cost of a trip to Washington, D.C., to observe the inauguration. This might include items such as mileage costs, hotels, meals, and incidentals. On a project that was done with third-grade students studying landmarks of the United States, one of the components was the calculation of the driving distance from the town where they lived to the landmark that the student chose. An inquiry project had students researching animals that lived in different biomes. After the animal was chosen, one of the tasks to accomplish was to create a graph of the different animals chosen from each of the biomes. Students voted on the animal they liked best and created a graph to present to the rest of the class. Projects could include using money, telling time, or any number of graphing situations. So, while school librarians usually tend not to include math in the mixture of the project, it is relatively easy to create projects that would include this component.

The connections are clear. School libraries are integrated into the Common Core Standards from the school library perspective. However, what school librarians need to do is make sure that the connection we see is also seen by administrators and teachers. School librarians have to paint that picture clearly so there is no doubt of the role they play in the Common Core implementation.

Resources/Works Cited

"Read the Common Core Standards." *Common Core State Standards Initiative*. Council of Chief School Officers and the National Governors Association. June 2, 2010. Accessed October 27, 2013. http://www.corestandards.org/the-standards.

Standards for the 21st-Century Learner. Chicago: American Association of School Librarians, 2007.

3

How Will the Common Core Impact the Administration of a School Library?

As with most major initiatives in schools, the impact of Common Core Standards on instruction is assumed. But, librarians also need to consider how this is going to impact the rest of the school library program. Some changes may appear more obvious than others. An opportunity to sit back and reflect on the program can be a very positive change that develops. School librarians all know that our plates are completely full. Adding a new initiative like Common Core Standards in addition to what school librarians are already doing isn't going to feel like it is feasible. Instead, school librarians need to think about what needs to change or be eliminated. What are some elements that can be eliminated to make way for new items that might align or support the Common Core Standards? Is a lesson that has been conducted for years appropriate with the new standards? Can that lesson be tweaked, or should it be eliminated altogether? Is a school librarian spending too much time conducting lessons on procedures that could be incorporated into another area? Does additional time need to be spent on sharing resources with teachers in the building to incorporate the new standards?

Another way to think about this is that there is a finite amount of hours in the day. Driving to school each morning, you likely ponder all the things that need to get done off of the to do list. School librarians all know that the odds of completing it are slim to nil as no day ever goes exactly as planned. But as you begin to prioritize that list keep this question in mind: "Is what I'm doing today going to impact student achievement?" Obviously our top job is helping kids learn. Keeping that question in mind—especially from the administration side—can help decide what gets dropped or what can wait.

Budgets

One of the first areas that the Common Core may impact is the budget and the collection development plan for the library. The economy over the last decade has taken a toll on library budgets. The need to implement the Common Core is an opportunity for librarians to make a case for some of that funding to be restored or additional funding to be given. It certainly is no guarantee, but it may be an opportunity for the school librarian to propose a budget to the administration and justify needs using the Common Core Standards.

The increase in student choice and inquiry means a collection, in both print and online, is going to need to cover a variety of topics and a variety of reading levels. In the past, standards project topics may have been easy for a librarian to predict and purchase resources for; the more open inquiry is going to require creativity in obtaining those resources, and at a variety of reading levels. In addition to a librarian's budget, support from other schools in the district, the local library, and interlibrary sources may be crucial.

First, survey teachers to see what topics they intend to cover in the upcoming year. If teachers have not decided, go through the standards and make intelligent decisions on what you think might be needed. Match that with the current collection (both print and online resources). Finally, create a report demonstrating additional needs that can be shown to administrators. See the example in figure 3.1. There is a blank form available in appendix B.

When working on a spreadsheet, be honest. Show what you can manage from your budget and what you can't. Make sure to include a document showing how you plan to spend the budget. Also, be realistic. This sheet can be used in two directions—for your administrators and budgeting, but also for you in planning instruction for the year.

As part of preparing the budget for administrators, consider creative methods for providing the resources that students need. For example, list possible places where resources can be interlibrary loaned (ILL) from other schools or from the public library. Demonstrate what can be found online versus what can be found in print and why the funds are needed for the projects you've requested.

While the examples are focused on nonfiction and research, there are ample places where fiction titles will be key to reaching the Common Core. There is no guarantee that it will result in any extra budget dollars, but you won't get anything if you do nothing. You've outlined the need, and it may spark some thoughts on the part of an administrator if funds become available down the road. Also, there may be an opportunity to use these figures in grant-writing opportunities or in requesting extra PTA funds. The well-prepared school librarian always finds that it is good to have money figures ready when an opportunity arises!

Collection Development

The Common Core Standards increase the push for nonfiction texts and reading. A heavier emphasis is placed on research and inquiry. School librarians will need to think about how to update the nonfiction collection—whether it be print or online.

No matter how much funding or from where it comes, school librarians need to prepare a plan of how they are going to update and maintain the nonfiction collections both online and in print. At the same time, neglecting fiction isn't an option. Every collection is going to be different based on the needs of the users. The school librarian needs to be attuned to what those needs are in the building.

Figure 3.1 Budget Justification

Project	Teacher/Grade Standards	Resources Currently Available	Additional Resources Needed & Cost	Budget Analysis and Comments
Social Studies: Native American Tribes	Mr. Woodlands/ Fifth Grade CCSS.W.7 CCSS.W.8 CCSS.W.9 State Standards for Social Studies	<u>Print Collection</u> 1–2 titles available on each tribe. Copyright dates are acceptable. <u>Online Collection</u> A few websites are available for students. Difficult to find online resources at appropriate reading levels.		Additional resources will be obtained via interlibrary loan as needed.
Health: Body Systems	Mrs. Heart/ Third Grade CCSS.W.7 CCSS.W.8 CCSS.W.9 State Standards for Science and/ or Health/ Wellness	<u>Print Collection</u> Old and not current. Materials need to be weeded. <u>Online Collection</u> Materials available in statewide database and in our Grolier Online database.	Print collection needs some new titles. May consider eBooks to replace the dated titles. Estimated cost is $350–400. The library will also need to consider in the future some mobile devices for reading eBooks until we go 1:1.	These costs can come from the current library budget.
Social Studies: Famous Americans	Mrs. Taft/First Grade CCSS.W.7 CCSS.W.8 CCSS.W.9 State Standards for Social Studies.	<u>Print Collection</u> Collection is dated and no titles at first grade reading levels. <u>Online Collection</u> None available and difficult to find for primary students.	Print collection needs to be updated. Estimated cost is $600–$700. Online database available— $400/ year yearly subscription.	The current library budget cannot handle adding these resources. Additional funding is needed.

Note: Prices are merely to provide examples and do not actually represent current prices from vendors.

The first things a school librarian needs to make sure they understand are the grade levels, ability levels, and subject content that is being taught. Too many times purchasing is done with a subject in mind, but not the expectation of what the teacher expects or the varying reading levels of the students involved.

So much time is spent on teachers making sure that students are reading at their reading level that the school librarian must be careful to purchase books on single topics at varying reading levels. A good example of this would be books on the topic of the *Titanic*. Although many books have been written at a higher level, younger children are also interested in this topic. A school librarian might purchase *Titanic Sinks!* by Barry Denenberg (Viking, 2011) and *Titanic* by Melissa Stewart (National Geographic Readers, 2012) for a lower reading level. The first example includes primary-source documents of newspaper articles written during the time, while the second example is on a lower reading level with fantastic pictures. A third choice on this topic might be a biography about one of the passengers on the ship in a picture book format. *Heroine of the Titanic: The Real Unsinkable Molly Brown* by Joan Blos (HarperCollins, 2001) would be an example of an entirely different approach.

Another good example of varied reading levels would be in the biography section of the school library. The Common Core State Standards lists reading in many areas and pushes students to read biographies. There is a fantastic array of great picture book biographies being published. A picture book biography gives a student a chance to read and find out about a person they know little about and eventually might entice them to read a longer book on that particular person.

Picture book biographies are a fantastic introduction for students of all ages. Refer to chapter 11 for a lesson plan and bibliography on picture book biographies. Couple these examples with a longer read, and the student has been stretched to a higher level. A longer read might be from an author such as Russell Freedman or Candace Fleming who both go into extreme detail when writing biographies for children.

Of course this poses a problem for the school librarian when purchasing because not only do you have to know the subjects and topics teachers are covering, but you must be familiar with students' reading levels and interests. Although all subject areas do not lend themselves to this thinking, publishers have been publishing many Common Core State Standards-aligned books. However, it is important to note that a book should not be boring and/or contain stilted language just because it is at a lower reading level. Students realize when they are being talked down to even in a book. The language in the book still needs to be rich and stretch the student's vocabulary. In their scramble to offer more CCSS-aligned materials publishers settle for materials that are lower level with stilted language. Gone are the days when students have to read "See Sally run. Run, Sally, run." Language needs to draw the student into the text of the content. Don't let students become bored with reading because the text is too easy or stilted. Rich language is the key to keeping each and every student reading and clamoring for more.

In his series of animal books (i.e., *Lizards*, Scholastic, 2010) Nic Bishop not only uses his fantastic photographs to draw students into the book, he also writes in two parts on the page. A student can get the meaning of the books simply by reading the larger print on the page and leaving the rest for when their reading level gets higher. Sleeping Bear Press also does this with their alphabet books on each state. Part of the words on the page are written in bigger print, and a reader can read just that to learn about a state or pursue the information on the same page with a bit more detail. This is a wonderful way to satisfy the younger student looking for state information while challenging the better or older reader to find more information in the finer print on the page.

Vendors are now advertising everything as "Common Core aligned," so it will be important to help teachers and administrators wade through those ads to find the best resources and products. The question school librarians must ask as they purchase books and materials is: will this really help the students achieve the standards?

As school librarians examine the school library collection, they must be able to identify what materials they have already that will fit into the framework of the Common Core Standards. This would be an excellent opportunity to analyze our nonfiction collections to search out the titles that will address specific standards. To do that school librarians must first identify specific Common Core Standards on which to focus. They must make sure they are familiar with the ten anchor standards for reading and writing. These are the building codes to help implement the curriculum. If school librarians are familiar with these anchors, the library collections will meet the needs of teachers and students getting ready for college and careers. One of the anchors focuses on themes within and across texts. School librarians should discuss with their teachers what these themes are and then develop a collection around those themes. Another one of the categories focuses on the integration of knowledge and ideas. In the areas of social studies school librarians want to make sure they have historical fiction, picture books, biographies, original primary sources, and diaries to be able to combine to give teachers. The same would go for science, where one might have picture books, experiment books, poetry books, and science concept books to group in units around themes. This will help teachers integrate social studies and science into their language and literature lessons. Giving teachers specific examples of books to use enables them to realize that collaboration is a key to implementation.

Just as librarians can build a print collection, they can also help students, teachers, and administrators to curate resources on a variety of topics using the web and online databases. These online resources and tools can be even more current and up-to-date then items found in a print collection. As inquiry standards in the Common Core may stretch a budget, curating these online resources can be a way to provide the resources that students need.

An example of putting together a collection of books on a particular topic or theme would be a unit that was prepared this past summer using primary sources. A topic taught in fifth grade in social studies is Jamestown. Combine a picture book entitled *Jamestowne; Struggle for Survival* by Marcia Sewall (Atheneum, 2001) with a biography of John Smith, an informational book about the settlement of Jamestown, a book incorporating John Smith's diary of exploration (*Captain John Smith's Big and Beautiful Bay* by Rebecca C. Jones, Schiffer Publishing, Ltd., 2011), and primary sources from the Library of Congress showing the original map of Jamestown that John Smith drew in 1607. Students can compare and contrast the map of 1607 with the present-day map of the area while reading about how John Smith was able to draw the original. Social studies standards along with Common Core Standards in Language Arts are covered. Additional materials could be added as the unit unfolds.

School librarians teamed with classroom teachers can create small collections like this on a variety of subject areas in both social studies and science. However, to do this well, the school librarian must be well versed in the standards at all grade levels and be familiar with the library collection. When creating these types of units, the classroom teacher must also be aware and rely on the expertise of the school librarian.

Policies

This would also be an excellent time to review your school's collection development policy to address changes that might need to be made. As the school librarian discusses with classroom teachers what they need to address in the Common Core areas, she can then develop a collection map to guide in purchasing materials needed. As budgets shrink, a plan for purchasing is the best route. In fact, a case could be made with the administration that the school library budget should be increased to supply the materials needed to address specific areas of the Common Core and work them into the curriculum.

eBooks

Another debate will be the purchase of eBooks or print collections or both. Probably the answer is both. Many schools are moving to a 1:1 initiative. This simply is developing a plan for each student in a school or classroom to have a device to use 24/7. Whether it is an iPad, Chromebook, or other laptop, the devices are provided by the school just as if they were textbooks. In other cases a school might decide that every student should bring their own device (BYOD) to use. In either case all students would have some type of electronic device to use in class. If your school has moved to 1:1 then you may lean more heavily toward eBooks. If your school is still waiting on 1:1, then you may want to lean more heavily toward print. However, neither type of material is going away soon, so having both options allows some flexibility for the users.

Access is key, so when deciding between print and eBook purchases, do you have enough devices for students to access these resources? Is your license multiuser to allow numerous students to have access to the same book at the same time? Purchasing decisions need to be based on both your environment and how they will best be used, so make sure to keep that in mind. However, eBooks are here, so instead of asking if you will provide them, the bigger question is how are you going to provide these resources. See figure 3.2 for some ideas of things to consider.

The ALA has been working for the last two to three years with major publishers to determine options for libraries. Some, like HarperCollins, will sell eBooks that only circulate so many times; others like Random House have raised prices significantly. There seems to be significant progress being made, but there is still work to do. You can keep up with the latest at the ALA Transforming Libraries website at www.ala.org/transforminglibraries/e-books-digital-content.

One of the major areas with eBooks is platform. Some publishers have created their own platform that a reader would use to access just the eBooks from that publisher (or just a few publishers). There are also vendors who primarily focus on the platform and then provide books from a variety of publishers. There are pluses and minuses to both

Figure 3.2 Considerations with eBooks

Purpose	Why are you having eBooks?
Devices/Portal	What devices will your students be accessing these eBooks on?
Content Decisions	Do your eBooks focus on recreational reading or curriculum/research or both? How many publishers work with the vendor?
Funding (Long Term/Short Term)	How will you pay for it? There is typically a subscription fee for most services.
Pricing	What is included in the annual fee?
Ownership of Content	Who owns the content? If you quit the subscription, do you lose the content?
Formats	What are the formats in which a reader can access the book? There are many different formats depending on the reader that students are using. Are there multiple formats?
Number of Circs	Some publishers limit the number of times you can circulate an eBook before you have to buy it again. You need to know this ahead of time before purchasing.
Number of Access at a Time	How many students can access a book at a time?
Enhancements	What additional features does the eBook provide? Is there media content? Are their links to additional information?
Roll Out Plan, Professional Development, and Publicity!	How will you promote this to your teachers, students, and parents? What will you need to train these various groups to access the eBooks? How will you garner interest and use of the resources?

of them, and a school librarian will need to do some research to determine the best path for their building.

Some of the major vendors eBook platforms common in schools are:

- Baker & Taylor's Axis 360
- Follett Shelf
- Mackin Via
- myON Reader
- Overdrive

Pricing varies from the vendor to the number of students in your school to the amount of materials you are buying. Check with each vendor to determine the specific costs for your school or district.

A lot of the K–8 informational text publishers are also setting up their own platform for their books. Some still publish books for the platforms mentioned above, and others just use their own. Some host the books for you and then put MARC records in the catalog. Others have their own system for accessing it. It varies greatly from publisher to publisher. The September issue of *School Library Journal* contained a useful Market Directory of eBooks (http://www.slj.com/resources/sljs-school-ebook-market-directory/).

With Common Core State Standards being a buzzword in education, additional funding from PTO, grants, or local organizations might be an avenue to pursue. Make sure to have the information and the connections needed to support your requests. There is no guarantee that money will be received, but nothing ventured, nothing gained. Again, can you justify what you need using the Common Core Standards?

Technology

Libraries will be forever intertwined with technology—not just eBooks, but a variety of resources for creating and sharing information. School libraries are transitioning from being a place where information is stored, to one where information is created. Technology is an integral part of this phenomenon. While often school librarians don't have as much input into technology needs as they might with the library budgets, they should be aware of what technology the library needs and why. What kind of spaces do libraries need for production? What kind of tools do students need (digital cameras, iPods, iPads, etc.)? What kind of access do students need for online resources for inquiry? Is a bank of computers sufficient, or is a complete lab needed? Do school libraries need mobile labs instead of stationary labs? A multitude of questions concerning technology should be analyzed. School librarians need to think in terms of what they might want to put into a proposal and connect it to the Common Core State Standards. Again, there are no guarantees in life, but school librarians need to be thinking ahead for possibilities and advocating for implementation.

Another question that needs to be addressed is if there are plans in your school or state for a technology conversion. Some schools are looking at bringing your own device (BYOD). Others are implementing 1:1 devices. What does this entail for the library? How does this impact instruction? Who will be making these decisions? Can students really use technology well, or do educators only assume that they know what to do? If the latter is the case, how do school librarians go about making sure that they educate students in the best use of the technology and also in the best way of finding the information they need? Do these additional resources help achieve the Common Core and how? The school librarian can be a leader in helping teachers best utilize various tools in instruction.

When thinking about technology, the school librarian needs to examine how students need to find information. Many believe that since students are digital natives, they automatically know how to access and find information. Many times the first place searched by students is Google. However, Google is not always the answer, yet students will believe that this is the only way to find information if they are not instructed. It is the savvy school librarian who lights the way for students and teachers to be aware of online encyclopedias, databases, primary source documents, and a myriad of other scholarly sources of information that cannot be found with a simple Google search or on Wikipedia.

The other piece of the technology puzzle that school librarians play a part in is working with teachers and students in presenting and manipulating information for either presentations or creating projects. Teachers today are scrambling to figure out how to embed technology into lessons. Many believe that using an app or writing a paper on a computer fulfills this command from administrators. However, this is a very low level of technology usage. Students must be able to use technology to explore, create, rearrange, and produce meaningful output for technology to have an impact on their education. Again, it is the school librarian who imparts and shares the knowledge of different approaches to presenting information. Whether it is a simple PowerPoint, an elaborate Prezi presentation, a Skype encounter, a podcast, or a demonstration of how to combine resources in Symbaloo, the school librarian can lead the way. Know a variety of avenues to share with teachers and students.

Since technology is constantly changing, it is difficult for a school librarian to keep abreast of all the different methods to use. But again, the knowledge of knowing where to look and what organizations will assist will place the school librarian in the forefront of technology knowledge. One of the best avenues to use is the International Society of Technology Educators (ISTE). Their publication *Entresekt: Where Learning, Technology and Community Meet* has excellent articles, and their conference held every summer is the premier gathering of vendors, presenters, and technology users. For more information about this organization, visit their website at https://www.site.org. As school librarians search for varied ways to present or to synthesize information to recommend to students and teachers, the array of opportunities is amazing. Publications, blogs, and articles are available to assist. For a listing of various programs and applications to be found on the web, refer to appendix F. Although this is not a complete listing, it is a good place to start in producing products in a variety of ways for projects.

Staffing

Odds are that the Common Core isn't going to lead to drastic changes in the way that libraries are staffed. However, as you become more integral in what is happening in the classroom, teachers and students may be better allies when it comes to increasing staff (especially with a librarian covering multiple buildings). It will be important to document and keep data on all that you are doing as it relates to the Common Core, but also at the same time track what could have been done had there been more staffing (whether that be an aide or another librarian). Paint that picture showing all the possibilities. Because dollars are driving decisions, there are no guarantees. School librarians have to be ready so that if funding becomes available, administrators will see the library as a potential place for additional spending.

The best advocacy is when others are speaking for the library and librarian. School librarians want parents and students to demand access to a school librarian to help them be successful with these new standards.

Facilities

Most people accept a library position and the facility is what it is when the school librarian takes it over. Options are sometimes limited in what can be done to change a facility. However, with the implementation of the Common Core this might be the opportunity to think about how the library is arranged. Is there furniture sitting around unused? Are there places where students can work in small groups? Are there options for multiple activities going on at the same time? Is there empty shelving that is not needed? Is there a need for additional shelving? Think in terms of how to best utilize the space to meet the students' needs. Think about small-group work areas as teachers plan projects. How are multiple classes handled? Are there areas that can be utilized differently?

David Loertscher has written on the concept of a Learning Commons model. In this model, the facility is much more flexible and nimble. Furniture can be moved around and open spaces created when needed. Small groups can be pulled together for working on projects. The library becomes the space the students need. Each of our facilities is different and options vary, but think in terms of how the facility can be set up to better meet the needs of students as they work with these new standards.

Facility updates or refreshes may be another great conversation to have with PTO/PTAs. Parent groups often like things that will have a lasting value and are a visible example of them spending PTO/PTA dollars. New, versatile, and movable furniture and shelving is often very appealing to parent groups and a good tangible, visible target for their fund-raising activities throughout the year.

Scheduling

There are many options for scheduling a library. Obviously best practice dictates the best way is a flexible schedule. It allows the school librarian and classroom teacher to co-teach the project and lesson. It provides the flexibility to schedule a project in a more compressed time instead of once every few days. If you don't have a flexible schedule, you can always lay the groundwork by explaining to the administration why a flexible schedule is better for students and the teachers when implementing the Common Core Standards, but you also must be a realist and realize that this might not happen.

The other option is a fixed schedule. Many school librarians have been forced into having fixed schedules within the elementary school setting, which simply means that some or all of the day is filled with scheduled classes, giving teachers planning times. Although this is not the ideal situation, it is a reality in many schools. If this is something that is happening in your library, what do you do?

First and foremost (no matter what schedule you have), you must be involved in the planning teams at the individual grade levels. Attend grade-level planning, Common Core implementation/planning, or any other meetings that grade levels might have to plan their curriculum mapping and instruction. Explain to the administration how important it is that you attend these meetings if they want the school librarian to be a part of a team of educators who will be teaching students the integrated skills needed for college and career readiness.

Once you have been invited and attend planning meetings, make sure you are ready to suggest topics of interest to the teachers, literature that they can use, and lesson plans that are adaptable. Once the teachers see you as an integral piece of the puzzle, they will be more than willing to collaborate and will be the best advocates when staffing cuts loom.

The planning must go on so that each participant knows what their job will be. Unlike the flexible schedule, in a fixed schedule you probably won't have both the librarian and the teacher together to do the team teaching, but the planning makes sure each participant will know what their responsibilities are and will carry them out. For example, on a unit concerning fairy tales and studying the different cultures and continents, the librarian can introduce the original fairy tale, followed by sharing the same story from another country to show the students how stories can change. The teacher then follows up in the classroom by sharing additional stories from different countries based on the original fairy tale. The next step is to compare and contrast the stories that have been shared by the teacher and the librarian. This could be done by one or the other, although the ideal situation would be both working together. This might be arranged if the school librarian has some flexible planning time of their own to meet additional times with the class. Students could then prepare a chart of their own showing how they would retell the story with different characters or settings. The writing could be done in the classroom or done in a computer lab with the librarian.

Although a fixed schedule is not the ideal scenario, it is possible to work at it to make collaboration a reality. Both individuals have put their input into the plan and taken on the responsibility to keep the project moving. The final assessment can be done by both individuals. The librarian can be responsible for the charts made, and the teacher can be responsible for the grading of the final written version (grammar, punctuation, spelling, etc.).

The beauty of a flexible schedule when doing this same unit is that instead of being separate, the teacher and school librarian would co-teach. Now the students have the advantage of having two educators working together at the same time, which is definitely a win-win situation for everyone involved.

Procedures/Access

Another area to consider is procedures and access to materials. Can students find the materials needed? Are they allowed sufficient numbers of books at one time? Procedures for checking out library materials vary greatly across the country. Each librarian tends to have his own plan or process that works. However, the critical idea to consider is student access to materials.

Consider the annual postings on LM_Net. Every year school librarians will post information concerning book limits for kindergarten students. The replies to the query bring all sorts of answers.

- Our kindergarten students don't check out until second semester.
- Our kindergarten students don't check out at all.
- Our kindergarten students only select from a few preselected titles on the table.
- Our kindergarten students only select from a certain area or shelf.

These are examples of the comments one might read. However, the option is to consider broader concepts and ask additional questions. Why can't kindergarten students check out books from the first day they visit the library? Why not expand the checkout area to include fiction and nonfiction? Why limit them to preselected books? Embracing the excitement our youngest students bring to the library should be foremost in a school librarian's mind. Make it a huge celebration that they can check out books! Share with them the behavior and expectations for circulation. Let them know that success will increase their access to materials. It has been proven that the more students read (or are read to) the better readers they become. So, if the goal of the library is to help students become better and voracious readers, increasing their access to resources is justified.

Consider all the standards in the Common Core that kindergarteners need to master. They need access to a plethora of reading materials, and the school library is a perfect place to get it. It will give them the resources needed to practice and master these standards.

For example, on week one (first visit), the student checks out a book. The librarian discusses the process, procedures, and care of a book. From there, begin to build on the number of books allowed, increasing not only the number of resources checked out, but allowing them to search different areas. It takes a little while until they are checking out the same amount of books and areas that other students are using based on their needs and wants. Having a liberal policy starts students off loving the library and respecting the resources within it.

Examine other grade-level policies. Are they limited to one or two items? Are they limited to a selected area of the school library? Then determine why these policies are in place. It is possible that the policies and procedures are valid due to staff limitations or collection limits. What are the benefits versus the negatives? For example, one librarian uses the idea that students can check out as much as they can be responsible for. So, for some students that might be one item at a time, and for others it could be four or five items. Discuss what responsibility means with students. Talk about five resources being the tipping point. The librarian jokes with students that five is that point where the students may fall over because their backpacks are going to tip them over. However, at the same time the librarian always makes sure to say that any student that can justify more than five items will be able to get what they need. Again emphasize that responsibility is the key.

The student also might need to have a conversation with the librarian to justify additional resources. The bottom line is that each student is different, so try to judge each case separately. This can be difficult when decisions are made district-wide on limits and procedures. Conversations need to be had with those decision makers concerning why local control of policies is important in the new education environment. Flexibility is key to ensuring students have access to the materials they need when they need them!

When policies are put into place, there must also be consequences. Students that demonstrate they can handle responsibility will have more privileges. Those that make poor choices will have privileges taken away. Policies like this give students more access to materials, make them want to access materials, and in the end helps with the Common Core implementation. Conversations of this type need to be implemented with all grade levels and personnel so that everyone understands the policies and procedures.

Programming

Programming can include guest speakers such as authors, or other special events for the school such as book fairs, parent nights, poetry groups, etc. Consider how the Common Core implementation might impact these events. For example, when choosing an author, consider a nonfiction author for a visit. Highlight a variety of complex-text type books at the book fair for parents to see. Highlight poetry books and additional lessons on different forms of poetry and poetry writing when hosting a poetry performance group. An author of informational text would be an excellent addition for a visit to demonstrate to students the type of effort it takes to write a nonfiction book. Certainly school librarians want to continue to be a primary resource and they don't want Common Core to take over everything they do, but where there are appropriate choices that could be made, why not take advantage of them?

Evaluation / Reflection

No matter where you fall on the Common Core debate, the concept of evaluating the school library program on a consistent basis is essential for its growth and development. The Common Core (or any new initiative or standards) provides an even more urgent opportunity to examine current practice and determine what is working, what isn't working, and what needs to be changed.

Evaluation can come from a variety of sources. It could be personal self-reflection. It could be a survey of students and staff. See appendix C for a sample of a survey to use. How one obtains the data needed to make the reflection matters little; time and thought about how to make it better the next time around is the critical element. Making the school library work efficiently is the bottom line since the school library is essential to a well-run school.

Changes

Obviously in an ideal world, every school would have a state-certified school librarian. Many places are a long way from being there; however, a point can be made from looking at the Common Core that a school librarian is essential to implementing the standards with fidelity.

Whether you are covering one school or multiple schools, the focus has to be on the implementation of the Common Core Standards and the instruction the school librarian can provide. School librarians have to paint a clear picture for teachers, administrators, school board members, and parents that what school librarians are doing clearly helps prepare students for these new standards and helps them become career and college ready.

If time is focused on this component, then many of the roles or jobs that school librarians have deemed important in the past need to disappear. School librarians can't worry if the cart of books doesn't get shelved. School librarians can't worry if there is a pile of resources that need book jackets. Certainly no one would disagree that these tasks need to be accomplished, but at the end of the day if you can't answer the question, "What did I do today to impact student learning?" then something was amiss with that day.

Resources/Works Cited

"A Primer on Ebooks for Libraries Just Starting With Downloadable Media." *The Digital Shift*. Accessed September 24, 2013, http://www.thedigitalshift.com/2012/04/ebooks/an-ebook

-primer-many-small-libraries-are-still-just-getting-started-with-ebooks-heres-a-helpful-guide-on-those-first-steps/.

Burns, Elizabeth, Sue Kimmel, and Kasey L. Garrison. "How Common Is Common? An Analysis of the Recommended Text Exemplars." *Teacher Librarian* 41, no.1 (2013): 23–27.

"Ebooks." *American Library Association.* Accessed September 24, 2013, http://www.ala.org/advocacy/ebooks.

"EBooks Are Beginning to Replace Textbooks in the Classroom." *WebProNews.* Accessed September 24, 2013, http://www.webpronews.com/ebooks-are-beginning-to-replace-textbooks-in-the-classroom-2012-02.

"Ebooks: You Have to Make Up Your Mind at the Very Beginning [chart]." *Ebook Friendly.* Accessed September 24, 2013, http://ebookfriendly.com/ebooks-you-have-to-make-up-your-mind-at-the-very-beginning-chart/.

Enis, Matt, and Sarah Bayliss. "SLJ's School EBook Market Directory." *School Library Journal* 59, no. 9 (2013): 34–37.

Guernsey, Lisa. "Are Ebooks Any Good?" *School Library Journal.* June 2011. Accessed September 24, 2013, http://www.slj.com/2011/06/ebooks/are-ebooks-any-good/.

Harris, Christopher. "Ebooks and School Libraries." *American Libraries Magazine.* January 2012. Accessed September 24, 2013, http://www.americanlibrariesmagazine.org/article/ebooks-and-school-libraries.

Harvey, Carl A., II. *The 21st Century Elementary Library Media Program.* Santa Barbara, CA: Linworth Publishing, 2010.

Johnson, Doug. "The E-reading Advantage—Home—Doug Johnson's Blue Skunk Blog." *The E-reading advantage.* N.p., n.d. Accessed October 23, 2013, doug-johnson.squarespace.com/blue-skunk-blog/2013/2/6/the-e-reading-advantage.html.

Johnson, Doug. *The Indispensable Librarian: Surviving and Thriving in School Libraries in the Information Age.* Santa Barbara, CA: Linworth Publishing, 2013.

Morris, Betty J. *Administering the School Library Media Center.* Santa Barbara, CA: Libraries Unlimited, 2010.

Valenza, Joyce. "Curation." *School Library Monthly* 29, no.1 (2012).

Woolls, Blanche. *The School Library Media Manager.* Santa Barbara, CA: Libraries Unlimited, 2013.

Young, Jr., Terrence E. "Always Open, Never Visible: Challenges and Opportunities in Marketing and Promoting Your Informational E-Books." *Library Media Connection* 31, no. 3 (2012): 48–52.

4
How Will the Common Core Impact Instruction In/Out of the School Library?

As teachers and school librarians examine the Common Core Standards closer, they will begin to notice that there is a shift in the way topics are addressed. Instead of simply teaching a lesson on similes, students might examine picture books containing similes, discuss what they do and have in common, and construct a definition of a simile. School librarians will find that what they have been teaching (information literacy, critical thinking, research skills, lifelong learning, and reading) is suddenly the focus for classroom instruction. Classroom teachers will realize that the school librarian makes the best collaborative partner in going forward. A global setting is now the focus of our teaching. No longer do the four walls of the classroom define the teaching environment. The world has been opened up with a vast array of materials and opportunities to bring learning alive. To teach well, the instructor will realize that it is no longer possible to stay isolated in a room. To make sure our students are making the most of their educational opportunities, teams of teachers and school librarians will work together to change the instruction in both the classroom and library.

One area that needs to be examined critically is the Language Arts standards. Changes in this arena impact instruction both in the classroom and the school library. For many years the entire focus of Language Arts instruction was on fictional text or literature. Common Core now puts a greater emphasis on nonfictional text. Educators not as familiar with this area need to be acquainted with good examples to use in the classroom. The Common Core looks at topics a bit differently.

Informational Text/Nonfiction Text

When talking about nonfiction reading or as the Common Core refers to it, informational text, there is an abundance of books published, but the school librarian needs to share and recommend quality text to teachers for instruction. For instance, one of the attributes of a good informational textbook is using vivid language with plenty of action words. A book must bring complex ideas and subjects to life. The nonfiction books that should be used are ones that make the topic exciting. Some examples of this could include:

- Nonfiction books that use comparisons to help explain unfamiliar ideas, complex concepts, and impossibly large numbers. For instance, a text might read "a blue whale has a tongue that weighs as much as an elephant," which gives a child much more insight into this fact than an impossibly large number. Steve Jenkins is a master at comparisons in his numerous books about animals. One of his books, *Biggest, Strongest, Fastest* (HMH Books, 1999), not only gives readers a comparison, but the pictures show this visual. He tells us that a shrew can sleep in a teaspoon and an ant can carry five times its own weight while a strong man can carry something about as much as he weighs. *Actual Size* by Jenkins (HMH Books, 2004) shows the actual size of the animal on the page. Simon Seymour and Nic Bishop are also authors who use this same concept. Nic Bishop's books include life-size photographs of some of his animals, such as lizards, marsupials, and moths and butterflies. Seymour Simon's vast amount of knowledge of science is demonstrated in his very readable science books and on his website (www.seymoursimon.com). Mr. Simon was a former science teacher and feels it is very important to excite young people about science. StarWalk Kids (www.starwalkkids.com), a website that he created, is a subscription service for accessing eBooks.

- Nonfiction text also must have strong verbs for a student to understand what is happening. After the scene is set, the student will be sucked into the action with engaging words. *Wolves* by Seymour Simon (HarperCollins, 1993) is a good example of using strong verbs in a science book. The book starts out by saying, "Imagine snow falling silently in the great woodlands of North America. The only sounds are from the trees creaking and tossing in the wind. Suddenly the quiet is broken by the eerie howling of a wolf. And all the frightening stories and legends that you've heard about the treacherous and sly wolf and the evil werewolf begin to race through your mind." This is not your typical nonfiction book with dry, dull facts.

- Good nonfiction text also must use photos and diagrams to enhance the words of the text and engage the student. Asking questions of the reader is another excellent way to engage the student. When informational text does this, the reader will want to read more. Straight facts and boring detail does not draw a reader into wanting to enjoy the information in the book. Recently there have been numerous books published that use a question and answer method of getting information across to the reader. A series called I Wonder by Kingfisher is an example. Anita Ganeri's book *I Wonder Why Camels Have Humps* (Kingfisher, 2003) takes readers through a series of questions explaining why different animals have unusual features. World Book Publishing also has a series of books that use one question per page followed by an answer. Scholastic Publishers has published a series of books entitled Question and Answer series. *Do Whales Have Belly Buttons?* (Scholastic, 1999) is an example of one of the books in this series. This book, for example, has a question such as "Do whales have belly buttons?" This is then followed by the answer, "Yes! Whales have belly buttons just like cats and dogs, lions and tigers, you and me."

- School librarians also want to look for informational text that tells a story. Does it have a flow that draws students to read it? Obviously, biographies tend to be organized that way, but school librarians need other nonfictional texts to fulfill these criteria. An example of nonfictional text that tells a story would be *Owen & Mzee: The True Story of a Remarkable Friendship* by Isabella Hatkoff (Scholastic, 2006). This is the story of a baby hippo separated from his mother during the tsunami of 2004 in Kenya and how a giant 130-year-old tortoise was able to befriend him. To extend this lesson, the teacher can share several versions of this story for comparison and contrast such as *Owen & Mzee: The Language of Friendship* by Isabella Hatkoff (Scholastic, 2007) or the picture books, *A Mama for Owen* by Marion Bauer (Simon, 2007) and *Mama: A True Story* by Jeannette Winter (Harcourt, 2007). Examining the corresponding website (www.owenandmzee.com) would be another way to address the standard of reading and analyzing text from different sources. In chapter 8 you will find a lesson plan developed around these particular books to use.

As the Common Core Standards emphasizes the importance of informational text throughout the grade levels, school librarians realize that this text weaves information about the arts, science, and social studies into the language arts experience. A wide range of text that is used to fulfill this requirement includes newspapers, magazines, trade books, eBooks, database articles, reference material, and textbooks. Included in appendix A are many examples of books that are appropriate to use. The books are divided into subject areas for ease of access.

Several sites that are subscription based are also good choices to use. Scholastic's TrueFLIX is an example of a site that takes books from the True Book series from Scholastic Library Publishing and puts them online for students to read or listen to and includes short videos and websites to enhance the content of the books. It includes subjects such as science, nature, people, places, and history to bring these books to life for students. It helps students' literacy skills while building knowledge of subject area content for inquiry purposes. Subscription information can be found at www.scholastic.com/trueflix.

Magazines

While searching for good informational text, magazines are another avenue. Children's magazines have changed a great deal from *Jack and Jill* and *Highlights*. Just as adults enjoy reading magazines so do children. The price of a magazine is not outrageous for a school library or even an individual teacher to afford, and it provides nine to twelve issues with up-to-date information.

There are many companies that publish great materials for children. Cricket Magazine publishes an array of great magazines. Additional information can be found on their website (http://www.cricketmag.com). Examples of magazines to purchase or borrow would be some of the following:

- *Appleseeds*, aimed at grades three through five, stimulates students with articles and photographs concerning culture and history.
- *Ask* contains all kinds of invention and science information in each issue that will fascinate grades two through five. This would definitely be a plus for STEM education.
- *Calliope*, a World History magazine for grades five through nine, helps students discover the mysteries of the past, concentrating on places and cultures around the world and throughout time.
- *Click*, concentrating on science for grades kindergarten through second grade, would also be excellent for STEM education.
- *Cobblestone* brings American history alive through primary sources, historical photographs, graphics, and maps.
- *Cricket*, a literary magazine for grades five through nine, features high-quality fiction and nonfiction articles on topics that include stories, poetry, and art.
- *Dig*, travels into the past with archaeologists and historians exploring the mysteries of ancient civilizations through a partnership with many museums.
- *Faces*, which shows how other people live in the world including their food, clothes, and activities, is geared toward grades five through nine.
- *Iguana* has a unique place in this magazine list as it focuses on students in grades two through seven who are Spanish speaking. It contains a wide variety of history, geography, science, technology, language arts, and math materials.
- *Ladybug*, with colorful illustrations and text, will assure that beginning readers will love the information that is contained within its pages.
- *Muse*, aimed at the past, present, and future, concerns history, science, and the arts. The nine New Muses, who are smart alecks, inhabit the margins of the magazine and give each article humor and commentary.
- *Odyssey*, which covers space, technology, environment, the human body, mathematics, and other areas of science, is aimed at grades five through nine.
- *Spider* has stories, poems, and nonfiction articles that are selected to encourage students in grades two through four to read on their own.

Types of Text

The Common Core Standards also state that there are four types of text: procedural, persuasive, expository, and literary nonfiction.

Procedural Texts

Procedural texts are easy to understand when you consider that they tell how to complete a task step-by-step. Books in this area might include a materials needed list and/or graphics showing how to complete a task or to conduct an experiment. Science fair experiment books would fit into this category, such as *Yikes! Wow! Yuck! Fun Experiments for Your First Science Fair* by Elizabeth Snoke Harris (Lark Books, 2008) or a book on creating paper airplanes or a book on origami such as *Easy Origami* by Dokuohtei Nakano (Puffin, 1994).

Argument or Persuasion Texts

Influencing people or changing the reader's belief would fit into this next category of reading. The reader would read these books to help shape his/her own ideas about a specific subject or topic such as global warming or the greenhouse effect. Students need to verify the author's credibility. Several texts that are good examples are *Energy Island: How One Community Harnessed the Wind and Changed the World* by Allan Drummond (Farrar, Straus, and Giroux, 2011) and *Global Warming* by Seymour Simon (HarperCollins, 2013).

Teachers need guidance in this area so that the materials used are not propaganda but legitimate with factual information for both sides of the argument. Guidance also needs to be given to teachers to make them aware of copyright dates, making sure the material is current.

In this age where anyone can publish anything, students will access resources and information that come from a variety of sources. Many of these sources could have a potential slant or angle depending on the author's thoughts and ideas. Instruction and guidance on how to determine for themselves what is useful and valid is crucial. A lesson on using the Internet and verifying sources would be very appropriate to conduct with students.

Expository Text

Expository texts done correctly are great reading material for students. These materials contain diagrams, tables, maps, data tables, indexes, table of contents, and other navigational tools that help direct the reader to the correct areas needed. Students need assistance in learning how to use these devices to make the book usable. Many of Bobbie Kalman's books published by Crabtree Publishers are excellent resources and include an example of these devices. Carefully detailed and labeled diagrams even in younger children's books start students on their journey of understanding the topic that they are pursuing. Various text structures are also utilized, such as description, cause and effect, comparison and contrast, problem and solution, question and answer, and sequencing.

Instruction by teachers and school librarians can be given that might include:

- Reading captions
- Using the table of contents
- Understanding boldfaced words
- Using a glossary
- Using an index
- Scanning material to find a starting place
- Skimming to find specific details
- Reading and interpreting maps, charts, graphs, and diagrams

An example of a lesson incorporating different book terms can be found in chapter 10.

Literary Nonfiction

Literary nonfiction, the closest to narrative fiction and many times written like a story, includes shorter texts like biographies, memoirs, essays, speeches, opinion pieces, informational picture books, or informational poetry. Authors that write well for this area include Seymour Simon, Dianna Hutts Ashton, Steve Jenkins, Lynn Cherry, Candace Fleming, Judith St. George, and Doreen Rappaport. For example, Dianna Hutts Ashton takes the subject seeds and writes *A Seed Is Sleepy* (Chronicle, 2007). Her premise is to write on two levels. An easy level, where the words on each page are larger, read "A seed is sleepy. A seed is secretive, A seed is fruitful." She then draws the reader deeper into the subject by having smaller words on the page that might say, "It lies there tucked inside its flowers, on its cone or beneath the soil. Snug. Still." Her books also include *An Egg Is Quiet* (Chronicle, 2006) and *A Rock Is Lively* (Chronicle, 2012).

Picture book biographies or autobiographies are an easy way to introduce students to literary nonfiction. A book like *Heroine of the Titanic* by Joan Blos (HarperCollins, 1991) intrigues a student into wanting to pursue more information about the *Titanic*, for example. This coupled with *Titanic; Voices from the Disaster* by Deborah Hopkinson (Scholastic, 2012) and *All Stations Distress! April 15, 1912: The Day the Titanic Sank* by Don Brown (Roaring Book Press, 2008) is a great combination for a study of the *Titanic*. Examining additional topics can create other combinations.

Informational poetry falls into this category. Several poets have outstanding books in this area, such as Douglas Florian, whose books *Poetrees* (Beach Lane Books, 2010) or *UnBEElievables* (Beach Lane Books, 2012) are excellent examples of poetry that weave facts into poems. *Ubiquitous: Poetry and Science about Nature's Survivors* by Joyce Sidman (Houghton Mifflin, 2010) includes poems in a variety of forms along with expository informational paragraphs about life-forms on our planet.

Informational alphabet books and counting books would also be useful because they allow authors to use a creative format to impart factual knowledge. *H Is for Hoosier* by Catherine Furlong Reynolds (Sleeping Bear Press, 2001) takes students on a trip through Indiana with factual information. This publisher has addressed all fifty states plus various other subjects (sports, habitats, countries) with the same basic alphabet format. Another author, Jerry Pallotta, uses the same strategies of writing alphabet books about a variety of topics such as dinosaurs, vegetables, jet planes, bugs, and reptiles. *The Butterfly Book* (Charlesbridge, 1995) is one example. The Declaration of Independence is covered in a book entitled *The Declaration of Independence from A to Z* by Catherine Osornio (Pelican Publishing, 2010). This book breaks the Declaration of Independence down into chunks to understand it better and conveys incidents to help students understand the time period. In appendix A, you will discover more examples of books to use for literary nonfiction. The bibliography is broken into broad subject areas to help the reader of this book find information that will assist in teaching the Common Core Standards.

Time Spent Reading

To emphasize the time to be spent in this area, the Common Core State Standards state that fourth graders should spend one half of their time reading informational text.

As you progress through the grades, additional focus is put onto informational text. Also realize that often students have limited exposure to this type of material through their classroom libraries, teacher read-alouds, basal texts, and teacher-guided instruction. As school librarians examine materials, it should always be foremost in our minds how to share these materials with our teachers and students. Creating bibliographies, sharing titles through e-mail, booktalking at teachers' meetings or grade-level meetings should become everyday occurrences if school librarians hope to make an impact on teachers' book selections. If school librarians are not actively recommending, sharing, and pushing books, teachers are going to choose books from a publisher's booklist as exemplary texts.

School librarians and teachers can create a plethora of lessons addressing these areas, which could include:

- Choosing "just right" books
- Deciding when to abandon a book
- Organizing book clubs—discussing books with others
- Comparing two characters
- Inferring or making inferences from the text
- Working on themes
- Reading aloud

Comprehension

Many students do love to read informational text more than fiction, but struggle with comprehension because of the reading difficulty of the material. As the Common Core Standards address these issues, teachers must realize that overemphasizing this area is not good either because students still need to develop the love of reading, which is not addressed by the Common Core. This has been a major criticism by educators who have not embraced the Common Core Standards. School librarians can guide teachers in making wise decisions with carefully selected trade books to fulfill the need for good reading material to encourage reading for pleasure and to build a lifelong habit.

A focus on text complexity is the hallmark of the CCSS. The standards focus is on developing students' reading skills so that they will be able to read grade-level specific text independently and proficiently. The road to get there is not established, but educators would be wise to hold discussions on a plan to have all students comprehend grade-level text. An additional focus of the CCSS is higher-level thinking skills.

To be college and career ready, students must be able to read and comprehend all types of texts and materials. Reading over the instructions on how to assemble a piece of furniture shows a "real world" application for the Common Core State Standards. The fear has been that students are not challenged or encouraged enough to accomplish this task and understand the reading they must do for a job or in an occupation.

Reading Standards/Reading Anchors

The Common Core emphasizes four reading standards and ten reading anchor standards. Below you will find an overview of these with several examples.

Key Ideas and Details (Anchor Standards 1–3)

Students must be able to read closely to determine what the text says and to make logical inferences from it. This requires them also to be able to write and speak in support of their conclusions. Central ideas and themes of a text must also be determined and proven by facts found in what they have read. Students must be taught to look closely at a text (literary or informational) to determine what the author means.

As the language arts standards are examined, notice that each grade level builds upon the previous level. First graders must "ask and answer questions about key details in a text (R1.1.1), while second graders expand upon this by "asking and answering questions as who, what, where, when, why, and how to demonstrate understanding of key details in a text" (R1.2.1). As third graders, they will "ask and answer questions referring explicitly to the text" (R1.3.2). Fourth grade students will "refer to details and examples in a text" and "draw inferences" (R1.4.1). Skills are expanded as they progress into fifth grade and students will "quote accurately from the text while drawing inferences" (R1.5.1).

Craft and Structure (Anchor Standards 4–6)

This set of anchor standards asks students to interpret words and phrases along with analyzing the structure of a text and examining the point of view and purpose of a text. School librarians will find books such as *Diary of a Spider* by Doreen Cronin (Joanna Cotler Books, 2005), *Diary of a Wombat* by Jackie French (Clarion, 2003), or *Letters from LaRue* by Mark Teague (Scholastic, 2002) fit the bill as examples showing point of view.

Integration of Knowledge and Ideas (Anchor Standards 7–9)

Synthesizing of information with more than one text is a key component of these anchor standards. Students will be expected to take two titles and compare and contrast the information that they find. An example of this might be during a study of George Washington using the book *Big George: How a Shy Boy Became President* by Anne Rockwell (Harcourt, 2009) combined with *Farmer George Plants a Nation* by Peggy Thomas (Boyd Mills Press, 2008). Both of these books examine Washington at different times of his life. Using a book *A Picture Book of George Washington* by David Adler (Holiday House, 1990) would anchor the two books together using a timeline that is included in this book. Students need to be directed toward materials from the same author and then branch out to information from different authors, but on the same topic to give different perspectives. Martin Luther King, Jr.'s speech (1963) "I Have a Dream" and President John F. Kennedy's "Civil Rights Address" (1963) would be another example of different perspectives on the same topic (www.loc.gov).

Range of Reading and Level of Text Complexity (Anchor Standard 10)

This anchor expects students to "read and comprehend complex literary and informational texts independently and proficiently." This is where it is important that teachers and school librarians explain to students how important it is to slow down while reading these types of texts. To read and understand informational text well is different than reading a fiction book. A student might be able to quickly read this material, but their comprehension level would not be what it should be. School librarians also must realize that students will struggle to comprehend informational text because of a lack of exposure to this material and their inability to comprehend. Students need much more practice to be proficient in this area.

Reading materials online would fall under this category as this is different reading than reading a book. Students need to be taught not only how to read online, but how to locate information easily. Even though students seem to be technologically literate at a younger age, they need assistance in comprehending and locating information in online sources. Students searching for information independently sometimes develop bad habits, so the wise educator should teach them to search efficiently in reputable areas.

Librarians with online reference sources find it necessary to spend time instructing students how to locate information on specific sites. Skimming, noticing boldface words, determining links and other online peculiarities will need to be taught.

Close Reading

Becoming familiar with the terminology *close reading* would also benefit school librarians. Close reading means reading to uncover layers of meaning that will lead to deep comprehension. Students must be encouraged to read thoroughly and methodically. This will enable them to reflect not only on the meaning of individual words, but the order of sentences, and finally the development of ideas, which hopefully leads to understanding text.

The Common Core Standards suggest traditional kinds of literature such as folktales, legends, myths, fables, poetry, and scenes from plays to use for close reading. Couple these with informational texts like short articles, biographies, personal narratives, and short, easier primary source material like Martin Luther King, Jr.'s "I Have a Dream" speech or the preamble to the Constitution. Close reading also asks students to look at imagery using similes, metaphors, personification, figurative language, word choice, tone, and voice.

As you can see school librarians have a wonderful opportunity to not only recommend materials for the teacher to use to teach these components, but to use the books themselves in collaborative instructional units that will help fortify specific skills. Using books like *Owl Moon* by Jane Yolen (Philomel, 1987) or *Baby Whale's Journey* by Jonathan London (Chronicle, 1999) to teach similes and metaphors is a wonderful lesson. Challenge students to find other books to fortify these concepts. Students, depending on age, could be provided books to find examples or be challenged to search for additional books themselves.

Close reading is a skill that takes time to teach. Students are not accustomed to having to "prove" their answer in language arts as they are in math. Nothing is more frustrating than talking with a student who cannot go back and prove where they found their answer. Close reading emphasizes this skill.

When planning strategies to introduce students and teachers to informational text, make sure that teachers realize that students must read entire books, not just excerpts or passages from informational text. Students cannot be college and career ready unless they read entire books. School librarians realize that there are numerous books on fascinating topics, books that are skillfully written and well researched with outstanding visual elements available to put into students' hands.

Graphics

Although it seems as if most of our time is focused on the written word, school librarians need to be aware that in informational text, graphics should not be underestimated. Graphics provide an alternate route when reading informational materials. Graphics not only help the struggling student understand the written word, but they push good students into deeper thinking about the subject they are reading.

Graphics can also explain more than the written word. Maps, graphs, and diagrams are prime examples of this. For example, take a book about tornadoes. If it contains maps showing what states have the most tornadoes, followed by a map of the United States showing Tornado Alley, it gives the student access to information that is not conveyed within the text. Using graphics will also assist the struggling reader. Graphics will help the student focus on the information being conveyed instead of a long passage of text.

Photographs in books also assist the reader in understanding in addition to just reading about it. In his book entitled *Lizards* (Scholastic, 2010), Nic Bishop takes photographs of the different lizards he describes. The close-ups of the animals are amazing. The statement "a photograph is worth 1,000 words" can be used while examining his books, which include *Frogs* (Scholastic, 2008), *Marsupials* (Scholastic, 2009), and *Snakes* (Scholastic, 2012).

Students need to be taught how to use and read graphics in different formats. Sidebars, inserts, and captions all play a part in extending the written text in a book. Give students time to examine a graphic. Ask them what they see. Lead them into examining it for a longer period of time after reading the caption below a picture. Discuss what a caption does for a picture versus a picture without a caption. Be sure that students are comprehending the graphics instead of just looking at them. Teaching them to see the importance of graphics and reading the graphics to understand the text is a skill that will take them far in their reading journey. Included in chapter 10 is a lesson plan on parts of a book and being able to identify a variety of graphics within a book.

Graphic Inquiry by Annette Lamb and Daniel Callison (Libraries Unlimited, 2012) addresses many of the ideas and problems of using graphics. Throughout the book, they give ideas, suggestions, and illustrations of what can be done using graphics. There is an extensive bibliography to pursue plus a variety of websites and examples throughout the publication. They also pose the problem of how illustrations and graphics or visual literacy have not been fully explored in the information inquiry maze.

In this day of digital photographs, students need to understand how hard it is to get the pictures that are in books. Nic Bishop is a prime example of the difficulty of taking pictures and the inordinate amount of time it takes. In his book on lizards, he relates that the basilisk lizard (Jesus lizard) walks on water, but he was hard-pressed to actually photograph it since the lizard did not want to walk on water in the pool he built in his garage. He puzzled over whether the lizard did not like being moved from the house into the garage to the pool, so although it took him many weeks, he built a pond inside the house. Much to his delight, the basilisk "buzzed across the water surface like a speedboat" the first time he picked him up. It had taken two months and now he was finally able to take the pictures that he needed. In another example he was driving in Australia looking for the elusive thorny devil. He drove for days and hundreds of mile searching when suddenly he found one beside the road staring at him! With information such as this in his book, he has captured the reader's attention, with not only words, but also with pictures.

Capacity, Stamina, Reading Aloud

As school librarians look at informational text in the primary and intermediate grades, they should be recommending high-quality literature to teachers to engage students, to expose them to rich vocabulary, and to help give them insights and ideas that they may not be able to comprehend on their own. Teachers who read only excerpts from textbooks to their students do not help students read better or independently. Reading aloud text that the students may not be able to read by themselves helps build their vocabulary.

However, many teachers confess to not reading informational text because they don't know where or how to find good examples, they don't feel confident in reading it to their students, and they are not sure how to have students respond to what they hear. What a fantastic opportunity for a school librarian to assist teachers in locating and modeling good techniques of reading aloud and suggesting activities to respond to the text!

Just as we look for hooks to engage students in listening to fiction, we must look for hooks in engaging informational text. Sometimes the title will pull the student into reading the book, such as *How They Croaked; The Awful Ends of the Awfully Famous* by Georgia Bragg (Walker, 2011). Sometimes the enticing photographs or diagrams will excite a student. Oftentimes it might be the first paragraph that catches the student when they open the book. *The Man That Walked between the Towers* by Mordicai Gerstein (Roaring Book Press, 2003) begins "Once there were two towers side by side. They were each a quarter of a mile high; one thousand three hundred and forty feet. The tallest buildings in New York City." Whatever it might be, the school librarian must be attuned to the books, the students, and the interest level of the material to bring them all together to satisfy the reluctant reader.

Also when reading informational text, the realization comes that many times the text might be filled with unfamiliar academic or content-specific vocabulary. Choose informational text that might have some new vocabulary, but not so much as to cause a person to stop every two minutes to explain. The beauty of nonfiction text is that you do not necessarily have to read the entire book as you do with a novel. Reading a selection that is well crafted works. The school librarian can compile lists of excellent reading materials in different subject areas to recommend to teachers. Examining the books in appendix A will give many suggestions to begin your search for exemplary examples.

Another area that school librarians should focus on is capacity and stamina. Stamina is the ability to read for long periods of time without getting distracted or distracting others. School librarians know that students in the lower grades may be able to read words; however, they lack the stamina, or the ability or willingness to keep on reading when the task is hard or long. School librarians have seen this with students who check out books and bring them back within a short period of time. When asked if they have read the book, they might answer "No, it was too long" or "No, it was too hard" or "No, it didn't interest me." These are students who cannot stay with reading a book because the length of the text stops them. School librarians can assist teachers in finding "just right" books for students like this and encourage them to stick with the book instead of returning it. Teachers need to have many books in their classrooms on interesting topics to assist students in finding something in which they are interested. The more books that the school librarian can give to the teacher to have available in the classroom, the more the students will choose to read. Rotating classroom libraries with a wide variety of books and topics engages the students in reading more.

For example, consider putting together tubs of paperback books to be loaned to the classrooms. Organizing them by genres, authors, subject areas, or just a variety of topics would give students a wide selection of avenues to choose. Teachers could come down and check out the tubs to supplement their classroom libraries. This would give a rotating selection of materials that were always available to those students that complain that they didn't have a book to read. Books could come from paperback copies from book fairs, donations, additional copies from state reading lists, etc. It provides teachers with a variety of materials for their classroom collection.

Silent reading time is a concept that should be addressed by the teacher and the school librarian. As the students go into second grade, the ratio of silent to oral reading should increase. Silent reading habits need to be modeled by the teacher and the school librarian so that the students realize what a focused silent reading period should look like. Just as a basketball player needs to practice his skills, students need to practice their reading habits or they will never become proficient. Students need to have opportunities to read widely to not only develop new ideas, but to increase vocabulary, background knowledge, and fluency. Teachers and administrators must come to understand that silent reading time is just as important as direct instruction if the student is expected to develop stamina in reading.

Writing and the Common Core

The school librarian must also focus on writing. Good literature whether it be fiction or nonfiction emulates the skills that students need to acquire. Authors of these texts model specific styles and techniques to show command of the written word. They connect with and hook readers as well as explain important concepts.

In the area of writing, the Common Core states three writing areas that are important. These are opinion pieces, information/experiences pieces, and narrative writing. Again, school librarians have excellent examples of this writing on the shelves ready to utilize. The table below helps to see what examples you might use.

Figure 4.1 Areas of Writing in CCSS

Opinion Pieces	Letters, responses to reading, book reviews, editorials, essays
Information/Expository	Informational books, videos, manuals, instructions
Narrative	Fictional stories, memoirs, biographies, autobiographies

School librarians also find that they are already teaching lessons to target examples of author's writing styles. These could include lessons on:

- studying authors and writing styles
- studying authors and opinion writing
- studying examples of authors who write narratives
- studying poets and poetry writing
- studying authors and where they get their ideas
- studying pattern writing in books, such as repetition, rhyming
- studying authors and use of voice in books
- studying introductions of books and how they entice readers
- studying how authors conclude their books

TeachingBooks.net is an awesome subscription website that assists in teaching these skills. It not only shows examples for students, but gives an abundance of lesson plans and ideas for educators to use.

Writing styles is an area that will entice students to read more just as it does for an adult reader. Writing styles can include areas such as strong introductions, sentence structure, figurative language, and strong conclusions. Now let's examine some examples of writing styles to introduce to students to motivate their reading habits.

Writing Styles

Strong Introductions

Just as school librarians show students how to find fiction books that "grab" a reader, they can also show students nonfiction books with introductions that "grab and excite readers" to read further into the book. Readers must feel a connection to the subject before they want to read further. Locate authors who help readers "see" from the beginning what is happening. Jean Fritz's biography on Paul Revere entitled *And Then What Happened Paul Revere?* (Coward, 1973) pulls the reader immediately into a typical day in Boston when she says, "In 1735 there were in Boston 42 streets, 36 lanes, 22 alleys, 1,000 brick homes, 2,200 wooden houses, 12 churches, 4 schools, 418 horses (at the last count), and so many dogs that a law was passed prohibiting people from having dogs that were more than 10 inches high. But it was difficult to keep dogs from growing more than 10 inches and few people cared to part with their 11- and 12-inch dogs, so they paid little attention to the law. In any case there were too many dogs to count." Additional books by Fritz are *Why Don't You Get a Horse, Sam Adams?* (1996), *Why Can't You Make Them Behave, King George?* (1996), and *Will You Sign Here, John Hancock?* (1997). With these books a fantastic study of the American Revolution can be accomplished simply by focusing on people that were key components of the rebellion of the colonists. Literacy circles can be formed within a classroom or groups of students can jigsaw and explain what is happening in their books.

Jim Murphy is another nonfiction author who will keep students reading; he portrays Philadelphia in 1793 with *An American Plague: The True and Terrifying Story of the Yellow Fever Epidemic of 1793* (Clarion, 2003). Written in a diary format, it begins, "Saturday, August 3, 1793. The sun came up, as it had every day since the end of May, bright, hot, and unrelenting. The swamps and marshes south of Philadelphia had already lost a great deal of water to the intense heat, while the Delaware and Schuylkill Rivers had receded to reveal long stretches of their muddy, root-choked banks. Dead fish and gooey vegetable matter were exposed and rotted, while swarms of insects droned in the heavy, humid air." This book can easily be paired with Laurie Halse Anderson's *Fever, 1793* (Aladdin, 2002), to entice students into discovering what it was like to live during this time. Anderson's book dovetails perfectly with Murphy's because it begins on August 16, 1793, and says, "I woke to the sound of a mosquito whining in my left ear and mother screeching in the right. Rouse yourself this instant!" The information in Murphy's book gives great background for students to be able to understand the fictional account that Anderson writes about in her book. Additional books that Jim Murphy has written are included in appendix A.

Richard Peck has some of the best opening lines in novels. He is a master at bringing a reader into a book. His opening in *The Teacher's Funeral* (Dial, 2004) has students clamoring to read more. The first line reads "If your teacher has to die, August isn't a bad time of year for it." Mentioning the words teacher, death, and August all in the same sentence is enticing for anyone who is not a big fan of school. In chapter 10, a lesson plan dealing with beginning paragraphs is included.

Varying Sentence Structure

Students must be shown how sentence length and structure needs to be changed. Students even at the youngest ages need to hear good literature being read and then be able to turn their own writing into the same structure. Books such as Mo Willems's Elephant and Piggy books can start students thinking of the interaction between characters, but longer and more fluent, rich writing needs to be shared.

If students do not see and hear expert writers, they will have a difficult time writing anything except short, choppy, boring sentences. Just as adults read aloud with expression in their voices, adults must also model writing in the same way. When modeling writing for students, write like an adult would write or else students will not see the need to use interesting sentence structure. Students must hear the thinking process happening as an adult writes.

Seymour Simon, who has the writing craft down well, shows in his books that sentences must vary in length to be interesting. An example from his book *The Heart* (Morrow, 1996) reads "Make a fist. This is about the size of your heart. Sixty to one hundred times every minute your heart muscles squeeze together and push blood around your body through tubes called blood vessels. Try squeezing a rubber ball with your hand. Squeeze it hard once a second. Your hand will get tired in a minute or two. Yet your heart beats every second of every day." The sentences of varied length drive home the point of what a heart does as it beats. The author could have just told us that the heart beats so many times per minute, but he vividly shows us the size of the heart compared to something that students know (the fist) and then demonstrates how it beats with an additional concept that is familiar (the rubber ball).

Similes and Metaphors

These two forms of writing are not just for fiction, but also play a huge part if done well in informational text. Seymour Simon also uses this technique frequently in his books as he explains concepts about the world and the universe. *The Eyes of the Gray Wolf* by Jonathan London (Chronicle, 1993) works with metaphors as the author writes "Gray Wolf stands alone and stares. His eyes burn like steady flames," and a little further he relates this as the wolves see each other again: "Even the trees seem to hold their breath."

Jane Yolen in her book *Owl Moon* (Philomel, 1987) uses both metaphors and similes as she describes a young boy and his father venturing out on a snowy night to observe owls. Another author to use for great examples of similes is Hanoch Piven. Her books *My Best Friend Is as Sharp as a Pencil* (Random, 2010) and *My Dog Is as Smelly as Dirty Socks* (Random, 2007) are completely filled with similes. *Crazy Like a Fox; A Simile Story* by Loreen Leedy (Holiday, 2008) is another good example of a book filled with similes. Students will need practice as they absorb these books and try to write examples of their own.

Vocabulary

Expanding vocabulary development is also important. School librarians can find themselves encouraging vocabulary development by creating vocabulary lists, having a word of the day posted in the school library and on the website, and various other ideas. Picture book use is heavy in elementary schools to encourage background knowledge and can be utilized for vocabulary development also. Books with rich language include *Fancy Nancy's Favorite Fancy Words* by Jane O'Connor (HarperCollins, 2008). This particular book is used in kindergarten to show students what a variety of words there are available to be used. Creating lists of vocabulary words from novels, picture books, or nonfiction text the teacher uses is one idea to create and expand vocabulary.

Vocabulary also includes using academic vocabulary with the students. Words such as analyze, topic, compare, contrast, and interpret are all words that can be used in all subject areas. Being consistent with vocabulary across the grade levels helps to develop the understanding all students need as high-stakes testing evolves.

Jane Yolen's *Welcome to the River of Grass* (Putnam, 2001) uses rich language to describe the Everglades when she writes, "Tree islands hump up over the grass, clump up into hummocky hammocks covered with vines: live oak, myrsine, pigeon plum-making green clouds of trees crowding the horizon. Islands of cabbage palm, willows, formed on top of rotting peat pillows." Teachers can spend time dissecting the unfamiliar words with students while discussing the picture that is being formed in the reader's mind.

Alliteration and Onomatopoeia

Having fun with language is what writing is all about, and good writers use these two forms in both narrative and informational text. The repetition of the text is what draws listeners in as a teacher reads aloud. April Pulley Sayre does this well in many of her nonfiction books. *Go, Go Grapes! A Fruit Chant* (Beach Lane Books, 2012) is an example of alliteration: "Blackberries. Blueberries. Bag a bunch. Strawberry season? Let's munch-a-munch!" A lesson plan is included for this book and her book *Rah, Rah, Radishes!; A Vegetable Chant* (Beach Lane Books, 2011) in chapter 8. *Ant, Ant, Ant, an Insect Chant* (NorthWord Books, 2005) is also an excellent example of the use of alliteration as she goes through name after name of insects with no explanation, just drawings. This book can be taken to a higher level as students examine insects and conduct research.

Additional books that are great to use for onomatopoeia are *Rattletrap Car* by Phyllis Root (Candlewick Press, 2001), *Red Sled* by Lita Judge (Atheneum, 2011), *Slop Goes the Soup* by Pamela Duncan Edwards (Hyperion, 2001), and *Roller Coaster* by Marla Frazee (Houghton, 2006). All of these are great fun to use with students to demonstrate sound words. Making their own sound word books, students could demonstrate their understanding of onomatopoeia. Additional books featuring alliteration and onomatopoeia can be found in appendix A.

Strong Conclusions

Conclusions that are clear and concise do more than just finish the book. They can motivate the reader into going out and doing something on their own, motivate the reader into wanting to learn more on a topic, or help the student wonder what conclusions might be formed by what they have read. For example, students who read *The One and Only Ivan* by Katherine Applegate (HarperCollins, 2012) may want to go beyond the fiction title and learn more by reading about gorillas or searching online to read about the real Ivan (http://theoneandonlyivan.com). After reading *Ghost Soldier* by Elaine Marie Alphin (Henry Holt, 2001), students could delve into informational books on the Civil War.

Readers/students must be able to understand and appreciate the author's means of conveying the knowledge they are seeking. The more the student is exposed to good informational books, the better educated the student becomes. School librarians are in a position to understand and be familiar with the literature to help guide teachers into making wise decisions in what to share with students. Left on their own teachers may gravitate to nonfiction books with straight facts. As school librarians, one must share with teachers the knowledge of well-written informational text that will showcase a writer's craft in nonfiction with rich language. All of the above elements are important to share with students as well as teachers in the walk toward better literacy and satisfying the Common Core State Standards.

Primary Sources

As lessons are being created after examining the Common Core Standards, teachers and librarians need to focus on and address primary sources in their lesson planning.

Although states might have used primary source documents in their original standards, teachers might not realize how much easier finding primary documents can be using the Internet. The Library of Congress's website (www.loc.gov) and its American Memory website (http://memory.loc.gov/ammem/index.ht) put primary documents literally at one's fingertips. Again, school librarians can take the lead in identifying, searching, and instructing students and staff in finding and using these sites to locate the documents they need. As a teacher and school librarian sit down to collaborate, the teacher brings to the table the topic or area they want to use. The school librarian can then demonstrate where to find the material. At this point, the two collaborators can decide if they want to print materials to use or whether the goal is for the student to find the material themselves on the above websites.

Teachers may not realize what a rich and easily accessible repository of primary sources the Library of Congress has become. When examining the Library of Congress webpage, there is a teacher link on the opening page in the middle that will lead to teacher resources, a newsletter to provide current ideas (*TPS Journal*), and a link to already created lesson plans tied to primary source documents. On the teacher page you will also notice that there is a search by Common Core Standards or by individual state standards and then by grade level in a drop-down menu. A link for professional development is also available.

With the link entitled Using Primary Sources an abundance of ideas can be generated on using primary sources in the classroom. The links found there show an analysis document for primary sources, how to create citations, and copyright of primary documents. All in all this site is a treasure trove of information. One more item that is important about this site is the link at the top of the page that is entitled Ask a Librarian. If you can't find the answer or are confused about where to go, click on this button and ask any question you want. A librarian will answer within five days. Several of the areas also have chat rooms to have questions answered immediately.

The Library of Congress also offers a weeklong institute in Washington, D.C., for educators each summer. This institute, presented four to five times during June and July, gives educators a hands-on experience on locating and using sources, demonstrates how to create lessons, and offers insight into other sources and materials at the Library, along with requiring the educator to create an original lesson plan and present it to their fellow workshop participants. This allows other educators to give valuable feedback on missing pieces in the plan plus allows access to twenty-nine additional lesson plans from fellow classmates. Besides developing a lesson plan, learning how to find resources, and becoming familiar with the Library of Congress website and its physical building, the workshop also creates a small PLN with other educators around the country. To find out how to apply for this wonderful learning opportunity, go to www.loc.gov/teachers/professionaldevelopment/teacherinstitute and see if this would be an avenue you might like to pursue. Learning to use primary source documents with students and teachers is a life skill for college and career readiness.

Inquiry

The Common Core Standards emphasize the connection between informational text and inquiry learning. Students will take high-level nonfictional text, and not only read it, but evaluate it, synthesize it, and turn that information into a new product. While inquiry should not be new to the librarian, it is possible that this concept isn't known or understood by the classroom teacher.

Inquiry can often be messy, and teachers aren't always sure that they are able to get in all of their standards and instruction when taking time for a project. But Common Core assessments from both PARCC and Smarter Balance have said these projects will be part of the assessment. Librarians have long been advocating for this type of learning, so this may be a huge boon to the school library program.

Teachers will need to design projects that allow students to take part of a subject or concept and explore it on their own. Using nonfictional text and other resources in order to come to their own conclusions will be a huge part of this piece. Students will be expected to use creative ways to share what they learned with their peers, incorporating their own thoughts created while pursuing the topic.

What Is Inquiry?

Inquiry is more than just the research portion that many of us think of when students come to the library. Although students need to realize and understand how to go about finding answers to low-level questions, true inquiry is much more than regurgitation of facts.

Inquiry requires students to seek deep understanding through their research. Inquiry assists students in becoming successful in research and in using differing media formats on the way to understanding the concepts required in the CCSS. Today, students want the fast, easy answer to their questions. When working with inquiry fast and easy is not the process that needs to be undertaken. Inquiry requires the student to continue questioning as they delve into the subject they have chosen. The answers they find must be arrived at from multiple sources and combined into meaningful understanding. This can be accomplished in multiple ways. A student needs to be encouraged by the school librarian and teacher through modeling, coaching, and direct instruction. Another important component during inquiry is having the teacher and school librarian meet with students to discover where they are in the process. In fact, this might be one of the most important points that can happen as this can be the catalyst for the student to keep searching and asking questions.

Too many times school librarians see students stop at a very superficial level when participating in research. If the questions can be answered easily then true inquiry is not happening and revamping of the topic might be needed. Discussion of the topics also needs to be done throughout the process. Meeting with students individually gives them the opportunity to articulate what they might be searching for and gives the educator a chance to probe the student to see if the understanding is there for the student to keep questioning. This takes practice for both the educator and the student. The school librarian is a perfect candidate to meet with students to determine where they are in their inquiry process. Suggestions can be given, additional ideas can be pursued, and both parties can participate in meaningful dialogue on the topic.

True inquiry also is taking the information that is found and turning it into more than just a report. It could be taking information about an animal (description, habitat, food) and showing how all of those components work together to determine how an animal adapts to the area in which they live. It could be comparing and contrasting two animals that live in the same habitat and how they coexist. Many teachers do not realize that this is the true meaning of inquiry.

Inquiry is the basis for many of our collaborative projects, so this is another logical connection where the school librarian and classroom teacher can sit down and plan together. What mini lessons are students going to need before beginning such a project? What kind of resources are available? What kind of additional resources are needed? How do school librarians want to instruct students throughout this process? How do school librarians want to divide up instruction? What kind of assessments are needed? How will the librarian and classroom teacher work together to assess the project? From an even larger perspective, how is this set up systematically?

The school librarian should be at the forefront for leading inquiry projects, setting up a systematic process for students to use throughout their experiences in school. That consistent and organized approach will work far better than students learning different procedures and processes every time they change classroom teachers. It truly can be a building-wide change in the concept and thinking that contributes to how teachers view the library program and the instruction it can provide. School librarians must take the lead in working with administrators to make that happen. Make no mistake, teachers will have to change the way they teach as dictated by the inquiry strand in the Common Core State Standards whether librarians are there or not, so this is the perfect opportunity to be ready and willing to be a part of the conversation and the solution.

If librarians work with administrators and administrators see the importance of having a building-wide initiative concerning inquiry, the path to success will be so much easier. Working with individual teachers or even grade levels can be a time-consuming endeavor for the school librarian to undertake. It can also be a losing battle if every teacher does not buy into this approach. Working one-on-one with teachers takes a very long time, especially in a large school. Making sure the administration understands and encourages teachers to work collaboratively with the librarian will make this a win-win situation. Mini lessons on some of the topics needed to succeed would be:

- designing good questions to guide inquiry
- looking for information in all the right places
- taking good notes
- accessing information in different sources
- paraphrasing information
- synthesizing information from several sources
- defining plagiarism
- asking good questions
- creating bibliographies

Project-Based Learning

Project-Based Learning (PBL) is based on students going through an extended process of inquiry. This is in response to a question, problem, or challenge that is presented. Educators plan projects that are rigorous while allowing for some degree of student choice. These projects are eventually assessed to assist students in learning key academic content; practicing twenty-first century skills such as collaboration, communication, and critical thinking; and creating authentic products and presentations. Revision, reflection, and presentation to a public audience are also key in project-based learning. For more information examine the website http://www.bie.org/.

For example, students could look for ways to improve their school. Depending on what students think needs improvement, they might come up with

- new ways to communicate
- changes to school rules/procedures
- additional programs such as recycling
- who knows . . . kids come up with amazing ideas!

The research develops from the impact of the changes, including costs as well as how some of these changes would be implemented. Students would need to present their results and ideas to the powers that be to see if they can be successful in getting changes implemented.

The Common Core Standards also call for students to build speaking and presentation skills, to organize and explain their ideas, to use visual aids, and to do this for various contexts and tasks; project-based learning therefore fits in perfectly. School librarians have always felt that these skills were important, but sometimes not ones that were emphasized in the classroom. In project-based learning, students use critical thinking skills, collaboration, and communication, skills that will be used for college and career readiness.

Again, the school librarian can collaborate with teachers to teach students how to develop effective presentations after researching their topics. Many times teachers do not take the time to explain or model presentation skills to students. At even an early grade level, students can be taught how to look at examples of well-done presentations to develop their own. Rubrics can be shared with the students to emphasize the items that are most important. Develop a planning guide to help students focus on the audience, content, organization, and visual components. Plan practice sessions where students have the opportunity to present before a few other students to get feedback on the positives and negatives of their presentation. The school librarian and teacher working together can develop a plan on how this takes place. More importantly, the school librarian can assist teachers at each grade level, giving them valuable feedback on the capability of students at each level so that a gradual, age-appropriate pace can be established over the years. This insight into each grade level is one of the most important components that can develop out of this marriage. The teacher and the school librarian will come to realize that this will be a key strategy for achieving the goals of the Common Core Standards. Project-based learning builds speaking skills along with thinking and application skills in whatever subject area the project is addressing.

Push Down to Younger Students

As has been a trend recently, the Common Core continues to push down standards to younger grades. The Common Core Standards were designed by looking at what students needed to know to be college and career ready at the end of twelve grades and then worked backward. This pushed down many standards from older grades to younger grades. The end result is that teachers will need to examine units of study and modify them (or even completely revise them) to include these new, more rigorous standards in their teaching.

For example, persuasive writing, which has been an area handled at the older grade levels, now drops down to a kindergarten and first-grade level. Examples of materials and/or books might need to be shared with students to get an idea of what this type of project should look like.

In a first-grade classroom a lesson on persuasive writing might develop this way. The school librarian reads the book *Can I Keep Him?* by Steven Kellogg (Dial, 1972) to the students. In this book a young boy keeps asking his mom for a pet. He brings home a different animal every day, but his mother tells him two to three reasons why he can't keep it. Each day, the boy finds another animal and tells his mother it doesn't have any of the characteristics she tells him he can't have. Finally he brings home a boy his own age, and his mother tells him he can't keep him, but they can be friends.

A variety of pet books can be displayed for the students to choose from. Each student then thinks up reasons why they can keep the pet after examining the books. In this particular lesson, iPads or any other device would work well. This lesson was done using iPads, and each child had to put together three to ten slides persuading their parent to keep the animal. The lesson could also be done using pencil and paper. However, the iPads worked well because the students could include pictures that would also tell the story. For example, one young student had a Labrador retriever and used a close-up of the dog with the words "isn't he lovable?" as a reason to keep him. Another student used a bunny and explained to her mom that "a bunny is soft, a bunny is cute, a bunny eats vegetables and we have those in the house." So with very simple sentences students worked at persuasion in an area that they could comprehend and understand.

How to Locate Great Nonfiction

Throughout this chapter it has been emphasized that there is a vast sea of great nonfiction books. School librarians must be aware of titles and the authors writing this literature. To do this well, school librarians must keep searching for the best. Reading reviews from the following sources is a great way to start.

- *Booklinks* (http://www.booklistonline.com/booklinks). This one is fantastic on linking books and the Common Core State Standards together.
- *Booklist* (www.booklistonline.com)
- *Bulletin of the Center for Children's Books* (bccb.lis.illinois.edu)
- *Library Media Connections* (www.librarymediaconnection.com)
- *Library Sparks* (www.librarysparks.com)
- *School Library Journal* (www.slj.com)
- *School Library Monthly* (www.schoollibrarymonthly.com/)
- The *Horn Book Magazine* (www.hbook.com)
- *VOYA—Voice of Youth Advocates* (www.voyamagazine.com)

However, there are other websites and blogs that will also assist in helping to select the best of the best in nonfiction writing. Try one of the following:

- Reading Rants: Out of the Ordinary Teen Booklists (www.readinggrants.org)
- Nonfiction Booktalker (blog written by Kathleen Baxter) (www.slj.com/author/kbaxter)
- The Nonfiction Detectives (blog written by two librarians, Louise Capizzo and Cathy Potter) (www.nonfictiondetectives.com)
- Nonfiction Monday (Bloggers submit reviews of nonfiction books) (http://nonfictionmonday.wordpress.com)
- Nerdy Book Club (nerdybookclub.wordpress.com/)

Last but not least don't forget the following organizations that honor outstanding nonfiction books! You can check the lists for the current year and also those of past years to select books that would fit into your library.

- Robert F. Sibert Informational Book Medal (www.ala.org/alsc/awards-grants/bookmedia/sibertmedal). This honors nonfiction books for children from birth to age fourteen.
- YALSA Award for Excellence in Nonfiction (www.ala.org/alsc/nonfiction-award). This honors the best nonfiction books for readers twelve to eighteen.
- NCTE Orbis Pictus Award for Outstanding Nonfiction for Children (www.ncte.org/awards/orbispicturs). Awarded for excellence in nonfiction writing for children.
- Notable Social Studies Trade Books for Young People (www.socialstudies.org/notable). This is a list from the National Council for Social Studies recommending nonfiction books in social studies for grades K–8.
- Outstanding Science Trade Books for Students K–12 (www.nsta.org/publications/ostb/ostb2013.aspx). These are outstanding trade books for K–12 in the science area that are listed by the National Science Teachers Association and the Children's Book Council.
- The AAAs/Subaru SB&F Prizes for Excellence in Science Books (www.sbfonline.com/Subaru/Pages/PrizesHome.aspx). This award recognizes outstanding science writing and illustration for children and young adults and is given by the American Association for the Advancement of Science.

Another reference that you might want to check is a publication called *A to Zoo: Subject Access to Children's Picture Books* (Libraries Unlimited, 2014). This is a thematic listing of picture books that help in planning units of instruction.

The website TeachingBooks.net was also mentioned earlier in this chapter as an excellent source of links to authors, books, and websites that will lead you to a plethora of information to use as you travel down the road of nonfiction books. This subscription website adds a multimedia dimension to reading experiences with thousands of resources about fiction and nonfiction books that will enliven and enhance the reading experience. It includes meet the author, book guides, lesson plans, Common Core Standards, award winners, and book readings plus many additional resources.

Literacy Isn't Just for English/LA Classes Anymore

Another issue about the Common Core is that emphasis placed on reading and literacy goes beyond the core subjects. While this isn't as much of an issue in an elementary school, it becomes a huge issue in the secondary world. While this book focuses on K–5, it is important to keep note of this concept. Elementary instructors have been incorporating social studies and science texts as part of their literacy instruction for years. As time during the school day is crunched more and more with all of the "extras" to teach, teachers will have no choice but to integrate topics together in order to cover all of the curriculum. Reading also isn't just for the regular classroom either. Art, music, and physical education can all play an integral part in helping our students learn how to read. Resources provided by the school librarian could even open the door to the potential for collaborative planned projects.

Common Core Math Standards

Although we have spent a good deal of time in this chapter discussing the way school librarians impact informational text for the Language Arts standards, we have spent little time discussing the impact of the Math standards. Math has been a topic that school librarians have sometimes avoided as math teachers in the middle school and high school settings seem to have little time for collaboration with the school librarian. However, on the elementary level where the teacher is teaching all subject areas, math should be a little easier to integrate. School librarians on the other hand have found our haven in the language arts area recommending and working with literature and informational text. A greater deal of time, though, should be spent on the math component.

As the Math standards are examined, it is relatively easy to see how books can be integrated. Looking just at first-grade Math standards in the Common Core, the topics of time, shape, adding and subtracting, and measurement are key components. All of these topics lend themselves to books that would assist with these concepts. As the standards are examined at each grade level, these concepts are still key components and additional topics are added, such as money and graphing (grade 2), fractions (grade 3), angles and symmetry (grade 4), volume (grade 5), and statistics and ratios (grade 6). Authors who write math concept books with rich language components can be singled out. Picture books can also be added to the math classroom, providing not only key concepts but enrichment activities to a math lesson.

Teachers who believe that math must be taught strictly out of the math book need to realize that additional books will appeal to students and the concepts that are being taught will stay with them longer. For instance, when large numbers are being taught, a million does not mean a great deal for a child who is struggling to count to 100, but a child reading a book that talks about millions and shows pictures of what a million will look like has a much better chance of understanding this concept. David Schwartz has developed a series of books that would be excellent to use. These include titles such as *Millions to Measure* (HarperCollins, 2002), *If You Made a Million* (HarperCollins, 1994), *How Much Is a Million* (HarperCollins, 2001), and *On beyond a Million*

(HarperCollins, 2002). Another book that would be excellent to use is one called *G Is for Googal* (Tricycle, 1998), a math alphabet book that defines math terms that students need to understand.

Another author who is excellent to use with a variety of math concepts is Stuart Murphy. He has taken math concepts and created readable books about each. For example, the book *Game Time* (HarperCollins, 2000) examines the concept of time and calendar usage. The book *Captain Invincible and the Space Shapes* (HarperCollins, 2001) and *Circus Shapes* (HarperCollins, 1998) both work with shape concepts starting with simple shapes and progressing to three-dimensional shapes. Combine these with the book *Shapes* by Lois Ehlert and a powerful lesson can be created. Check out the lesson plan in chapter 6 dealing with shapes. Teachers would do well examining all of Stuart Murphy's books to see how they can be incorporated into their math lessons. The school librarian who is aware of the concepts in his books could team with a classroom teacher to introduce these to the students to use.

Another author, Cindy Neuschwander, works with the concept of shapes, ratio, and geometric concepts. She has written a series of books about Sir Cumference and his knights of the round table dealing with the above math concepts. So as you can see, there are authors who use a very readable style for teachers and students to access.

Again, it cannot be emphasized enough that the school librarian should be well versed in books and materials that would work well for the teacher in conjunction with the topics covered in the Common Core Standards. Besides covering the topic they are teaching, the teacher is also using the rich language that the Common Core emphasizes throughout the Language Arts standards. Although math may not be a subject area the school librarian has worked with before, this area will blossom with additional ideas as the school librarian searches for "just the right" book for the teacher to use to enhance the concept being taught.

Quality Implementation of Math Standards

The other aspect that needs to be realized when addressing the Mathematics standards is that quality implementation must be grounded in understanding the main core shifts. If educators do not focus on this premise, then time planning implementation of the standards will be spent spinning wheels on alignment on grade levels and where the standards have changed.

The first premise that needs to be understood for the Math standards is that the greatest focus of the Common Core Standards is on fewer topics. In the past the standards were a mile wide, but only an inch deep. The switch is that the standards are now much narrower, but deeper in each of the clustered grade levels. For instance in grades K–2, concepts, skills, and problem solving are emphasized when it is related to addition and subtraction. The same holds true for grades 3–5, but the concepts, skills, and problem solving are now related to multiplication and division. For once educators can throw out some of the material they were shallowly covering year after year and focus more deeply on the topics that need to be mastered at each grade level. This erases the myth that the Common Core is adding additional topics to the curriculum.

The second premise is that there needs to be more linking of topics and thinking across the grade levels. Teachers must understand that the topics introduced need to focus and link all topics to the major work of the grade. In third grade, for example, bar graphs need to be able to aid in solving word problems using addition, subtraction, multiplication, and/or division. The bar graph must demonstrate how this focus works. School librarians can assist in this aspect by locating books that focus on creating bar graphs in an everyday situation. For example, two books concentrating on this concept—*The Best Vacation Ever* by Stuart Murphy (HarperCollins, 1997), which discusses data collection and problem solving skills on where to go on a vacation, and *The Great Graph Contest* by Loreen Leedy (Holiday House, 2006), which focuses on students having a contest to see who can make the best graphs, would work well. Again the teacher is combining math and language arts.

The third premise is that rigor needs to be accomplished by a deep, authentic command of mathematical concepts. Math is not just a series of memorization of facts; students must understand how the facts happen and their importance. Students must understand the basic concept of "why we learn math." If students do not understand why something happens, they are not going to be able to do more than memorize facts and hope that the rules will always hold true.

School librarians can step up to the plate and help teachers understand the shifting of thought when it comes to these standards. By understanding the standards ourselves, school librarians determine what types of materials teachers will find useful and again embed ourselves into their teaching and learning process. The school librarian who can readily hand a teacher a book on bar graphs or symmetry at the right moment will go far in making sure that the teacher will turn to them the next time they need help. The school librarian who can teach a lesson on measurement using tools that can be found in the school library will again be the person whom the teacher will call on when help is needed. Teachers are used to teaching math on their own, but understanding of the above premises will enable them to approach math in a different manner.

Collaboration

Probably no time in history has the door to collaboration been so wide open as with the implementation of the Common Core State Standards. Teachers will dramatically re-create their units of instruction. For many of the topics and standards they'll be teaching, educators will be starting from scratch. To do this well, teachers and librarians need to sit down and discuss collaboration at the beginning of a new topic or concept.

What is collaboration? Let's go back and make sure that everyone understands what true collaboration is in the library setting. Shared creation is one way to look at this endeavor. When two people get together to plan a lesson or a unit and define the responsibilities of each individual they truly collaborate. Usually the people who plan together have the same way of thinking so that as a lesson comes together, they realize that it takes each of them to make this plan work well. Jean Donham, in her book *Enhancing Teaching and Learning: A Leadership Guide for School Librarians* (Neal-Schuman, 2013), suggests what true collaboration means for library media specialists and teachers. She states: "When teachers and library media specialists work together to identify what students need to know about accessing, evaluating, interpreting, and applying information; when they plan how and where these skills will be taught and how they relate to content area learning; when they co-teach so students learn the skills at a time when they need them; and when they assess the students' process as they work with information as well as the end product, they have truly collaborated" (21).

The thing that school librarians like best about collaboration is that with shared goals and vision for a project, a climate of trust, respect, and shared risks also develops. In a collaborative project between a school librarian and a teacher, each of these individuals brings a different set of knowledge skills to the table. The teacher brings an understanding of the students in his classroom along with the content being taught, whereas the librarian brings the understanding of information literacy skills, the best ways to integrate those into the content area, and a vast knowledge of the literature needed.

A definition for collaboration proposed by Toni Buzzeo in her book *Collaborating to Meet Standards: Teacher/Library Media Specialist Partnerships for K–6* (2002) provides a guide for practitioners. It defines collaborative planning "as two or more equal partners who set out to create a unit of study based on content standards in one or more content areas plus information literacy standards, a unit that will be team-designed, team-taught and team-evaluated."

As is typical when building relationships with teachers, the school librarian takes on the larger part of the collaboration process (like 80/20) until eventually the trust is there and the partnership can move to a more 50/50 balance. This is something that develops over time. The idea of working with a classroom teacher and the Common Core Standards brings our knowledge of literature and information literacy skills into the forefront instead of teaching skills in a vacuum.

Kicking in the Door

For librarians, the opportunity to help break down those doors to collaboration is going to fall under two main areas: research and inquiry. This doesn't mean there won't be other options, because school librarians are working with people and that means there are always other ways. But, for the most part, the door can be wedged open when it is known that the school librarian is a willing partner to work with these two huge concepts.

As mentioned earlier in the book, these standards are rich with students using informational text. Teachers are going to search out sources for mentor texts and examples they can use in instruction. An astute librarian will already be ahead of the game, beginning to pull those resources together along with potential ideas for collaborative projects.

Resources/Works Cited

Alberti, Sandra. "Making the Shifts." *Educational Leadership*, December/January 2013, 24–27.

Boss, Suzi. "Are School Librarians Part of Your PBL Dream Team?" *Edutopia*. October 28, 2013. Accessed October 30, 2013, http://www.edutopia.org/blog/school-librarians-part-pbl-team-dream-suzie-boss.

Boyles, Nancy. "Closing in on Close Reading?" *Educational Leadership*, December/January 2013, 36–41.

Buzzeo, Toni. *Collaborating to Meet Standards: Teacher/Library Media Specialist Partnerships for K–6*. Worthington, OH: Linworth, 2002.

Calkins, Lucy, Mary Ehrenworth, and Christopher Lehman. *Pathways to the Common Core: Accelerating Achievement*. Portsmouth, NH: Heinemann, 2012.

Callison, Daniel. "Common Core for Mathematics." *School Library Monthly* 29, no. 5 (February 2013): 21–24.

Corsaro, Julie. "Common Core: It's Not Happening without the Librarian." Blog post. *NovelList Blog*. EBSCO, September 12, 2012. Accessed October 30, 2013, http://www.ebscohost.com/novelist-blog/novelist-article/common-core-its-not-happening-without-the-librarian.

Donham, Jean. *Enhancing Teaching and Learning: A Leadership Guide for School Librarians*. Chicago: ALA Neal Schuman, 2013.

Duke, Nell K. "Starting Out Practices to Use in K–3." *Educational Leadership*, November 2013, 40–44.

Fontichiaro, Kristin. "Nudging toward Inquiry: Re-Envisioning Existing Research Projects." *School Library Monthly* 26, no. 1 (September 2009).

Hallermann, Sara, John Larmer, and John R. Mergendoller. *PBL in the Elementary Grades: Step-by-Step Guidance, Tools and Tips for Standards-Focused K–5 Projects*. Novato, CA: Buck Institute for Education, 2011.

Hiebert, Elfrieda H., and P. David Pearson. "What Happens to the Basics?" *Educational Leadership*, December/January 2013, 49–53

Kaaland, Christie, with input from Jean Littrell-Kwik. *School Library Monthly*, November 2013, 26–29.

Lamb, Annette C., and Daniel Callison. *Graphic Inquiry*. Santa Barbara, CA: Libraries Unlimited, 2012.

Larmer, John, and John R. Mergendoller. "Speaking of Speaking." *Educational Leadership*, December/January 2013, 74–76.

Miller, Donalyn. "The Dazzling World of Nonfiction." *Educational Leadership*, November 2013, 22–27.

Moreillon, Judi, and Susan D. Ballard, eds. *Instructional Partnerships: A Pathway to Leadership*. Chicago: American Association of School Librarians, 2013.

Norman, Rebecca R., and Kathryn L. Roberts. "Not Just Pretty Pictures." *Educational Leadership*, November 2013, 62–65.

Schmidt, William H., and Nathan A. Burroughs. "How the Common Core Boosts Quality and Equality." *Educational Leadership*, December/January 2013, 54–58.

Young, Terrell, and Barbara A. Ward. "Common Core and Informational Texts." *BookLinks*, September 2012, 31–36.

5
Common Core, Professional Development, and Advocacy

One of the biggest concerns for school librarians as they begin this trek with the Common Core Standards is to decide where to start, how to find ideas, and how to connect with others who might have the answers. School librarians must find outlets on their own to make sure that their learning does not stop. In addition, school librarians need to be an active part of providing professional development to teachers. This is a natural leadership role for the school librarian as they build collaborative partnerships with teachers.

Professional Development for the School Librarian

To begin with, each person might want to build their own personal learning network (PLN) to assist them in finding the help they need. Reach out to other school librarians through conferences, social networking outlets, or informal meetings. Webinars, online resources and classes, and blogs are easy ways for the school librarian to learn more about the Common Core and can be done in the comfort of your home. Belonging to local, state, and national organizations is another way to keep abreast of information about the Common Core. Reading the latest educational books and magazines on the topic also will keep you abreast of the news. The following are some suggestions to start examining for information.

Blogs

- Diane Ravitch (for another perspective about Common Core) at http://dianeravitch.net/http://dianeravitch.net/
- Edutopia has a multiple list of blogs to read at http://www.edutopia.org/blogs/tag/common-core-standardshttp://www.edutopia.org/blogs/tag/common-core-standards
- School Improvement Network at http://www.schoolimprovement.com/common-core-360/blog/

- Paige Jaegar at http://librarydoor.blogspot.comhttp://librarydoor.blogspot.com/
- Great Kids Book—Common Core IRL (In Real Libraries) at http://networkedblogs.com/QloiN

Twitter

- @INFOlit4U
- @ccedtech at https://twitter.com/ccedtech
- @WisDPITech at https://twitter.com/WisDPITech
- @ASCD

Facebook Groups to Like

- https://www.facebook.com/CommonCoreMathResources
- https://www.facebook.com/SCCOECommonCore

Pintrest

- http://www.pinterest.com/edutopia/common-core/
- http://www.pinterest.com/officialascd/common-core-state-standards/
- http://www.pinterest.com/esheninger/common-core/

Webinars/Discussion Groups

- edWeb.net—There are several communities and webinars available for free on this site with a variety of topics including Common Core.

In Print

- Check out titles published by ABC-Clio, American Library Association, American Association of School Librarians, Neal-Schuman Publishers, and the Association for Supervision and Curriculum Development.

Conferences

- American Association of School Librarians (every two years in the fall)
- American Library Association (annual each summer is full of programming)
- Association for Supervision and Curriculum Development (ASCD) (annual conference and also quarterly conferences)
- International Society of Technology Educators (ISTE) (annual conference every summer for four days)

The resources above are just some of the many options for learning more about the Common Core State Standards. Opinions cover both sides of the issue, which will give you a variety of perspectives.

A PLN can be a lifeline as you are dealing with new initiatives or searching out new ideas. Face-to-face or virtually the connections a PLN can provide a school librarian are immeasurable. Because school librarians are often the only librarian in our buildings, connecting with others is key. For example, the two authors of this book live in completely different cities and yet keep in touch several times a week sharing the successes and failures of our libraries. Each has borrowed many good ideas from the other, and our conversations led to this book. Everyone needs a person who relates to what you do to have as a sounding board.

Attending conferences is a prime example of a great avenue for professional development. It cannot be emphasized enough that attending conferences not only educates, but enlightens you to new ideas, concepts, and materials, plus energizes and excites by putting life back into you. Attending conferences is like a breath of fresh air when you think you cannot do one more activity. Many school librarians may say that they do not have the opportunity or time to attend, yet it is these conferences that give us a shot of adrenaline for our programs. It is the belief of the authors that attending conferences should be a requirement in our jobs, because without these opportunities, the job becomes stale and lifeless.

State conferences and national conferences for school librarians are fantastic places to acquire new ideas, new concepts, and information on implementation of programs such as Common Core State Standards. However, don't turn down opportunities to attend technology conferences or conferences pertaining to subject areas such as science, social studies, language arts, or math. These conferences give the opportunity to interact with those outside our field of expertise. Better yet, decide to present at a conference. Besides sharing ideas with others, you will also discover others who will interact with you. Both of the authors find it refreshing to attend conferences and also to present. It not only expands our horizons to new materials and ideas, but also allows us to connect and share with others we do not know. Lifelong professional friendships can be established and a virtual PLN can be started.

Professional Development Provided by the School Librarian

After learning about the Common Core requirements, school librarians must not be timid in leading teachers to the areas and materials needed to teach the standards. School librarians can lead seminars or workshops on technology usage, connect students with good books to read, choose the best informational text to study, plan collaborative lessons for researching purposes, and use informational texts.

As you look back over the chapters in this book, articles you've read, or other topics you've learned via your PLN, there is a treasure trove of information a school librarian can share about the Common Core State Standards.

For example, school librarians have ways of finding high-quality "complex texts" that is a key component in the Common Core Standards. One of the concerns that librarians have is that publishers are simply making lists of available titles they think fit the Common Core Standards. School librarians realize it is more difficult to find good quality texts that will engage students and build rigor. Texts of this nature need to be discovered and purchased. Spending time reading reviews and examining books will be crucial for this component.

If you examine appendix B in the Common Core Standards, it identifies titles in grade bands. Many titles are dated and/or out of print. The question school librarians should ask is: who chose these titles? Teachers and administrators are going to assume that these references are the materials that are needed. Students will not be engaged by many of the older choices. This list completely leaves out the expertise school librarians have in finding the texts needed to teach a particular standard well. It is our mission to make sure school librarians step up to the plate and identify titles to demonstrate how teachers can use these to teach the standards. School librarians cannot wait until teachers ask us! Being proactive in this scenario is the most important piece school librarians can provide. Offer short workshops, bibliographies with annotations and applications, and one-on-one guidance to teachers. Make sure administrators are aware and support your efforts. Demonstrating to administrators that school librarians have the expertise and knowledge of literature to guide teachers in conducting great lessons will show us in a most favorable light.

Another avenue might be to look at some of the writing and research standards. There is a great deal of focus on digital resources and using digital tools for sharing student work. What a perfect place for the school librarian to introduce new digital tools and provide ways to integrate these with the classroom curriculum. Many of the professional development opportunities may lead to collaborative projects as teachers may want/need additional support working with their students! You might want to check out appendix F for ideas of apps to share with teachers.

Remember, professional development doesn't have to be a face-to-face workshop. It could be short video clips posted online or e-mailed. It could be a monthly newsletter with a section including titles great for teaching Common Core Standards. It could be a simple e-mail with an idea or a website to use. Better yet, it could be a conversation at the mailboxes with a teacher. All of these are forms of professional development.

After giving information to teachers about a topic, offering your services is the next step. Using digital tools for the first time can intimate even the best instructor. Having two heads working together is an excellent way to begin. You will find if one doesn't know the solution the other person might. It is also less scary to work with another educator when starting with a new format or tool.

Professional development also dovetails perfectly into the next topic of advocacy, because by providing professional development you have an open forum to share the amazing and wonderful activities that are happening in the school library. It is a perfect opportunity to demonstrate what the library and school librarian can offer to ensure that both stay intact.

Common Core and Advocacy

School libraries and librarians have always been near the top of the hierarchy when it comes to discussions about budget cuts. Especially in this technology-rich world in which society lives, administrators and school boards wonder about the necessity of a school librarian, and in some cases even a school library. Obviously school librarians know this to be a bunch of nonsense. The reality is, school librarians and libraries are needed now more than ever.

However, school librarians must also realize that not everyone knows or believes this premise. Each school librarian must be proactive in embracing the Common Core and the role school librarians play in its implementation. With the heavy focus on inquiry, technology tools, and informational text, there are a plethora of places where a school librarian is a critical and vital partner to teachers. Schools where the librarian is a leader are going to succeed in making their students successful with the new standards.

All of us realize that everyone is busy with work, commitments inside and outside of school, and family. Nevertheless, the school librarian must find time to become an advocate for the school library program and the role school librarians play in implementing the Common Core State Standards within the school environment. The school librarian who ignores this crucial aspect of the job may find themselves replaced when the next round of budget cuts occur. Although it seems self-serving to "toot our own horn," it is essential if the position of school librarian is to stay intact. The reality is that it can't be just us being proactive. School librarians have to make sure that students, teachers, and parents have a clear understanding of the position and the job, so they are the ones at the podium fighting for why the school librarian and the school library program is crucial in their school.

Advocacy with Administrators

Advocacy must start with our administrators, because they must be aware that the school librarian is an important component in teaching the Common Core Standards. School librarians need to make sure that they talk directly with administrators to show that they do understand what is needed to help students succeed. Oftentimes the busy administrator is not aware of the role of a school librarian, and so it is up to the school librarian to educate them. Education of administrators is the first step in advocacy for a program. This can be done in a number of different and effective ways.

Communicating through e-mail and memos, sharing bibliographies and articles are ways to share with administrators, especially if you realize they are always busy. One of the most dramatic avenues school librarians can use is through invitations to observe what is happening in the school library with students. Showing instead of telling makes a bigger impact.

Another vital step is sharing with administrators information gleaned from conferences, workshops, or webinars that school librarians might attend concerning Common Core. It is always useful to bring back helpful materials and information; however, this information needs to be shared in either a one-on-one chat or through e-mail or memo. One of the ways to share with administrators is by passing on books or articles that they would be interested in reading, usually with a short note attached. Administrators would be very appreciative of this information and would probably share with the teachers, especially if the information is relevant to discussions or topics at recent meetings or discussions.

Many times school librarians will say, "I don't like to bother my principal" or "I feel like I am tooting my own horn when I tell them I have attended a workshop or conference or telling them I have worked with this teacher or another." However, school librarians have found that if they don't do this, many times it is not known how important the role of a school librarian is, and when it comes time for cuts, it might be your job on the line. Make it a goal to share at least one article or book a month with your administrator. Coordinate the topic with what was discussed at the last teacher's meeting or professional development seminar.

Set up a regular way of communicating with your principal. One colleague set up weekly formal meetings because that worked best. Others made sure to check in periodically. Still others used e-mail or a monthly report-type format. Whatever vehicle you use, the important thing is to try and communicate as best as you can so there is no doubt in the principal's mind as to what is happening in the library. Sharon Coatney, past AASL president, said, "My former library director used to tell me that if I had not had an instructional conversation with my principal that week I was not doing my job."

An annual report is another wonderful tool to use with building and district administrators to recap the activities and teaching components that happened throughout the year. However, it has been proven that most school librarians do not take the time to create an annual report. This report can also show what was accomplished for an entire year. The annual report can be done on paper, through an e-mail or memo, or as a presentation. Any of these means can also be used to share with school board members to advocate for the school library.

Advocacy with Teachers

Just as the authors have discussed earlier in this book how important it is to collaborate with teachers, it is just as important that school librarians lay the groundwork for our collaborative role. Teachers need to be aware of how they can team with school librarians to make teaching easier as implementation of the Common Core Standards take place. School librarians have to realize that even though they think it should be intuitive that our role is important, many teachers do not understand this concept of collaboration. Schools of education do not advocate the school librarian's role to pre-service teachers. Teachers within a school who do not have a school librarian don't realize our crucial role. A school librarian must take a proactive role in demonstrating what they can do. This can be done in various ways.

If you are new in a school, get to know the staff so that they can understand your role. Bibliographies, memos, and e-mails are one approach that you might like to try; however, remember, these paper avenues are ones that people can lay aside and never look at again. Direct contact is a better way. This can be done in a whole group setting, at a teacher's meeting, or during a Professional Learning Committee meeting. One-to-one contact is another avenue, and although more time consuming, it is sometimes the most productive way. Inviting staff into the library will lure many in, especially if the word "food" is mentioned. Books can be shared that would work to address standards. Visiting individual teachers in their rooms is also a powerful avenue. Sharing with them and answering their questions about our role in the Common Core Standards will demonstrate that they have found a willing partner in collaborative projects.

Read the teachers' newsletters to students to be aware of what they are teaching at the moment. Many times you can suggest titles of books or other materials to use. These materials can be routed to the teachers with a note suggesting that they may want to use this material to support their instruction on whatever topic the material might be on. Another good method is to deliver the materials personally and demonstrate how the materials will work with their topic. Use this information as a springboard to suggest a lesson with the class or a way to work together. Using a one-on-one approach makes the teacher feel special and appreciated.

Sometimes it is easier to work with one or two teachers at a grade level to demonstrate what can be accomplished. Let word of mouth spread the information to others! Teachers are always watching what their colleagues are doing. They don't want to be left out, so they think that if one teacher is doing something they might be missing out on an opportunity. Highlight an activity that has gone well in one grade level to other grade levels. This might be done through a monthly newsletter or casually through an e-mail. E-mails sent out weekly to all grade levels is an easy way to share information about what is working for others.

Associations Advocacy

Advocacy by either local librarian associations or national associations is powerful if the information is delivered in a timely manner. First, it is important for the school librarian not only to be familiar with state and national associations for school librarians, but that they become members. It cannot be emphasized enough that there is power in numbers when it comes to advocacy. One person speaking out and endorsing a cause will get little attention; however, an association that has thousands of members will make people sit up and take notice.

School librarians should naturally become a member of their state librarian association. Why? The state association provides information, professional development, and helps its members in a number of different areas and concerns. School librarians are sometimes the only librarian in a school or district and a state organization assists this person in locating information on issues that are important. The state association also can become the lifeline for the lonely school librarian in a district. There is nothing more exhilarating to a person than to be able to discuss topics of interest and concern with a fellow school librarian. Even when not employed within the same district, school librarians can glean valuable information by discussing topics of interest with other school librarians. Being able to pick up a phone or send an e-mail to someone when a question or problem arises is the most comforting feeling to have. Discussing Common Core implementation with others from different schools gives valuable information for your own implementation.

National associations like the American Association of School Librarians and its parent organization the American Library Association often are overlooked because the building level librarian does not understand what they do for the profession on a daily basis. Both of these associations are advocates for the school librarian nationally. They provide the knowledge and expertise to become knowledgeable about a variety of topics including information about Common Core Standards. By checking the websites of these organizations and attending meetings either in person or virtually, information can be obtained that will help in promoting the jobs that school librarians do. These organizations also promote school librarians as leaders in schools. Reading the literature that is published by these associations gives credibility to ideas and actions that school librarians might promote in our own schools. Sharing an article with the administration goes a long way in the advocacy of the profession. Both authors of this book have long been members of their national and state organizations, and while it is an investment of dollars, it has been dollars well spent.

One thing to be clear on is what professional organizations can and can't do in regard to advocacy. Whether at the state or national level, organizations are working to influence policy and legislation that impact school libraries and school librarians. While they certainly do all they can to help at the local level, there are limits to what they can do. They can provide a wealth of tools and knowledge and information that you as the librarian can do at the local level in regard to advocacy. There is always a cry for AASL or a state organization and what they are doing in regard to jobs and positions and budgets. Be assured, they are working on it for you. But, the question to ask back is, "What are you doing for school library advocacy in your own backyard?"

Advocacy with Parents

One group that school librarians sometimes forget when it comes to advocacy and the Common Core are parents (and really it can be the most important group!). According to an Achieve report (2012), 79 percent of regular voters knew "nothing" or "not much" about the Common Core Standards, yet it is an area that many who have children are already seeing since Common Core should be started in kindergarten, and first and second grades. More and more information is coming out about these standards, yet parents know little to nothing about them.

There are many ways to present information to parents. One place to start is by communicating with the PTA or PTO or parent group of the school, always making sure that your administrator knows about it first. After explaining what the Common Core Standards are and how the school librarian is a key component in implementation, the parent group president might ask you to present at a formal meeting for parents. If the group does not have meetings that are well attended, another avenue to examine would be the creation of a pamphlet explaining Common Core and the school librarian's role. Pamphlets are sometimes not read, but these could also be given out at a Back to School or Open House night, during parent-teacher conferences, or any other night that parents would come to the school for meetings or programs. A small presentation planned in the library during a parent night inviting parents in and not only explaining what Common Core is but also showing them materials that will be used in implementing the standards could be done. Booklists or bibliographies of books to share with their children would be appropriate. Websites or databases used might be another resource that could be shared. Although not all parents will be reached, you will make an impression on the ones that attend, and word of mouth always helps publicity. Posting information on social media outlets is an additional way to reach parents with this important information.

Remember, if you do give a small presentation, make it clear, using everyday language and not a series of acronyms and catchy educational phrases. Demonstrate to parents that these standards will help prepare their child for college and the workplace by giving them practice in using informational materials, using higher-order thinking skills, and practicing oral communication skills. Conducting research and making deductions are vital skills that should be emphasized when sharing an overview of the standards. Parents need to realize that educators are working very hard to make sure that all of our students finish high school ready to go onto college or enter the workforce. Actually showing materials and sharing a small lesson plan with parents will help them understand what their child is encountering in school.

Advocacy with Students

Students are the most important element in our endeavor as school librarians implementing the Common Core Standards, yet they are often overlooked when implementation takes place. Even elementary students realize that what is being taught is different than what they were learning before. Middle and high school students see a more in-depth implementation of information. As school librarians emphasize the standards, students can be a strong ally in impressing parents and decision makers that the school library and the school librarian is an important component.

Students must see school librarians as an active force in promoting literature and informational text. If the only job students witness is a school librarian checking out books, shelving books, and ordering materials, they will not understand our teaching role. Students that observe school librarians in the classroom teaming with their classroom teacher or instructing in the library will realize that school librarians are teachers. Observing school librarians instructing and assessing their projects will demonstrate to students that school librarians are teachers, too. Nothing can gain us more recognition then a student seeing us in public and pointing out to their parents that school librarians are their library teachers. This not only validates our existence in the school, but shows that a school librarian has an extremely important role in the student's education.

Advocacy with State Government Officials

Belonging to our state and national associations helps enlighten our government officials on the crucial role that school librarians assume in the school. However, it is the individual person talking, e-mailing, or writing legislators that makes a difference in the end. Elected officials do listen as cards, letters, e-mails, and voice messages flood their office on an issue. (Remember that most of them are all about getting reelected, so they take the voters' thoughts very seriously!) It is the individual that makes the most difference in swaying a legislator's mind. A good example of advocacy toward state legislators is the case of the school librarians in Washington State. It was a group of parents and school librarians who were able to sway legislators' minds on the crucial role of school libraries and librarians in the school. Call legislators, write letters, send pictures of projects, and invite them into the school library to demonstrate what really happens on a day-to-day basis. Many times school librarians talk among themselves about what they do but fail to share the stories and day-to-day operations with the people in charge. These are the people who control the money and make our jobs possible. If school librarians stay hidden or do not show what they do, no one else will take up our cause.

Conclusion

As you can see, school librarians have a job to do! Advocacy is extremely time consuming and has to be repeated over and over. As teaching staff, administration, parents, students, and legislators change, our job of educating a new field of people starts over again. Never take for granted that the public and your patrons know what happens in a school library. Many of them did not have a school library. Some might have had a person who didn't do much more than check out books. Some might have had a school librarian who had the responsibility of multiple schools. Whatever the situation, school librarians have the opportunity to showcase the school library as a vibrant, constantly changing, dynamic environment where students are encouraged to explore the world around them!

Resources/Works Cited

DelGuidice, Margaux, and Rose Luna. "Common Core—Connecting with Parents." *School Library Monthly* 29, no. 7 (April 2013): 30–32.

Harvey, Carl A., II. *Adult Learners: Professional Development and the School Librarian*. Santa Barbara, CA: Libraries Unlimited, 2012.

Harvey, Carl A., II. "The Coach in the Library." *Educational Leadership/ASCD*, October 2011. Accessed October 30, 2013, http://www.ascd.org/publications/educational-leadership/oct11/vol69/num02/The-Coach-in-the-Library.aspx.

Harvey, Carl A., II. "Putting on the Professional Development Hat." *School Library Monthly* 29, no. 5 (2013): 32–34.

Levitov, Deborah D., ed. *Activism and the School Librarian. Tools for Advocacy and Survival*. Santa Barbara, CA: Libraries Unlimited, 2012.

Murvosh, Marta. "Follow the Leaders: Washington State's Stellar Advocacy Model." *School Library Journal*, October 2013. Accessed October 30, 2013, http://www.slj.com/2013/10/advocacy/follow-the-leaders-washington-states-stellar-advocacy-model/.

Common Core, Professional Development, and Advocacy 67

In the chapters that follow, there are a variety of lesson plans that librarians can adapt, change, or garner ideas for their own instruction. Throughout the lesson plans, there are references to resources. In order to make it easier to read, below is detailed information about where to learn more about several of these resources that are used numerous times in many of the lesson plans.

- Britannica—Online encyclopedia from Britannica. Britannica School has three levels of learning: elementary, middle, and high school. It is accessible for any technology. It is aligned to the Common Core and state standards. The text selections are written, edited, reviewed, and updated by content experts. It also has a lesson plan builder to create interactive activities for groups. There is audio capability (http://info.eb.com).
- Grolier Online—Online encyclopedia from Scholastic Library Publishing. This encyclopedia has over 120,000 articles that are leveled using Lexiles and correlated to national and state standards, web links, 1,100 world newspapers in 73 languages representing 195 countries, and GOTube videos. It also has the following interfaces: elementary, middle school, high school, adult, and Librarians/Educators. Another new feature on Grolier Online are GOTube videos (http://teacher.scholastic.com/products/grolier/).
- Image Quest—Online database of images from Britannica. This site has three million rights-cleared images from fifty of the best collections in the world, including the Bridgeman Art Gallery, Dorling Kindersley Images, Getty Images, the National Portrait Gallery of London, and the National Geographic Society. Images can be quickly found for all types of activities, and each photo or illustration comes with citations and complete data, including source, copyright holder, caption, and keywords (http://info.eb.com/products/image-quest/).
- PebbleGo Database—Online databases geared toward students in K–3 from Capstone Publishing. These include Pebblego Animals, PebbleGo Earth and Space, PebbleGo Biographies, and PebbleGo Social Studies. The databases include leveled text and navigation designed for beginning researchers and video clips, audio, and text highlighting. There is audio capability (http://www.pebblego.com/).
- Rosen Science Databases—These three databases focus on science for upper elementary students. PowerKids Science includes Life Science, Earth and Space Science, and Physical Science. Included are text and video to cover a variety of topics under three major headings. For more information go to http://www.rosendigital.com.
- TeachingBooks.net—TeachingBooks.net is an easy-to-use website that adds a multimedia dimension to the reading experiences of children's and young adult books. The online database is developed and maintained to include thousands of resources about fiction and nonfiction books used in the K–12 environment, with every resource selected to encourage the integration of multimedia author and book materials into reading and library activities (http://teachingbooks.net).

- World Book Online—Online encyclopedia from World Book. World Book is designed and written by experts for a variety of different reading levels, kindergarten through adult. It can be used with all types of technology. It contains illustrations, maps, audio, videos, eBooks, primary source documents, a dictionary, and an atlas. It has audio capability (http://worldbookonline.com/).

6

Sample Lesson Plans—Kindergarten

GRADE LEVEL: Kindergarten

Lesson Topic/Theme: Farm Animals

Standards

Common Core: RI.K.1, RI.K.10, W.K.6, W.K.8, SL.K.4, SL.K.6
AASL: 1.1.3, 1.1.6, 1.1.8, 1.1.9, 1.3.1, 2.1.3, 2.1.6, 3.1.3, 3.1.6, 3.2.3

Resources

- PebbleGo Database
- Blabberize: http://blabberize.com/
- Nonfiction Text
  - Farm Animal series from Bellwether Media, 2007.
  - *Animals That Live on the Farm* by Gareth Stevens, 2010.

Instructional Roles

Librarian's Role

- Model researching with the topic of duck
- Model using PebbleGo Database
- Provide support for research stations in the classroom
- Guide students in creating a blabberize with their research

Teacher's Role

- Provide support for research stations in the classrooms
- Guide students in creating a blabberize with their research

Project Description

For the first lesson, students will come to the library and will walk through the process of researching a farm animal, which will be a duck.

Introduce the concepts and process of looking for information. Brainstorm what do school librarians want to know/need to know? Why are the animals important on the farm? Some potential questions might be:

What does the animal look like?
What does it eat?
What is the duck's name?
How does it help the farm?
How does it help people?

Model how to use PebbleGo Database from Capstone to obtain information. Discuss how students can find specific answers to some of the questions directly from the text. Other questions require us to think about some of the information students find and draw our own conclusions.

For the next several lessons, as part of their stations in the classroom, students will use PebbleGo Database to locate the information they need for their farmyard animal. Options: If the librarian's schedule permits, they could go to the classroom to provide additional support for students researching, or this could be part of the activity monitored by the classroom teacher.

Next students will create a photo of their barnyard animal talking about the research they found. Blabberize is a site where you can make an image look like it is talking. Students will upload a picture of their animal. They will record the information they learned about their animal during their research.

The blabberize videos can be used for students to learn about other animals that they hadn't researched.

Assessment

Assessment will be a rubric, as well as observations of students during their process of work.

Figure 6.1 Farm Project Rubric

	3	2	1	0
Research	Student found lots of information that supported their opinion.	Student found enough information to support their opinion.	Student did not find very much information.	Student did not find any information.
Opinion/ Sharing	Student shared why their animal was important on a farm.			Student did not share why their animal was important.
Blabberize	Student's blabberize worked.			Student's blabberize did not work.

GRADE LEVEL: Kindergarten
Lesson Topic/Theme: Research: Frogs

Standards

Common Core: W.K.2, W.K.5, W.K.8, W.K.6, W.K.8, RI.K.9, RI.K.10, RF.K.1, SL.K.2, SL.K.3

AASL: 1.1.1, 1.1.2, 1.1.6, 1.2.3, 2.1.1, 2.1.2, 2.14, 2.1.6, 3.1.1, 3.2.3

Resources

- Bishop, Nic. *Frogs*. New York: Scholastic, 2014.
- London, Jonathan. *Let's Go, Froggy!*. New York: Scholastic, 1994.
- London, Jonathan, and Frank Remkiewicz. *Froggy's Baby Sister*. New York: Viking, 2003.
- London, Jonathan, and Frank Remkiewicz. *Froggy Bakes a Cake*. New York: Grosset & Dunlap, 2000.
- London, Jonathan, and Frank Remkiewicz. *Froggy's Best Babysitter*. New York: Viking, 2009.
- London, Jonathan, and Frank Remkiewicz. *Froggy's Best Christmas*. New York: Puffin Books, 2002.
- London, Jonathan, and Frank Remkiewicz. *Froggy Builds a Tree House*. New York: Puffin Books, 2013.
- London, Jonathan, and Frank Remkiewicz. *Froggy's Day with Dad*. New York: Viking, 2004.
- London, Jonathan, and Frank Remkiewicz. *Froggy Eats Out*. New York: Puffin Books, 2003.
- London, Jonathan, and Frank Remkiewicz. *Froggy's First Kiss*. New York: Puffin, 2000.
- London, Jonathan, and Frank Remkiewicz. *Froggy Gets Dressed*. New York: Puffin Books, 1994.
- London, Jonathan, and Frank Remkiewicz. *Froggy Goes to Bed*. New York: Scholastic, 2000.
- London, Jonathan, and Frank Remkiewicz. *Froggy Goes to Camp*. New York: Puffin Books, 2010.
- London, Jonathan, and Frank Remkiewicz. *Froggy Goes to Hawaii*. New York: Viking, 2011.
- London, Jonathan, and Frank Remkiewicz. *Froggy Goes to School*. New York: Puffin, 1998.
- London, Jonathan, and Frank Remkiewicz. *Froggy Goes to the Doctor*. New York: Scholastic, 2002.
- London, Jonathan, and Frank Remkiewicz. *Froggy's Halloween*. New York: Penguin, 1999.

- London, Jonathan, and Frank Remkiewicz. *Froggy Learns to Swim*. New York: Puffin Books, 1997.
- London, Jonathan, and Frank Remkiewicz. *Froggy Plays in the Band*. New York: Scholastic, 2002.
- London, Jonathan, and Frank Remkiewicz. *Froggy Plays Soccer*. New York: Puffin Books, 2001.
- London, Jonathan, and Frank Remkiewicz. *Froggy Plays T-ball*. New York: Puffin Books, 2009.
- London, Jonathan, and Frank Remkiewicz. *Froggy Rides a Bike*. New York: Puffin Books, 2008.
- London, Jonathan, and Frank Remkiewicz. *Froggy's Sleepover*. New York: Puffin Books, 2007.
- London, Jonathan, and Frank Remkiewicz. *Froggy's Worst Playdate*. New York: Viking, 2013.
- Frog website: http://www.kidzone.ws/lw/frogs/http://www.kidzone.ws/lw/frogs/
- Frog website: http://www.kiddyhouse.com/Themes/frogs/http://www.kiddyhouse.com/Themes/frogs/

Instructional Roles

Librarian's Role
- Share frog books
- Discuss fiction and nonfiction books
- Brainstorm frog information
- Examine frog pictures

Teacher's Role
- Share additional frog books with class
- Assist in brainstorming frog information

Project Description

Day 1
Put the question up on the board: What is a frog? Write student's answers. Read *Froggy Goes Swimming* by Jonathan London. Ask students what kind of book this is. Then read and share pictures in Nic Bishop's book *Frogs*. Ask students the difference between these two books. Discuss fiction and nonfiction books. Brainstorm a list of facts that the students learned after reading Nic Bishop's book.

Day 2
Review the two different kinds of books to see if students remember the difference. Discuss with the students the differences between fiction and nonfiction again. Have a variety of books to hand out to students. Have two signs labeled Fiction and Nonfiction. Students will walk to the side of the room that their book falls under. Assess how they did. Exchange books among students; have them do the activity again. Assess them again.

Day 3
Teacher will have been sharing nonfiction frog books in classroom. Brainstorm what the students have learned about frogs and write the discussion items on a large sheet of paper or on the computer that is projected on a SmartBoard or screen so that all of the class can see what is being written. Go over the facts that they have written.

Day 4
A class book on frogs can be composed, or the teacher can have them write frog facts themselves. A class book can be written by going around the room and everyone composing one sentence with a frog fact. Another suggestion is to give each child one of the words/thoughts on the brainstormed list and have them compose one sentence. Sentences are written for the whole class to see. With both instructors working together, it is easy to accomplish. The story is then read aloud. Have students give suggestions for a title. If there are several good titles, let the students vote on the one they like best.

Pictures can be drawn by the students in the classroom or real pictures can be added. If real pictures are used to illustrate each sentence, PowerPoint is an easy method to use to put picture and sentences together.

The book was bound so that the class could read it. Slides can be condensed on one page so that each student can have a copy to take home and read.

This lesson could also be done with a variety of topics that the teacher would choose. After this particular lesson, a follow-up lesson with another topic to see how the students improved should be done.

Assessment
Each student was given a check or a minus on his sentence that he/she composed. Look at the sentences with the following criteria:
- Did it make sense?
- Did it have a subject and a verb?
- If they wrote it themselves, did it begin with a capital and end with a punctuation mark?

Students that elaborated on their sentence were given a check plus.

The teacher and librarian also assessed the second topic when it was undertaken and compared the students to see if they improved on their second attempt.

Additional Follow-up
Another lesson completed was on the topic of spiders. Using the book *Diary of a Spider* by Doreen Cronin (HarperCollins, 2005) and Nic Bishop's book *Spiders* (Scholastic, 2007), as main components, a similar lesson was created. The finished book this time was in the form of a diary. There is a variety of diary books listed in the bibliographies in appendix A in the back of this book.

GRADE LEVEL: Kindergarten
Lesson Topic/Theme: Healthy Eating/Nutrition

Standards
Common Core: R.I.7, R.I.10
AASL: 1.1.4, 1.1.6, 1.1.9

Resources
- Book Series
  - Eating Right with MyPlate: Bellwether Media, 2012.
  - Health Eating with MyPlate: Heinemann Library, 2012.
  - MyPlate and Healthy Eating: Capstone Press, 2012.
- http://www.choosemyplate.gov/

Instructional Roles
Librarian's Role
- Lead discussion about finding information from pictures
- Assist students in locating and making their list

Teacher's Role
- Assist students in locating and making their list
- Connect activity to other learning in the classroom about MyPlate

Project Description
This is a one-visit lesson to focus on teaching young readers that information can also be found from the pictures in a text. Students are reminded about the connection to learning about MyPlate and healthy eating in the classroom. Discussion continues about how information from pictures can be as helpful as information students get from the text of a book. Students use the various series of books to make a list of foods from each of the food groups on their MyPlate.

Option:
- Students work in groups with each doing a different food group and then share responses.
- Each student creates their own list based on the pictures they find for the various food groups.
- Students could follow up this activity by picking something from each of the groups to help design a meal for themselves.

Assessment
A quick scan of the students' work making sure they have foods from the books in the various food groups will verify that they completed the activity.

GRADE LEVEL: Kindergarten
Lesson Topic/Theme: Shapes

Standards

Common Core (Math): K.G.A.1, K.G.A.2, K.G.B.5, K.G.B.6
AASL: 1.1.2, 1.1.6, 1.1.8, 1.1.9, 2.1.4, 2.2.4, 3.1.4, 3.1.6,

Resources

- Ehlert, Lois. *Color Farm*. New York: Lippincott, 1990.
- Ehlert, Lois. *Color Zoo*. New York: Lippincott, 1989.
- Hall, Michael. *Perfect Square*. New York: Greenwillow, 2011.
- iPod, iPad, or some sort of digital cameras

Instructional Roles

Librarian's Role
- Read the story
- Guide Group 1

Teacher's Role
- Guide Group 2
- Extend the instruction about shapes in the classroom.

Project Description

Prior to reading the books, talk about looking for shapes all around. Tell students that the books to be shared will identify shapes in the illustrations. Read *Color Zoo*, *Color Farm*, and *Perfect Square*. Make a list of the shapes found in the stories.

Now, look for shapes all over the school. Review procedures and directions for using the digital cameras. Ideally it would be good to have several per group, but any number will work. Walk throughout the school and/or outside and have students take pictures of the different shapes.

Option: Another option would be that the librarian could take smaller groups to complete the shape search activity while others remain in the room with the teacher doing another activity.

In the next lesson, print out the pictures students found and have them cut out the shapes in each picture. They can build a new illustration. Remind them of the shape illustrations seen in *Color Farm*, *Color Zoo*, and *Perfect Square*. Students can write a story to go with the new illustrations.

Assessment

Students can identify their shapes and share their stories.

GRADE LEVEL: Kindergarten
Lesson Topic/Theme: Snowflakes

Standards

Common Core: RI.K.1, RI.K.9, W.K.7, W.K.8
AASL: 1.1.5, 1.1.6, 1.1.9, 2.1.2

Resources

- "Wilson 'Snowflake' Bentley Snowflakes in Motion" Trailer (http://www.youtube.com/watch?v=Y97z0anO1uM#t=11).
- Cassino, Mark, Jon Nelson, and Nora Aoyagi. *The Story of Snow: The Science of Winter's Wonder.* San Francisco: Chronicle, 2009.
- Fritts, Mary Bahr, and Laura Jacobsen. *My Brother Loved Snowflakes: The Story of Wilson A. Bentley, the Snowflake Man.* Honesdale, PA: Boyds Mills, 2002.
- Martin, Jacqueline Briggs, and Mary Azarian. *Snowflake Bentley.* Boston: Houghton Mifflin, 1998.

Instructional Roles

Librarian's Role
- Read aloud
- Timeline development
- Observe students for understanding

Teacher's Role
- Assist with timeline development
- Observe students for understanding
- Expand/extend instruction based on classroom theme of winter

Project Description

Day 1
Begin by making connections to what students have already been talking about in the classroom about snow and snowflakes. Tell students that the school librarian is going to read a biography about someone connected to snowflakes, a man by the name of Wilson Bentley. Tell them to listen for details about his life, because after reading, students are going to make a timeline of his life. Read aloud *Snowflake Bentley* by Jacqueline Briggs Martin. Pull out the main events from his life and create a timeline with the class. Librarian and/or teacher may need to reread sections with students to help fill in the timeline. It may also help for the teacher to write on the timeline on the dry erase board, chart, or a GoogleDoc as the librarian leads the class in coming up with the major events.

Day 2
Begin by refreshing the students' memories about what they learned about Snowflake Bentley. Review the timeline as well. Then, read *My Brother Loved Snowflakes* by Mary

Bahr. Compare the timeline and add additional information or see if there is information that differs from the book. If there is conflicting information, talk about why that might be and ask for suggestions for solving the conflicts. If the information is the same, talk about the authors using many of the same sources.

End with reading/viewing *The Science of Snow* by Mark Cassino. Students can now see what Bentley's photos looked like. Another possibility might be to watch the video on YouTube entitled "Wilson 'Snowflake' Bentley Snowflakes in Motion" trailer.

Assessment

Student self-assessment would be asking students to think about the timeline. Is there enough information? Was there more to know? Did students do their personal best job of getting the information? Were the library procedures being followed during the read-aloud and lesson?

Assessment is done by the school librarian and classroom teacher via observation during the lessons. The two educators make mental notes of areas that were hard for students and revisit those again in the next project.

7

Sample Lesson Plans— First Grade

GRADE LEVEL: First Grade

Lesson Topic/Theme: Famous Americans

Standards

Common Core: W.5, W.6, W.7, W.8, R.I.1, R.I. 2, R.I.3, R.I.10
AASL: 1.1.1, 1.1.3, 1.1.4, 1.1.6, 1.1.8, 1.1.9, 1.2.1, 1.3.1, 2.1.1, 2.1.2, 2.1.4, 3.1.3

Resources

- PebbleGo Database
- Informational text on Famous Americans
- Large sheets of paper
- Book Creator (www.redjumper.net/bookcreator/)

Instructional Roles

Librarian's Role
- Talk about text features when using informational text in the library

Teacher's Role
- Talk about text features when using informational text in the classroom

Project Description

Day 1

Begin by telling students that they will be writing a nonfiction book about a famous American. Discuss what kind of information is needed for a book. Students will work in groups of three or four.

Students will go through a research or inquiry process to find basic facts about the person. They will also need to answer some "thinking" type questions like why is this person important? or why are they famous? Students can take notes on index cards to keep track of the information.

Following the research, students will take the facts and turn them into a story for a book. This writing activity could be done in the classroom or in the library depending on schedules.

This would be a good opportunity to talk about the major nonfiction text features. Students can use nonfiction books as models to see what should be in their own book such as a table of contents, index, title page, and copyright page.

When they have the writing complete, the other sections of the book need to be created. The classroom teacher and librarian can decide how best to do that, but one successful strategy is to divide the class in half. Half can work with the teacher to create the table of contents, and the other half can work with the librarian on the index. The groups can then switch to complete the other part of the book. Repeat this for other sections of the book.

There are several options for creating a book

- The book could be made using big sheets of paper stapled together.
- The book could be made using a simple word processing program.
- The book could be made using online apps such as Book Creator.

The final product will include hand-drawn images or images found online and cited appropriately.

These lessons could vary in length and number of days needed depending on the class and the teacher's schedule.

Assessment

The final book is assessed with a rubric.

Figure 7.1   Famous American Rubric

	2	1	0
Research	Students found a lot of information about their person.	Students found some information about their person.	Students found no information about their person.
Book	Students created a nonfiction book about their person that contained all the major parts—index, table of contents, and chapters.	Students created a nonfiction book, but did not have all the major parts.	Students did not complete the nonfiction book about their person.
Images	Students were able to draw or locate images and included captions and sources for them.	Students were able to draw or locate images, but did not include captions and/or sources.	Students did not locate or draw images.
Groups	Students worked well in their group.	Students worked okay in their group.	Students did not work well as a group.

GRADE LEVEL: First Grade
Lesson Topic/Theme: Insects

Standards

Common Core: W.7, W.8, R.I.4, R.I.5, R.I.6
AASL: 1.1.1, 1.1.4, 1.1.6, 1.1.9, 2.1.2, 2.1.4, 3.1.4

Resources

- PebbleGo Database
- Insect Nonfiction Books
- Series from publishers like Capstone, Rosen, Scholastic Library Publishing, etc. would all be excellent for this type of project.
- Haiku Deck (https://www.haikudeck.com)

Instructional Roles

Librarian's Role
- Lead the instruction on research

Teacher's Role
- Lead the instruction in the classroom on insects
- Assist with research

Project Description

Students are learning about insects in their classroom. As part of the investigation, the students explore more in-depth information about a specific insect of their choosing. Students work in teams of three to four to locate basic information about their insects such as:

- Size
- Shape
- Color
- Food
- Enemies
- Benefits to the World

Use a mini-journal to help students keep the information organized. See figure 7.2 for a sample mini-journal.

Students can use online resource such as PebbleGo Database or print materials to locate the information.

Students will use the information and the app Haiku Deck to explain why their insect is important and needs to not be squashed by humans. The research should help provide the answers why.

Assessment

Teacher and/or librarian will be able to assess the final project based on the discussion with the chart.

Mini-Research Journal

Researching for Insects using the Big6!

What am I researching?

Where can we look for information?

Where are we looking for information?

What do I need to find?
How many kinds of your insect are there?
What color is your insect?
What does your insect look like?
How long does your insect live?

Who are your insect's enemies?

What does your insect eat?

What is the project?

What part of the project did you do your personal best?

GRADE LEVEL: First Grade

Lesson Topic/Theme: Long Ago and Today

Standards

Common Core: R.I.2, R.I.3, R.I.5, R.I.6, W.7, W.8
AASL: 1.1.2, 1.1.4, 1.1.6, 1.1.9, 1.3.4, 1.3.5, 2.1.2, 2.1.4, 3.1.4

Resources
- PebbleGo Database
- GoogleDocs

Instructional Roles

Librarian's Role
- Lead the research

Teacher's Role
- Assist with research

Project Description

Group students into partners and then put two sets of partners at each table. Don't use more than five groups, so some sets of partners may need three students in them. Navigate to PebbleGo Database, go to the Social Studies databases, and then navigate to Long Ago and Today. Each class will pick two main topics to research (communication, games, schools, farming, etc.). Each table is assigned one tab of the five time periods. Each team of partners is to read the text at least twice and then decide together which is the most important piece of information to share with all the other students. The two groups of partners at each station share their most important fact and then have to agree as an entire table on the singular most important fact.

Teacher creates a GoogleDoc like the chart below.

Figure 7.3 Long Ago and Today GoogleDoc

	Colonial	Frontier	1900s	1950s	Present
Communication					
Games					
Schools					
Farming					
Etc.					

Share the document so that all students have the link and can edit. Students in each group could open the GoogleDoc and add their fact to the chart. When it is completed, the chart can be shared with all the first-grade classrooms in order to see what new knowledge has been acquired in various topics.

The chart can be used to foster discussion with the students, such as

> What topic has seen the most change over the years?
> What time period would you like to live in the most and why?
> Why do you think things have changed over the years?

Assessment

Observations by the teacher and librarian of student conversations would be used as assessment.

GRADE LEVEL: First Grade

Lesson Topic/Theme: Measurement and Data

Standards

Common Core (Math): 1.MD.C.4
AASL: 4.1.1, 4.1.3

Resources

None

Instructional Roles

Librarian's Role
- Share stories
- Keep chart

Teacher's Role
- Share stories
- Keep chart

Project Description

Send three or four students out to the shelves and ask them to pick a book that looks interesting to them. (This could be done ahead of time during a check-out time so you don't have the whole class waiting on students that are slow.) Before reading the books, tell the students that they are going to listen to the stories in your stack and at the end will have to decide which one they like best. In order to help us decide which one is best, students need to make a list of things that make a good book. While the list will vary from class to class, it may look something like this:

Figure 7.4 Book Rating Chart

	Great characters	Excellent pictures	Interesting story	Made me feel part of the story	Want to read it again	Total votes
Title 1						
Title 2						
Title 3						

After reading each book, ask students to vote on each element. Then add them up at the end to get a total score for the book. After reading all the books (which you would not do all at once . . . read one every day or so until coming to the end of the stack), students can discuss the data you collected.

Data could be collected using a GoogleForm and added to all year long.

- Which book got the most votes for great characters?
- Which book got the most votes for an interesting story?
- Which story got the most votes? What part of that story made it the best?

This could be a good activity to use the titles from the state reading book award list. It could also be a great way to introduce students (and teachers) to books they might miss.

Assessment

Teacher and librarian observation during class discussion.

GRADE LEVEL: First Grade

Lesson Topic/Theme: Mem Fox Author Study

Standards

Common Core: RL.1.1, RI.1.6, R1.1.10, W.1.2, W.1.8, L.1.1

AASL: 1.1.1, 2.1.2, 2.1.4, 2.1.5, 2.1.6, 3.1.1., 3.2.1, 3.2.3, 4.1.1, 4.2.4. 4.1.5

Resources

- Fox, Mem. *Boo to a Goose*. Puffin, 2001.
- Fox, Mem. *Koala Lou*. HMH, 1994.
- Fox, Mem. *Possum Magic*. HMH, 1991.
- Fox, Mem. *Where Is the Green Sheep?* HMH, 2010.
- Map of the world
- Website: www.teachingbooks.net
- Website: www.memfox.com
- Books containing animals that live in Australia (this will depend on what is available in your school library). A good list of animals that live in Australia are the following: kangaroo, Tasmanian devil, bandicoot, bilby, cassowary, numbat, wallaby, echidna, platypus, lorikeet, wombat, koala, thorny devil, quoll, emu, dugong.
- Map of the world
- Books about Australian listed below although there may be different ones in your library
- Berendes, Mary. *Welcome to Australia*. Welcome to the World series. Mankato, MN: Child's World, 2008. Blue Dot Book.
- Bingham, Jane. *Australia*. Exploring Continents series. Chicago: Heinemann, 2007.
- Grupper, Jonathan. *Destination*. Destination Books series. Washington, DC: National Geographic Society, 2000.
- Heiman, Sarah. *Australia ABCs*. Country ABCs series. Minneapolis, MN: Picture Window Books, 2003.
- Hovanec, Erin M. *An Online Visit to Australia*. Internet Field Trips series. New York: Rosen Pub. Group's PowerKids Press, 2001.
- Kalman, Bobbie. *Australian Outback Food Chains*. Food Chains series. St. Catharines, ON: Crabtree, 2007.
- Kalman, Bobbie. *Explore Australia and Oceania*. Explore the Continents series. New York: Crabtree, 2007.
- Kalman, Bobbie. *Spotlight on Australia*. Spotlight on My Country series. New York: Crabtree, 2008.
- Lewin, Ted. *Top to Bottom Down Under*. New York: HarperCollins, 2005.
- Paul, Tessa. *Down Under*. Animal Trackers around the World Series. New York: Crabtree, 1998.

- Rose, Elizabeth. *A Primary Source Guide to Australia*. Countries of the World: A Primary Source Journey series. New York: Rosen Pub. Group's PowerKids Press Primary Source, 2004.
- Sayre, April Pulley. *G'Day, Australia!*. Our Amazing Continents series. Brookfield, CT: Millbrook Press, Inc., 2003.
- Scillian, Devin. *D Is for Down Under*. Ann Arbor, MI: Sleeping Bear Press, 2010.
- Vierow, Wendy. *Australia*. The Atlas of the Seven Continents series. New York: Rosen Pub. Group's PowerKids Press, 2004.
- Wojahn, Rebecca Hogue. *An Australian Outback Food Chain*. Minneapolis, MN: Lerner, 2009.

Instructional Roles

Librarian's Role
- Introduces author
- Read several books by the author
- Locate Australia on map
- Discuss Australian animals

Teacher's Role
- Shares additional books by Mem Fox
- Research on Australian animals
- Write story based on format of one of Mem Fox's books; *Where Is the Green Sheep* or *Boo to a Goose* are two excellent pattern books to use as models.

Project Description

Lesson 1
The librarian introduces Mem Fox to the class by showing her picture and linking to TeachingBooks.net where she explains and pronounces her name. The students will listen and hear the accent. Then they will discuss that she lives in Australia. Look at Australia on the SmartBoard map and then find Australia on a large world map hanging on the wall. Read *Possum Magic*, which is the first book she wrote. Share the book *Koala Lou*, examining the different animals of Australia that she includes in the book. Brainstorm other animals the students think live in Australia. Pass out animal books to students to locate animals that live in Australia. Compose a list of these animals as the students find them.

Lesson 2
Review from the first day. Look at several more of her books. Read *Where Is the Green Sheep?* and *Boo to a Goose*. Teacher will follow up with writing pattern books in the classroom modeled on the above books. Books can be displayed in the library after students write and illustrate them.

Lesson 3
Have each student choose one animal from Australia that was listed in lesson 1. Using animal books, they will find five facts about this animal. Students will be instructed to

write their facts on a sheet. From this sheet they will write a paragraph to share with their classmates. A picture of their animal can also be located using online sources and combined with the paragraph.

Assessment

Educators will assess how many books by this author are checked out to students. A short checklist will be used to assess the student's short research paragraph on an Australian animal that they choose to share with the class.

Questions for Self-assessment

Did you find five facts?
Did you use bullets when putting down your facts?
Did you make sure you did not use sentences when writing facts?
Is your paragraph written in complete sentences?

Extend This Activity

Other authors can be studied in the same way with the students. Books can be located and shared with students. Information about the author can be shared. This will make students aware of many different authors, why they write, and the motivation they may have for sharing information with students. Searching TeachingBooks.net is an excellent way to find different authors and what might need to be emphasized. Some of the authors will have short videos explaining how they create illustrations, for instance, or how they get their ideas. These will encourage students to read more from these authors or try drawing and illustrating themselves. Above all emphasis needs to be placed on why writers write and how they go about their craft. Emphasis to students should be:

1. the importance of reading and
2. what it takes to be a good writer.

Skype Visits

Another inexpensive way to connect with authors is by conducting Skype visits. Many authors are now doing this, and the cost is inexpensive. For example, Avi does one-hour visits with thirty students for only $100.00. J. Patrick Lewis, poet laureate, also Skypes for forty-five minutes for $350.00. Skype visits can be located by searching on Google, putting in "Children's authors who do Skype visits." One site that would be good to use is http://www.katemessner.com/authors-who-skype-with-classes-book-clubs-for-free/. There is also a good article to read at the following link to prepare for Skype visits: http://childrensbooks.about.com/od/readingresources/tp/Top-Ten-Tips-For-Successful-Author-Skype-Visits.htm.

Figure 7.5 gives other examples of authors to share with first-grade students. These authors have short autobiographies about themselves or biographies to share with students that you would find in your own library. Each also has a wide variety of books to share with students.

Figure 7.5 Authors to Use for First Grade

Name of Author	Something about These Books	Illustrator	Author
Tedd Arnold	Excellent short video on how to draw and illustrate on www.teachingbooks.net	X	X
Mary Jane and Herm Auch	A husband and wife author and illustrator team. Great website showing how they make their stories and illustrations (http://www.auchbooks.com)		
Jan Brett	Good author to use for how authors do extensive research before writing (http://www.janbrett.com/index.html)	X	X
Norman Bridwell	Clifford books; Indiana author	X	X
Marc Brown	Arthur books (http://marcbrownstudios.com/)	X	X
Eve Bunting	A variety of topics including areas like self-esteem, homelessness, Holocaust, family problems.		X
Doreen Cronin	Good for reading aloud; Her stories use voice (http://www.doreencronin.com)		X
Kevin Henkes	Great author to use for first grade (http://www.kevinhenkes.com)		X
Steve Jenkins	Author and illustrator of animal and science book and has a nice video on how he makes his books (http://www.stevejenkinsbooks.com)	X	X
Steven Kellogg	Great author to use for fairy tales. His illustrations are great (http://www.stevenkellogg.com/)	X	X
Helen Lester	Tacky the penguin books Tacky is a penguin that definitely likes to make life interesting. Nice website to use (http://www.helenlester.com)		X
Margie Palanti	Just fun books that make you laugh (http://www.margiepalatini.com)		X
Patricia Polacco	Many personal stories based on happenings in Polacco's life (http://www.patriciapolacco.com)		X
Cynthia Rylant	A variety of topics but likes to concentrate stories on life in Appalachia (http://www.cynthiarylant.com)		X
Rob Scotten	Splat the cat and Russell the sheep are two of his lovable characters. (http://www.robscotton.com/www.robscotton.com/RobScotton.com.html)	X	X
David Shannon	Famous for his David books. Kindergarten students LOVE him.		X
Janet Stevens	Has several books based on folktales; discussion of what folktales are; also *The Little Red Pen* is an excellent choice to use for personification (http://www.janetstevens.com)	X	X

(*continued*)

Figure 7.5 Authors to Use for First Grade (*Continued*)

Name of Author	Something about These Books	Illustrator	Author
Mo Willems	Good to use for Reader's Theatre; excellent website about himself (http://www.mowillems.com)	X	X
Don and Audrey Wood	Husband is illustrator and wife is writer; illustrations many times modeled on real people; *Heckley Peg* has the witch modeled on Don and the woman in the story is Audrey (http://www.audreywood.com)	X	X
Chris Van Allsburg	Strange stories with lots of deep meaning (http://www.chrisvanallsburg.com/flash.html)	X	X
Jane Yolen	A variety of books to use (http://janeyolen.com/)		X

8

Sample Lesson Plans—
Second Grade

GRADE LEVEL: Second Grade
Lesson Topic/Theme: Writing/Animals

Standards

Common Core: W.1, W.2, W.5, W.7, W.8
AASL: 1.1.1, 1.1.2, 1.1.3, 1.1.4, 1.1.6, 1.2.3, 1.3.1, 2.1.6, 3.1.3, 3.1.4

Resources

- Buzzeo, Toni. *One Cool Friend*. New York: Dial for Young Readers, 2012.
- Kellogg, Steven. *The Mysterious Tadpole*. New York: Dial, 1977. Print.
- PebbleGo Database
- Amazing Animals Online Encyclopedia (part of Grolier Online)
- Animal Nonfiction Books

Instructional Roles

Librarian's Role
- Read the stories
- Lead the research instruction
- Provide assistance while writing

Teacher's Role
- Lead the writing instruction
- Discuss components of good writing
- Provide assistance during the research

Project Description

Lesson 1
Read the two stories by Kellogg and Buzzeo. Students need to choose an animal they would like to take home (it should not be an animal that is typically a pet). A variety of choices could be pulled from books for the students to explore before making choices.

Lesson 2
Students then need to think about what they would need to know in order to bring the animal home. Students could use the research journal in appendix E as a way to organize their information. What questions do they have about the animals' needs in order to have them in their homes? Once they have their list of questions, they would then set out to find the answers using print and online resources.

Questions the students would need to know about their animals:
- Food
- Habitat
- Enemies
- Adaptations

Lesson 3
Students will continue working on locating answers to questions about their animals. They will continue using online and print resources to locate answers. Teacher and school librarian will assist when needed.

Lesson 4
With the information they have found students write their own crazy story about taking their animal home and what they would have to do to keep it alive (and away from their parents).

Lesson 5
Finish writing story. Discuss creating good sentences using descriptive words. Discuss that each story must have a beginning, middle, and end.

Assessment
Final project will be assessed with a rubric.

Figure 8.1 Animal Follows Me Home Rubric

	2	1	0
Research	Students located all the information they needed for their writing.	Students located some of the information they needed for their writing.	Students located none of the information they needed.
Writing	Students wrote a story with a beginning/middle/end.	Students wrote a story, but it did not have all the main elements.	Students did not complete writing a story.
Survival	The story included how the animal would survive and stay hidden from their parents.	The story included either how the animal survived or how they hide it from their parents.	The story does not include either how the animal survives or how it is hidden from the parents.

GRADE LEVEL: Second Grade

Lesson Topic/Theme: Nutrition/April Pulley Sayre Author Study

Standards

Common Core: R.I.1, R.I.5, W.2, W.5, W.7, W.8
AASL: 1.1.1, 1.1.4, 1.1.6, 1.1.9, 1.4.2., 1.4.4., 2.1.2, 2.1.6, 3.1.3, 3.1.4

Resources

- http://www.aprilsayre.com/
- http://www.choosemyplate.gov/
- Sayre, April Pulley. *Go, Go, Grapes!* New York: Beach Lane, 2012.
- Sayre, April Pulley. *Let's Go Nuts!: Seeds We Eat.* New York: Beach Lane, 2013.
- Sayre, April Pulley. *Rah, Rah, Radishes!: A Vegetable Chant.* New York: Beach Lane, 2011.
- Online encyclopedia
- Nonfiction books about foods

Instructional Roles

Librarian's Role

- Read-aloud books
- Lead research/inquiry instruction
- Help with writing composition

Teacher's Role

- Nutrition/Food Group unit in the classroom
- Support students during research
- Lead writing instruction

Project Description

As part of unit on nutrition, a perfect connection is to read books by April Pulley Sayre such as *Let's Go Nuts*; *Rah, Rah, Radishes!*; and *Go, Go, Grapes!*. Pulley has created these books with chants about fruits, vegetables, and nuts. The following are two different approaches for utilizing these books.

Approach 1
Students can dissect the books that Sayre has written by asking the following two questions: Why are the items she included in her book important to our nutrition? Is one food more important than another for our nutritional needs?

> Lesson 1—Read the books to the class. Brainstorm with the students a list of foods included in the books. Discuss what nutritional needs are. Determine what they think is important about each food item to nutritional needs. Have

students work with a partner to research what each food's nutritional value is to the body. A variety of books would be available to explore along with online encyclopedias. Remind students how to find information in the online encyclopedias to assist them in taking notes on each food that is being researched. One food can be used as a model to show students how to find the information needed in an online encyclopedia.

Lesson 2—Students continue research on the foods. Remind students to read for details.

Lesson 3—Each group can add to a chart about the foods to determine how many different answers they were able to discover.

Approach 2

Since the students have researched fruits, vegetables, and nuts from the books, have them concentrate on other nutritional foods. Using the MyPlate model from the USDA, have the students research the grains, proteins, and dairy groups in the same manner as stated above.

Lesson 1—Examine the MyPlate model and brainstorm a list of foods that would fall into the grains, proteins, and dairy groups of food. Decide what types of information would be needed to be able to write a book like April Pulley Sayre did. Reread her books so the students are familiar with the format. Students can be divided into pairs again to complete their research. Groups can choose one or two of the foods in the list to research.

Lesson 2—Groups need to finish their research using online encyclopedias and books. Again remind students how to best conduct their research using the encyclopedias. As groups finish, they can begin writing their chants.

Lesson 3—Students should concentrate on writing their chants and reading them to each other to make sure they make sense.

Lesson 4—Practice reading their chants aloud with expression. The chants will be filmed to be shared with others via morning announcements or posted online on their website or the school library website.

Assessment

Assess the finish products with a simple rubric.

Figure 8.2 Rubric of Chant

	2	1	0
Chant	Chant clearly covers the food group.	Chant has a few examples of the food group.	Chant does not cover the food group.
Chant Writing	Chant uses describing words and is interesting to read.	Chant is readable.	The chant does not use describing words.
Research	Students were able to successfully find all the information they needed for the chant.	Students were able to find some of the information they needed for the chant.	Students were not able to find any information.
Sharing	Students successfully presented their chant to be recorded using expression.		Students did not successfully present their chant to be recorded. Little or no expression was used.

GRADE LEVEL: Second Grade

Lesson Topic/Theme: Friendship: Owen and Mzee

Standards

Common Core: RL.2.3, RL.2.9, RI.2.1, R1.2.5, RI.2.9, SL.2.4, L.2.1
AASL: 1.1.1, 1.1.2, 1.1.3, 1.1.4, 1.1.6, 2.1.3, 2.3.1, 3.1.1, 3.1.3

Resources

- Hatkoff, Isabella, Craig Hatkoff, P. Kahumbu, and Peter Greste. *Owen & Mzee: The True Story of a Remarkable Friendship*. New York: Scholastic, 2006.
- Hatkoff, Isabella, Craig Hatkoff, P. Kahumbu, and Peter Greste. *Owen & Mzee: The Language of Friendship*. New York: Scholastic, 2007.
- Bauer, Marion Dane, and John Butler. *A Mama for Owen*. New York: Simon & Schuster, 2007.
- Owen and Mzee website (http://www.owenandmzee.com/omweb/)
- Individual maps of the world for each student
- Online encyclopedias
- Lesson plan website (http://www.scholastic.com/browse/collection.jsp?id=669)
- Lesson plan website (http://esllearningbydesign.com/resources/owen-and-mzee-complete-pdf-version.pdf)

Instructional Roles

Librarian's Role

- Read Owen and Mzee books to the class
- Discuss some of the key character concepts in the book, i.e. friendship, resilience, caring

Teacher's Role

- Talk about friendship in the classroom with teacher
- Discuss the word "resilience" in the classroom

Project Description

The story about Owen and Mzee is a story about friendship and also resilience. Students should realize that all people are unique and special, but that they also have many things in common. Owen and Mzee is a story about caring.

Day 1

Share with students that they will be reading and discussing a nonfiction book about a very unusual friendship between a tortoise and a baby hippopotamus. This story will make them listen closely to details about the sequence of happenings. After reading the story *Owen & Mzee*, have students complete some of the following activities.

Visualizing

Explain that visualizing is a strategy readers do to picture in their heads what is happening in the story. Students have a difficult time understanding nonfiction texts. They have a difficult time with concepts such as size, weight, length, and distance. Give each student a small map of the world. Have them find where the story takes place and label it. Have them label where Owen and Mzee finally ended up together.

Have students pick out facts in the story that show a concept like size, weight, length, and/or distance (i.e., Owen weighed 600 pounds as a baby and he will weigh around 8,000 pounds when fully grown, or Mzee is 120 years old). See if they can do some kind of a comparison to make others see and understand these concepts better.

Graphic Organizer

Have students use sticky notes to record major happenings in the book. Place these sticky notes on large chart paper. The class needs to decide what order the sticky notes should go in. Sequence them in the correct order.

Research

Have the students do simple research about different parts of the story to understand it better. Students could use World Book Kids Online Encyclopedia or their own online encyclopedias. They could also use their online catalog to find books in their library. Try topics such as:

- typhoons
- hippopotamus
- tortoise
- India
- Haller Park
- tsunami
- Kenya

Official Website of Owen and Mzee

Go to the official website (http://owenandmzee.com/omweb/) using a projector or a Smart Board so that all of the students can see the website together. Examine the different aspects of the site. Watch the documentary about Owen and Mzee. After spending some time on the site as a class, take the students to the computer lab, or have a set of laptops or iPads to use for each student so that they can explore a bit more.

Day 2

Read the sequel to this book, which is called *Owen & Mzee: The Language of Friendship*. This continues the life of these two characters who live in Haller Park. Have the students decide what this place really is and why they live there. Research Haller Park and show the students what it looks like today (http://www.owenandmzee.com/omweb/hallerpark.html).

Day 3

Discuss typhoons and how they occur. There are other typhoons around the world that cause a great deal of damage. Read more about typhoons, why they are caused, what happens during one, and where they occur. Have the students search the library for books about this topic. Also have them search encyclopedias or the online encyclopedias for information. Students can create a map of where these deadly storms take place. Discuss what the United States has that is similar to a typhoon.

Day 4

The teacher can have the students do writing in the classroom about typhoons.

Assessment

Informal assessment of students by school librarian and teacher as students work through the information together. Teacher and school librarian can assess students on the simple research project upon completion.

Figure 8.3   Owen and Mzee Assessment

Name _____

Did the student find facts about their topic?	Yes	No
Did the student use bullets for each fact recorded?	Yes	No
Did the student write short phrases when taking notes?	Yes	No
Did the student write a good paragraph about their topic with periods and capital letters?	Yes	No
Did the student have a good beginning sentence?	Yes	No
Did the student have a good concluding sentence?	Yes	No

GRADE LEVEL: Second Grade

Lesson Topic/Theme: Reading: Poetry with Douglas Florian

Standards

Common Core: R.L. 1.10, RF. 2.4.6
AASL: 4.1.1, 4.1.2, 4.1.3, 4.2.1, 4.2.4, 4.4.6

Instructional Roles

Librarian's Role
- Discuss Douglas Florian with the students
- Read his poetry to students
- Discuss shape poems, which are sometimes called concrete poems
- Choral reading of poems ("Army Ants" and "Boll Weevils" out of *Insectopedia*)

Teacher's Role
- Follow up in the classroom with writing poetry

Resources

- Various poetry books by Douglas Florian
- Website (http://www.douglasflorian.com)
- Florian, Douglas. *Autumnbling: Poems & Paintings*. New York: Greenwillow Books, 2003.
- Florian, Douglas. *Beast Feast*. New York: Scholastic, 1994.
- Florian, Douglas. *Bing Bang Boing: Poems and Drawings*. Orlando, FL: Harcourt Brace, 1994.
- Florian, Douglas. *Bow Wow Meow Meow: It's Rhyming Cats and Dogs*. San Diego, CA: Harcourt, 2003.
- Florian, Douglas. *Comets, Stars, the Moon, and Mars: Space Poems and Paintings*. Orlando, FL: Harcourt, 2007.
- Florian, Douglas. *Dinothesaurus: Prehistoric Poems and Paintings*. New York: Atheneum, 2009.
- Florian, Douglas. *Handsprings*. New York: Greenwillow Books, 2006.
- Florian, Douglas. *Insectlopedia: Poems and Paintings*. San Diego: Harcourt Brace, 1998.
- Florian, Douglas. *Laugh-eteria*. Scholastic, 1999.
- Florian, Douglas. *Lizards, Frogs, and Polliwogs*. San Diego, CA: Harcourt, 2001.
- Florian, Douglas. *Mammalabilia*. Florida: Harcourt, 2000.
- Florian, Douglas. *Omnibeasts: Animal Poems and Paintings*. Orlando, Fla: Harcourt, 2004.
- Florian, Douglas. *A Pig Is Big*. New York: HarperCollins, 2000.

- Florian, Douglas. *Poem Runs: Baseball Poems and Paintings*. Boston: Harcourt, 2012.
- Florian, Douglas. *Poetrees*. New York: Beach Lane Books, 2010.
- Florian, Douglas. *Summersaults*. New York: Greenwillow Books, 2002.
- Florian, Douglas. *Vegetable Garden*. San Diego: Harcourt Brace, 1996.
- Florian, Douglas. *Winter Eyes Poems and Paintings*. New York: Greenwillow Books, 1999.
- Florian, Douglas. *Zoo's Who: Poems and Paintings*. Orlando, FL: Harcourt, 2005.
- Michael J. Rosen. *Food Fight: Poets Join the Fight against Hunger with Poems to Favorite Foods*. San Diego: Harcourt Brace, 1996.

Project Description

Day 1
Librarian introduces poetry to the students. Introduce Douglas Florian the poet by linking to his website and showing his artwork and sharing the reasons he writes poetry. Read and share several poems that he has written.

Day 2
Review information about Douglas Florian. Discuss how poetry is good for reading out loud and also for choral reading. Discuss reading with expression. Choral read several of his poems ("Army Ants" and "Boll Weevils" are two good examples to use out of the book *Insectlopedia*). Challenge students to examine his poetry books and find several poems that they enjoy reading.

Day 3
Practice reading the poems they found out loud. Have them share their poem with the class, reading with expression. Some students might enjoy memorizing the poems for the class.

Day 4
Explain that shape or concrete poems are poems that take the shape of whatever the topic is explaining. Douglas Florian uses shape poems throughout his books to entice kids to read more. Find those poems in his books that are written in a shape. Then challenge students to write their own shape poems. Teacher will assist in helping students write shape poems in the classroom.

Assessment
Teacher and school librarian will assess the student on their oral reading of the poem.

GRADE LEVEL: Second Grade
Lesson Topic/Theme: Telling Time

Standards

Common Core: W.6, W.7, W.8
AASL: 1.1.1, 1.1.9, 2.1.1, 2.1.2, 2.1.3, 2.1.4, 2.1.5, 2.1.6, 3.1.3, 3.1.4

Resources

- Fraser, Mary Ann. *I.Q., It's Time.* New York: Walker &, 2005.
- Oxlade, Chris. *Animal Infographics.* Chicago: Raintree, 2014.
- Oxlade, Chris. *Environment Infographics.* Chicago: Raintree, 2014.
- Oxlade, Chris. *Population infographics.* Chicago: Raintree, 2014.
- Oxlade, Chris. *Weather Infographics.* Chicago: Raintree, 2014.
- Rowell, Rebecca. *Forces and Motion through Infographics.* Minneapolis: Lerner Publications Co., 2014.

Instructional Roles

Librarian's Role
- Read the story

Teacher's Role
- Telling Time unit in the classroom

Project Description

Read *I.Q., It's Time* to students as part of an extension of a unit in the classroom on telling time. Talk about the ways that I.Q. kept time during his day and what he did based on what time it was. Then share with the students the following scenario:

Mr. Principal has decided that there is too much "free" time at school when students are not learning. He is considering removing recess to gain more time for students to learn.

Students will need to brainstorm what could be done to help convince Mr. Principal to retain their recess time because they are doing a good job of spending the rest of their day learning. Part of the discussion should lead back to I.Q. and how he kept track of his day. Students will need to keep data on how they spend their days. Because data is important to have, spend several days collecting data.

Working with the class, design a GoogleForm to fill out how they spend their day. Depending on technology available, a classroom computer, iPad, or any device that has access to Wi-Fi could be used to collect data from students. Several students should record information. The Infographics book series by Lerner could be used as examples for students.

Students return to the library after collecting data for several days to analyze. Using information from multiple days they could design an infographic that shows how they spend the majority of each time block at school. This could be a large poster made out of paper or online tools could be used to create an infographic such as:

http://piktochart.com/

http://infogr.am/

http://www.easel.ly/

Students then present their findings to Mr. Principal. He weighs in on the issue with his final verdict (which of course is retain recess!).

Assessment

One self-assessment opportunity would be to have the students think about the data they've collected and pick one part of their day that they think they get the most done and why. Have them write out the reasons they chose this particular activity.

The infographic could also be assessed using a rubric.

Figure 8.4 Telling Time Rubric

	2	1	0
Text and Images	Text and images share the data collected.	Text and images are included but do not share data collected.	Text and images are not included.
Organization	The infographic is well organized.	The infographic contains data, but is confusing.	The infographic is not well organized.
Persuasive	The infographic convinces the reader to save recess.	The infographic doesn't completely convince the reader to save recess.	The infographic does not convince the reader to save recess.

9

Sample Lesson Plans— Third Grade

GRADE LEVEL: Third Grade
Lesson Topic/Theme: Biomes

Standards

Common Core: RL.3.1, RI.3.1, RI.3.4, RI.3.7, W.3.4, W.3.5, W.3.2b, W.4.2d, W.3.6, W.3.8, W.3.4, W.3.5, L.3.1, L.3.2, SL.3.4

AASL: 1.3.3, 1.3.1, 1.4.1, 1.4.2, 1.4.3, 1.4.4

Resources

- Folder for each student with outline of project (use old or new file folder, graphic organizer pages, map of the world, Venn diagram, evaluation sheet, bibliography page included)
- Websites for animals. These will vary, but Enchanted Learning is an excellent site to use (http://www.enchantedlearning.com/Home.html). This site is free to use, but a membership is only $125.00 and gives you access to more resources they offer.
- Online encyclopedias or print encyclopedias
- Books for different animals will be provided for students to use. Books will be dependent on what might be available in the school library. Make sure that you have a least one book for each student on different animals.
- Books for teachers for habitat overviews
- Graphing program (Microsoft Excel can be used)
- PowerPoint

Instructional Roles

Librarian's Role
- Teach note-taking
- Teach parts of books: index and table of contents
- Teach research skills
- Assist in writing reports
- Assist in drawing maps

Teacher's Role
- Introduce biomes/habitats
- Read appropriate books for biomes/habitats to class
- Teach writing topic sentences
- Follow up on writing paragraphs
- Compare and contrast animals

Project Description
This is a unit that can be done with all third-grade students near the end of the year as a culmination of skills taught. Each classroom does a different biome. All biomes could be done in one classroom by dividing up the students into the different biomes. Traditionally used biomes are desert, polar regions, savannah, mountains, ocean, rain forest, and forest.

Day 1
The teacher will introduce the concept of biomes in the classroom. The teacher and class will also decide on the biome they will research. After doing this, the teacher will begin by reading and sharing several books on that particular biome. This might include a book on a general overview of the biome, the food chain of the biome, and/or plants and animals of the biome.

Books about the biome are in each classroom so that students can examine them during silent reading time. Students choose animals from their region after the overview from their teacher. Students brainstorm places they can find information with the school librarian. (Refer to figure 9.1.) Each student gets a file folder that will contain all of their notes. They also receive a book or find a book about their animal. Librarian reviews using the table of contents and index. Students identify both features and examine them in their own book about their animal. A graphic organizer is discussed and students are shown how to use it. There are four pages for the graphic organizer so that students can develop four paragraphs. (Figures 9.2–9.5 are examples of a graphic organizer.) A review is held on taking good notes (correct spelling, no sentences, looking for key words, using bullets for each fact).

Day 2
A short review is given on items discussed the previous day. Librarian models note-taking again. Students spend time taking notes on their graphic organizer. Librarian checks students as they are working. Students are reminded how to locate books. Students locate other books on their topic.

Day 3
A review is given on using online encyclopedias. Students spend time using online encyclopedias to find information.

Day 4
The librarian does a mini lesson on bibliographies. Students will provide author, title, publisher, and year the book was published for their citation. Students will provide information on online encyclopedias by copying and pasting the given citation in their bibliography. Students write in their folder the materials they have used thus far. Refer to a sample bibliography sheet by looking at figure 9.6.

Day 5
Students locate their animal on a map of the world that is in their folder. Students finish taking notes. As students finish taking notes they are divided into pairs to compare and contrast their animals using a Venn diagram. See figure 9.7.

Day 6
Teacher spends time discussing a topic sentence, which the students compose on their graphic organizers. Writing about their animal is done in their classroom. Adding rich detail to their writing is important. The teacher will spend time reviewing the writing process. A topic sentence will be written on each graphic organizer sheet.

Day 7
Students continue writing about their animal. The teacher discusses using detail and descriptive words. The librarian works with them on typing their information. Their reports can be done in a word processing program or in PowerPoint. PowerPoint might be preferable because it gives the student a better chance of including illustrations on each page. There will be four paragraphs written. One will be on the description of the animals using rich detail. There will be a paragraph on prey and predators; one on habitat, which will include adaptations the animal makes to their habitat; and one on other facts such as how many babies they have, how they communicate, how long they live, and other information the student might find.

Day 8
Discussion is led by the librarian on inserting pictures into their PowerPoint and how important pictures are to words. Students are shown how to insert pictures and how to include captions. Students spend time on finishing their project.

Day 9
Students write an evaluation of the project and their work. Self-evaluation is important for students to be critical of the work they have produced. See figure 9.8 for sample evaluation questions.

Day 10
Students will use the editing checklist and make sure they have all the components they need. They will also check for spelling and grammar errors. Students also will present their project in class to other students when finished. This will probably take at least two days.

This project can take as long as the two collaborators want. Evaluation is done on the note-taking and folder work by the school librarian. The writing of the report is done in class, and the teacher grades it. Another twist in this project is adding some additional work on graphing. Students could poll other students and other classrooms to see what animal is their favorite and compose a graph from that data.

Assessment

There is a rubric to assess the entire project. Informal observation can be done throughout the project to see how students are progressing. See figure 9.9.

Paragraphs include:
- Paragraph one should include description of their animal.
- Paragraph two should include predator and prey of the animal.
- Paragraph three should include the habitat of their animal, including any adaptations.
- Paragraph four should contain any other information about their animal such as how many babies they have, life expectancy, communication, etc.
- Paragraph five should be an evaluation of their work.

Figure 9.1   Research Journal

Name:	Class:

What is the topic of your project?

Where can you look for information?
1.
2.
3.
4.
5.
6.

Figure 9.2

- Color
- Weight
- Other descriptive facts
- Height
- Description of ___
- Tail
- Length
- Ears
- Eyes
- Nose

Topic Sentence

Figure 9.3

```
┌─────────────────┐   ┌─────────────────┐   ┌─────────────────┐
│ What eats it    │   │ What eats it    │   │ What eats it    │
│ _____   │   │ _____   │   │ _____   │
│ _____   │   │ _____   │   │ _____   │
│ _____   │   │ _____   │   │ _____   │
│ _____   │   │ _____   │   │ _____   │
└─────────────────┘   └─────────────────┘   └─────────────────┘
         ↖                    ↑                    ↗
┌─────────────────┐         ╱─────╲         ┌─────────────────┐
│ Other facts     │        │       │        │ Other facts     │
│ _____   │ ←──────│Food of│──────→ │ _____   │
│ _____   │        │  a    │        │ _____   │
│ _____   │        │ ____  │        │ _____   │
│ _____   │         ╲─────╱         │ _____   │
└─────────────────┘         ↙  ↓  ↘         └─────────────────┘
         ↙                    ↓                    ↘
┌─────────────────┐   ┌─────────────────┐   ┌─────────────────┐
│ Food it eats    │   │ Food it eats    │   │ Food it eats    │
│ _____   │   │ _____   │   │ _____   │
│ _____   │   │ _____   │   │ _____   │
│ _____   │   │ _____   │   │ _____   │
│ _____   │   │ _____   │   │ _____   │
└─────────────────┘   └─────────────────┘   └─────────────────┘
```

Topic Sentence:

Figure 9.4

- What kind of habitat
- Why do they live there
- Other location
- Habitat of a _____
- How does it adapt to its habitat
- Location
- Other information

Topic Sentence: _____

Figure 9.5

- What are babies called?
- Other information
- How long does it live?
- How many babies?
- Other information (center)
- Other facts
- Other information
- Other information
- How does it communicate?

Topic Sentence:

118 Leading the Common Core Initiative

Figure 9.6 Research Journal

My Information Came From: Title: _____ Author's first and last name: _____ Publisher: _____ Place published: _____ Date published _____	**1**
My Information Came From: Title: _____ Author's first and last name: _____ Publisher: _____ Place published: _____ Date published _____	**2**
My Information Came From: Title: _____ Author's first and last name: _____ Publisher: _____ Place published: _____ Date published _____	**3**
My Information Came From: Title: _____ Author's first and last name: _____ Publisher: _____ Place published: _____ Date published _____	**4**

My Information Came From: Database Name (if Web): _____	**5**
My Information Came From: Database Name (if Web): _____	**6**
My Information Came From: Database Name (if Web): _____	**7**
My Information Came From: Database Name (if Web): _____	**8**
My Information Came From: Database Name (if Web): _____	**9**

120 Leading the Common Core Initiative

Figure 9.7

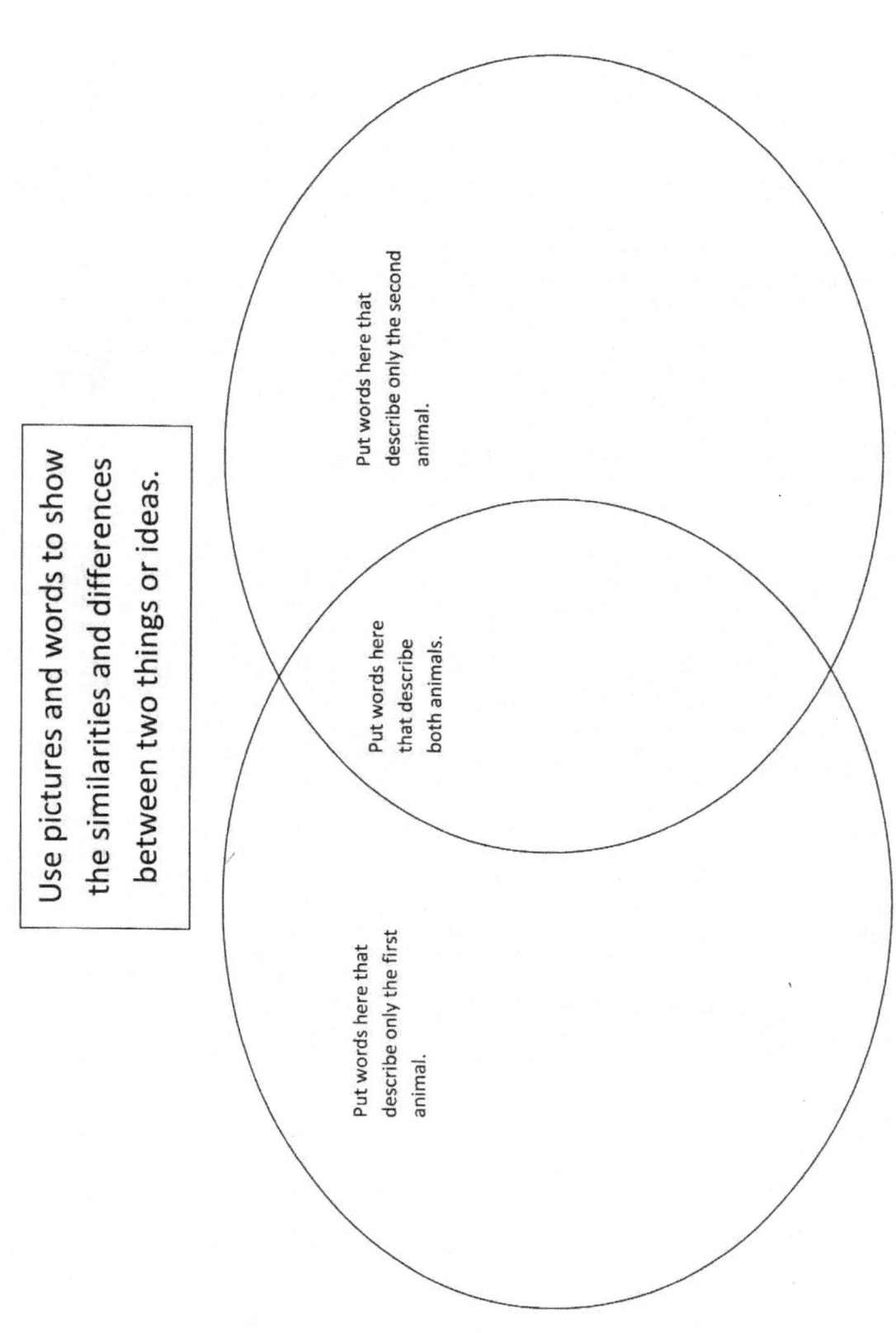

Figure 9.8   Editing Checklist for Biome Paragraphs

Do you have five paragraphs?	Yes	No
Have you indented each paragraph?	Yes	No
Have you started each sentence with a capital letter?	Yes	No
Have you ended each sentence with a period or a question mark?	Yes	No
Look at paragraph 1. Did you tell what group of animals your animal belongs to? (mammal, reptile, amphibian, insect)	Yes	No
Look at paragraph 2. Did you tell us where they live?	Yes	No
Look at paragraph 2. Did you tell us how your animal adapts to their habitat?	Yes	No
Look at paragraph 3. Did you tell us what your animal eats?	Yes	No
Look at paragraph 3. Did you tell us who eats your animal?	Yes	No
Look at paragraph 3. Did you tell us how your animal protects itself from predators?	Yes	No
Look at paragraph 4. Did you tell us how many babies your animal has?	Yes	No
Look at paragraph 4. Did you tell us if your animal was endangered?	Yes	No
Did you include other interesting facts in paragraph 4?	Yes	No
Did paragraph 5 tell us if you liked your project and what you might do that would be different next time?	Yes	No

Figure 9.9 Assessment Rubric for Biomes

	3	2	1	0
Searching	A list of 3 places to look for information is written.	A list of 2 places to look for information is written.	One place to look for information is written.	No places to look for information are written.
Searching	Student completely filled in the bibliography.	Student filled out most of the information for all sources.	Student filled out one place to look for information.	Student did not fill out any places to seek information.
Notes	Notes were written in the student's own words very neatly.	Notes were written in the student's own words but were very messy.	Notes were written, but copied straight from the source.	Few or no notes were written.
Map	The map shows where the habitat is and where the animal lives.	The map shows where the habitat is or where the animal lives, but not both.	The map is incorrect on where the animal lives.	The map is not finished at all.
Project	Each paragraph has a topic sentence that is well composed.	Each paragraph has a topic sentence, but they are very similar.	Half of the paragraphs have a topic sentence.	Only one or less of the paragraphs has a topic sentence.
Project	The final project is clearly written and has many facts.	The final project is written but not very interesting.	The final project is very hard to understand.	The final project is incomplete.
Project	The PowerPoint slides are completely finished with pictures and words.	The PowerPoint is finished, but the pictures do not match the words on the page.	The PowerPoint is written but has no pictures.	The PowerPoint is not finished.
Evaluation	The student completely answered all of the evaluation questions in sentences.	The student answered the questions, but not in sentences.	The student answered less than half of the questions.	The student did not answer any of the questions.

GRADE LEVEL: Third Grade

Lesson Topic/Theme: Writing/Opinions

Standards

Common Core: W.1, W.4, W.5, W.6
AASL: 4.1.1, 4.1.2, 4.1.3, 4.1.7

Resources

- Variety of books
- Online catalog

Instructional Roles

Librarian's Role

- Booktalks
- Brainstorm writing a book review
- Instruction for adding to the online catalog

Teacher's Role

- Lead the writing instruction

Project Description

Prior to starting booktalks, ask students to listen carefully to what is shared and not shared about a book. Tell them to focus on what might make someone else interested in reading.

Share a variety of different genres and highlight the items most interesting about the book. Why did you want to read it? What did you like about it?

Brainstorm with students about what is important to include when writing book reviews. Make a poster chart highlighting the important elements. See figure 9.10 as a good sample. The final results will vary depending on each class, but this is a good basic list.

Students are going to work on creating book reviews to entice others to want to read the books. Talk about the important items in writing a book review. Grammar, spelling, and complete sentences are all going to be components to work with.

If your automation system allows it, students can publish reviews electronically. Once the reviews are approved, they can be attached to the book record and students who are using the online catalog will be able to read them. This should help students make better selections.

Assessment

The review can be assessed with a rubric.

Figure 9.10

Title

Author / Illustrator } Grammar, Punctuation, Spelling

Setting Characters

Summary
↓
"Quotes" — BUT - <u>Do</u> <u>NOT</u> <u>GIVE</u> <u>THE</u> <u>ENDING</u>

Recommendation - opinion
⇓
Why?

Genre

Rating ★★★★★

Is it a series?

Books by the author?
  "If you like this book, you might also..."

Figure 9.11 Book Review Rubric

	2	1	0
Summary	The book review includes a detailed summary without giving away the ending.	The book review gives a brief summary of the book.	The book review does not give any summary of the book.
Details	Uses many details from the book to describe feelings.	Uses some details to describe feelings about the book.	Does not use details to support feelings about the book.
Recommendation	Forms opinion on book and uses reasons to support opinion.	Forms opinion on book, but uses few reasons to support opinion.	Does not form any opinion about the book.

GRADE LEVEL: Third Grade
Lesson Topic/Theme: Fairy Tales

Standards
CCSS: R.L.1, R.L.2, R.L.3, R.L.4
AASL: 4.1.1, 4.1.2, 4.1.3, 4.1.5, 4.1.7, 4.1.8

Resources
- Different versions of Cinderella stories (bibliography of examples are at the end of this lesson).

Instructional Roles

Librarian's Role
- Read original Cinderella story
- Read one adaptation of Cinderella from another country
- Do a compare and contrast sheet
- Develop a graphic organizer for their own story

Teacher's Role
- Read as many different versions as possible in the classroom
- Write story with the class

Describe Project

Lesson 1
Discuss the definition of fairy tales. Have the students brainstorm a list of different fairy tales that they know. Explain how fairy tales came to be. Share the original story of Cinderella. After reading this version, share at least one different version of the Cinderella story. The teacher will share other versions in the classroom. Students can compose a list of different countries these Cinderella stories represent.

Lesson 2
Have students fill out the Compare/Contrast sheet to show students the differences in the story from each country. Refer to figure 9.12 for a sample sheet. Compare the different versions to the original Cinderella story.

Lesson 3
The students will create a graphic organizer for their own Cinderella story. Figure 9.13 will help in organizing a story for the student. The teacher can work with the students in the classroom to finish writing these stories. They also can type them on the computer and illustrate them when finished.

Assessment
The teacher will grade the stories written on a rubric they create.

Figure 9.12 Compare and Contrast Sheet for Cinderella

Story title	Country	Cinderella's name	Something different in story

Figure 9.13 Cinderella Graphic Organizer

To develop a good story, you must know the main characters, setting and background, and other components of your story before you start writing. Decide how you are going to change the Cinderella story. Choose names for your characters, a setting, problems she or he will face, and other problems that will come up in your writing.

Cinderella character name (main character)	
Stepmother's name	
Stepsisters names	
Prince's name	
Fairy Godmother's name	
The setting of your story	
What type of a celebration will they be having in the story?	
What will your main character lose at this celebration?	
What kinds of magical items are involved in your story?	
What is the climax of your story?	
What will happen at the end of your story?	

Cinderella Bibliography

Auch, Mary Jane. *Chickerella*. New York: Holiday House, 2005.

Brown, Marcia. *Cinderella*. New York: Charles Scribner's Sons, 1954.

Climo, Shirley. *The Egyptian Cinderella*. New York: Crowell, 1989.

Climo, Shirley. *The Korean Cinderella*. New York: HarperCollins, 1993.

Climo, Shirley. *The Persian Cinderella*. New York: HarperCollins, 1999.

Coburn, Jewell Reinhart. *Angkat*. Arcadia, CA: Shen's Books, 1998.

Coburn, Jewell Reinhart. *Jouanah, a Hmong Cinderella*. Arcadia, CA: Shen's Books, 1996.

Coburn, Jewell Reinhart. *Domitila*. Auburn, CA: Shen's Books, 2000.

Daly, Jude. *Fair, Brown & Trembling: An Irish Cinderella Story*. New York: Farrar, Straus and Giroux, 2000.

De Paola, Tomie. *Adelita*. New York: G. P. Putnam's Sons, 2002.

Edwards, Pamela Duncan. *Dinorella*. New York: Hyperion, 1997.

Fleischman, Paul. *Glass Slipper, Gold Sandal*. New York: Henry Holt, 2007.

Gilani-Williams, Fawzia. *Cinderella*. Markfield, England: Islamic Foundation, 2011.

Guarnaccia, Steven. *Cinderella*. New York: Abrams, 2013.

Hennessy, B. G. *The Once Upon a Time Map Book*. Somerville, MA: Candlewick Press, 2010.

Hickox, Rebecca. *The Golden Sandal*. New York: Holiday House, 1998.

Hughes, Shirley. *Ella's Big Chance*. New York: Simon & Schuster, 2004.

Jackson, Ellen B. *Cinder Edna*. New York: Mulberry Books, 1998.

Karlin, Barbara. *James Marshall's Cinderella*. New York: Puffin Books, 2001.

Ketteman, Helen. *Bubba the Cowboy Prince*. New York: Scholastic, 1997.

Lattimore, Deborah Nourse. *Cinderhazel*. New York: Blue Sky Press, 1997.

Louie, Ai-Ling. *Yeh-Shen*. New York: PaperStar, 1996.

Lowell, Susan. *Cindy Ellen*. New York: HarperCollins, 2000.

Manna, Anthony L. *The Orphan*. New York: Schwartz & Wade Books, 2011.

Martin, Rafe. *The Rough-Face Girl*. New York: Scholastic, 1992.

McClintock, Barbara. *Cinderella*. New York: Scholastic, 2005.

Meddaugh, Susan. *Cinderella's Rat*. Boston: Houghton Mifflin, 1997.

Minters, Frances. *Cinder-Elly*. New York: Viking, 1994.

Pollock, Penny. *The Turkey Girl*. Boston: Little, Brown, 1996.

San Souci, Robert D. *Cinderella Skeleton*. San Diego, CA: Harcourt, 2000.

San Souci, Robert D. *Sootface*. New York: Bantam Doubleday Dell, 1997.

San Souci, Robert D. *Cendrillon*. New York: Simon & Schuster Books, 1998.

San Souci, Robert D. *Little Gold Star*. New York: HarperCollins, 2000.

Schroeder, Alan. *Smoky Mountain Rose*. New York: Dial, 1997.

Sierra, Judy. *The Gift of the Crocodile*. New York: Simon & Schuster, 2000.

Silverman, Erica. *Raisel's Riddle*. New York: Farrar, Straus and Giroux, 1999.

Singer, Marilyn. *Mirror, Mirror*. New York: Dutton, 2010.

Thaler, Mike. *Cinderella Bigfoot*. Happily Ever Laughter series. New York: Scholastic, 1997.

Whipple, Laura. *If the Shoe Fits*. New York: Margaret K. McElderry Books, 2002.

GRADE LEVEL: Third Grade

Lesson Topic/Theme: Research: Landmarks of the United States

Standards

Common Core: RL.3.1, RI.3.4, RI.3.7, W.3.2b, W.3.2d, W.3.8, W.3.7
AASL: 1.1.1, 1.1.3, 1.1.4, 1.1.6, 2.1.4, 2.1.2, 2.1.1, 3.1.1., 3.1.4, 3.1.16

Resources

- Mileage calculator (http://www.symsys.com/mileage/index.php)
- Online encyclopedias such as World Book Online or Britannica
- Map program (Google maps)
- Poster board
- Construction paper
- Paper cutter
- Websites of landmarks

Instructional Roles

Librarian's Role

- Introduce online encyclopedias
- Gather books on landmarks (These can vary depending on what books are available in the school library)
- Find and instruct students in the use of websites of different landmarks
- Instruction on map program
- Teach note-taking

Teacher's Role

- Introduce landmarks
- Teach a definition of landmarks
- Brainstorm different landmarks
- Assist in putting posters together

Project Description

Day 1

The teacher introduces landmarks in the classroom. Students decide on the landmark that they want to research. A short review is given on using the online library catalog. Students find a book on their landmark and read about their landmark for background information before next class meeting. A list of potential landmarks could be:

Bryce Canyon National Park
The Capitol
Death Valley National Park
Devils Tower National Monument

Empire State Building
Everglades National Park
Franklin D. Roosevelt Memorial
Glacier National Park
The Golden Gate Bridge
Grand Canyon National Park
Jefferson Memorial
Korean Memorial
Martin Luther King Jr. Memorial
Mount Rushmore
Mt. St. Helens National Monument
The Pentagon
Redwood National Park
Rocky Mountain National Park
Statue of Liberty
Vietnam Veterans Memorial
Washington Monument
Lincoln Monument
The White House
World Trade Tower Memorial
Yellowstone National Park
Yosemite National Park
Zion National Park

Day 2
Instruction is given on using an online encyclopedia. Students search for their landmark. Note-taking is modeled, reminding students that they do not write whole sentences, only phrases. Information can be taken from the online encyclopedia or from books. Students will take notes about their landmark.

Day 3
Teacher will lead students in using their notes to construct several paragraphs about their landmark. The librarian will assist.

Day 4
Students will locate their landmark on a map of the United States. A mapmaker program will be located and used to make the map. They will mark on the map the location of the landmark and also where they live. Maps will be printed. If no map program is available, a paper map of the United States can be printed and the students can mark the two places on their maps. They may use their books, online encyclopedia, or an atlas to assist them in finding the location. Using a mileage calculator, they will also calculate how far it is from their home to their landmark. Another step could be added

here if map skills need to be added. The students can make a set of directions how to get to their location and also make an agenda of how long it would take to get there and how much it might cost.

Day 5

Students locate and print a picture of their landmark using Imagequest (copyright free pictures, but since this program is subscription based, Google Images could also be used). Students are shown how to create titles for their poster. Print those. Students choose their poster board and arrange their materials attractively on poster board. Design techniques are discussed.

The poster will include:

- report
- picture(s) of landmark
- map
- mileage and/or agenda/directions
- title/name

Day 6

Students will present their landmark poster to the class. Teacher and librarian assess the project.

Assessment

Assessment will be done continuously throughout this project on each step to see if students are understanding each component. The teacher will assess the paragraph writing. The school librarian will keep a checklist of skills on whether students are using the skill well (online encyclopedia, searching for books, taking notes). This can then be followed up at a later date if more instruction is needed. See figure 10.1.

Note: This project could also be created using Prezi (www.prezi.com) or Glogster (http://edu.glogster.com/) with the same results but using digital means.

Figure 9.14 Assessment Tool for Landmarks

Name _____

Category	3	2	1	0
Notes	No sentences. Used bullets. Very neat handwriting.	No sentences. Used bullets.	Did not use bullets. A few sentences used. Not very much information.	Used sentences. Did not use bullets. Cannot read writing.
Topic Sentence	Topic sentence is there.	Did not use correct punctuation or capitals.		No topic sentence.
Ending Sentence	Used an ending sentence.	Did not use correct punctuation or capitals.		No ending sentence.
Content of Paragraph	Used all of their facts. Each fact is a different sentence. Paragraph makes sense.	Left out one or two facts that they took in their notes.	Left out more than two facts from their notes.	Content of paragraph does not make sense.
Sentences/ Capitals/ Punctuation	Complete sentences. Every sentence has a capital and ending punctuation.	Missing one or two capitals or ending punctuation.	Many sentences do not have ending punctuation. Misspellings.	No sentences. No capitals. No ending punctuation.
Pictures	Has two or more pictures. Pictures are clear and big.	Has two pictures.	Has one picture.	No pictures.
Map	Has a map. Landmark is spelled correctly and in correct location.	Has a map but has incorrect spelling on their landmark.	Has a map, but has an incorrect map.	No map.
Mileage Page	Has included mileage. Complete sentence, ending punctuation, and picture.	Does not have ending punctuation or capital.	Does not tell where landmark is located.	No mileage page.
Heading for Poster	Heading is nice and big and colorful. Easily read.	Heading is small and cannot be read to well.	Heading is not spelled correctly.	No heading.

GRADE LEVEL: Third Grade
Lesson Topic/Theme: U.S. Presidents

Standards

Common Core: W.1, W.5, W.7, W.8

AASL: 1.1.1, 1.1.3, 1.1.4, 1.1.5, 1.1.6, 1.1.8, 1.2.2, 1.3.1, 1.3.5, 2.1.2, 2.1.3, 2.1.5, 2.1.6, 3.1.3, 3.1.4, 3.1.6

Resources

http://www.ipl.org/div/potus/
http://www.whitehouse.gov/about/presidents/
http://memory.loc.gov/ammem/odmdhtml/preshome.html
http://memory.loc.gov/ammem/odmdhtml/preshome.html

Instructional Roles

Librarian's Role
- Leads instruction on research/inquiry process
- Provides support for final project

Teacher's Role
- Provides support for research/inquiry process
- Guides students with final project

Project Description

During the first visit, students are given time to explore a variety of books about the U.S. presidents. Tell students to think about what president they would like to know more about. Students can choose their top three choices. Examine their choices and divide up the presidents so that each student is researching a different president.

Once the presidents are assigned, have students brainstorm individually what they want to know about the presidents. After they have time to do that, have the class share. Record the questions on a whiteboard or large sheets of paper. Students will realize that many of the questions are the same. The librarian and the classroom teacher will help guide students in creating good questions.

Often they will come up with some basic fact questions like:

1. When/where was he born?
2. When/where did he die?

But, the school librarian wants students thinking of higher-level questions such as:

3. Was he an effective president?
4. What were some of the traits that made him a successful (or not successful) president?

Once the list is developed, students can brainstorm where to look for the information they need. This is also a great time to discuss keeping information organized as they are researching, as well as an opportunity to have a conversation about copyright and citing sources. Many schools use a research journal to help keep students organized. An example of a research journal is included in appendix E.

After finding information concerning how they were an effective president and the president's strengths, explain to students they will create a campaign to reelect their president. The campaign could include a website, campaign logos, posters, or a TV commercial. Students will also write a speech for the president announcing his reelection campaign.

Assessment

The librarian will assess the research journals to see the student's process in working through research. (See the rubric on the research journal.) The teacher and librarian together could assess the final project using a rubric.

Figure 9.15 Famous American Rubric

	2	1	0
Information	The student found information to prove (or not prove) if the president was effective.	The student found some information, but it did not prove if the president was effective.	The student did not locate any information.
Campaign	Student's campaign highlighted the president's strengths.	Student's campaign mentioned some of what the president did.	Student's campaign contained little to no information.
Persuasive	The student was able to convince folks to reelect the president.	The student was able to convince a few folks to reelect the president.	No one was convinced to reelect the president.

10

Sample Lesson Plans— Fourth Grade

GRADE LEVEL: Fourth Grade

Lesson Topic/Theme: Writing: Good Beginnings

Standards

Common Core: W.3, W.4, W.5
AASL: 4.1.1, 4.1.2, 4.1.5, 4.1.8

Resources

- Booktalk Titles

Instructional Roles

Librarian's Role

- Booktalk the titles to share good beginnings

Teacher's Role

- Connect this to writing good beginnings in the classroom

Project Description

Often the opening line in a story is the hook that pulls in a reader. For example, Richard Peck is the master. *The Teacher's Funeral* (Dial, 2004) has one of the best opening lines for young readers ever! But, there are lots of ways to start off a piece of writing.

Beginning with a Sound Effect

- Christopher, Matt. *Olympic Dream*. Boston: Little, Brown, 1996.
- Hoeye, Michael. *Time Stops for No Mouse: A Hermux Tantamoq Adventure*. New York: G.P. Putnam's Sons, 2002.

Beginning with Thoughts

- Bunting, Eve. *The Summer of Riley*. New York: Joanna Cotler Books, 2001.
- Clements, Andrew. *Frindle*. New York: Simon & Schuster, 1996.
- DeFelice, Cynthia C. *The Ghost and Mrs. Hobbs*. New York: Farrar, Straus and Giroux, 2001.
- Hale, Bruce. *The Hamster of the Baskervilles: From the Tattered Casebook of Chet Gecko, Private Eye*. San Diego, CA: Harcourt, 2002.
- Kochenderfer, Lee. *The Victory Garden*. New York: Delacorte Press, 2002.
- Langton, Jane. *The Time Bike*. New York: HarperCollins, 2000.
- Naylor, Phyllis R. *The Great Chicken Debacle*. New York: M. Cavendish, 2001.
- Snicket, Lemony. *The Bad Beginning*. New York: HarperCollins, 1999.
- Willis, Patricia. *The Barn Burner*. New York: Clarion Books, 2000.

Beginning with Dialogue

- Adler, David A. *Andy Russell, NOT Wanted by the Police.* San Diego, CA: Harcourt, 2001.
- Clements, Andrew. *The Landry News: A Brand New School Story.* New York: Simon & Schuster Books, 1999.
- Fields, Terri. *Missing in the Mountains.* Flagstaff, AZ: Rising Moon, 1999.
- Gutman, Dan. *The Kid Who Ran for President.* New York: Scholastic, 1996.
- Haddix, Margaret P. *The Girl with 500 Middle Names.* New York: Aladdin Paperbacks, 2001.
- Petersen, P. J. *White Water.* New York: Simon & Schuster, 1997.
- Sleator, William. *The Boxes.* New York: Dutton, 1998.
- Walter, Mildred P. *Suitcase.* New York: Lothrop, Lee & Shepard Books, 1999.
- Wiles, Debbie. *Love, Ruby Lavender.* San Diego: Harcourt, 2001.

Beginning with Action

- Clements, Andrew. *The School Story.* New York: Simon & Schuster, 2001.
- DiCamillo, Kate. *Because of Winn-Dixie.* Cambridge, MA: Candlewick Press, 2000.
- Franklin, Kristine L. *Grape Thief.* Cambridge, MA: Candlewick Press, 2003.
- Greenwood, Barbara. *The Last Safe House: A Story of the Underground Railroad.* Toronto: Kids Can Press, 1998.
- Kehret, Peg. *Don't Tell Anyone.* New York: Dutton, 2000.
- Naylor, Phyllis R. *Shiloh.* New York: Atheneum, 1991.
- Park, Linda S. *The Kite Fighters.* New York: Clarion Books, 2000.

Beginning with Description

- Cleary, Beverly. *Ramona's World.* New York: Morrow, 1999.
- Creech, Sharon. *Ruby Holler.* New York: Joanna Cotler Books, 2002.
- Cummings, Priscilla. *A Face First.* New York: Dutton, 2001.
- Eccles, Mary. *By Lizzie.* New York: Dial, 2001.
- Giff, Patricia R. *Pictures of Hollis Woods.* New York: Wendy Lamb Books, 2002.
- Park, Linda S. *Project Mulberry: A Novel.* New York: Clarion, 2005.
- Peck, Richard. *The Teacher's Funeral: A Comedy in Three Parts.* New York: Dial, 2004.
- Skurzynski, Gloria, and Alane Ferguson. *Cliff-hanger.* Washington, DC: National Geographic Society, 1999.

Booktalk these with students as they prepare their own writings.

Assessment

Teacher and librarian read students writing to see if they incorporate these beginning strategies in their writing.

GRADE LEVEL: Fourth Grade
Lesson Topic/Theme: Force/Motion

Standards

Common Core: W.2, W.6, W.7, W.8, W.9
AASL: 1.1.1, 1.1.3, 1.1.4, 1.1.5, 2.1.2, 2.1.4, 2.1.6, 3.1.1, 3.1.3

Resources
- Rosen's PowerKids Databases
- Nonfiction Text
- Fourth Grade Science Textbooks

Instructional Roles

Librarian's Role
- Guide the research instruction
- Assist with the writing and creating of the comics

Teacher's Role
- Assist with the research instruction
- Lead the writing and creating of the comics instruction

Project Description

Students are learning about common terms that accompany the concept of motion and force. Using the standards and science textbooks, a list of terms associated with this subject can be shared with students. Students can explore their textbook and nonfiction books to help brainstorm a list.

Possible Force/Motion terms

- Move
- Speed
- Friction
- Mass
- Weight
- Push/Pull
- Balance
- Gravity
- Buoyancy
- Acceleration
- Force
- Motion
- Equilibrium
- Momentum

Students will research various terms to get a better understanding of the concepts. They will choose two or three of them to use effectively in a comic strip. The research will take several visits.

The writing of the comic strip text would be next. A storyboard is an effective way to map out what they will write.

Once the text is complete, students can use a variety of tools to create their comic books.

- Pen/paper
- Comic Life (software) (http://plasq.com/)
- Read Write Think (http://www.readwritethink.org/files/resources/interactives/comic/)

Assessment

Assess this project with a rubric such as the one shown in figure 10.2.

Figure 10.1 Storyboard for Planning Script

Figure 10.2 Comic Book Rubric

	2	1	0
Comic Book	The comic book contains two characters and the dialogue is written well.	The comic book contains a character and is written with few errors.	The comic book is missing characters and the writing has many errors.
Terms	The comic includes at least 4 scientific terms from the list and they are used correctly.	The comic includes at least 2 of the scientific terms and they are used correctly.	The comic does not include any of the terms used correctly.
Research/ Notes	The student completely researched the terms to use in their writing.	The student researched some of the terms used in the writing.	The students did not research the terms used in the writing.

GRADE LEVEL: FOURTH GRADE

Lesson Topic/Theme: Nonfiction Feature Search

Standards

Common Core: RI 4.7, RF 4.4
AASL: 1.1., 1.1.2, 1.4.1

Resources

- Use figures 10.3 and 10.4 as guides for this lesson.
- Use a variety of nonfiction or informational text books to hand out to the students. Bobbie Kalman's books from Crabtree Publishers are good examples of books with many of these features.
- Sticky notes
- Laura Robb's book *Complete Resources for Reading, Grades 4–6*. Scholastic, 2006.
- Handout entitled Nonfiction Feature Search listing different nonfiction features of books
- BINGO cards

Instructional Roles

Librarian's Role

- Supply stack of books from the library
- Explain nonfiction terms with teacher (i.e., index, table of contents, glossary, map features, copyright, etc.)

Teacher's Role

- Follow up with additional discussion of the text features that are listed on our Nonfiction Feature Search handout

Project Description

Lesson 1

Students are given a list of features found in nonfiction books. See figure 10.3. Each student is given a book and a stack of sticky notes. Students look through their books first. Have them compare their book with the person next to them. As each feature is discussed by the teacher and the librarian, the students are instructed to place a sticky note on a page they find an example. Have students write a definition of each term. Have students find another student in the class that has the same feature in their book as they do.

Lesson 2

On the second day, a BINGO game will be played for assessment. Students will get a different book to search and a BINGO card. As each term is called, students look for the feature in their books. If they have it, they put a sticky note on the page and a marker on their BINGO card. See figure 10.4.

Assessment

Librarian and teacher will observe as the students are finding the features. Students that need assistance will be shown what to do. Teacher may want to follow up with a test in the classroom on these features.

Figure 10.3   Nonfiction Feature Search

Name _____

Feature	
About the Author	Found in the front or the back of the book or sometimes the back cover, it gives information about the author's life and why they wrote the book.
Appendices	This can be a variety of information that is included at the back of the book that the author does not want to include in the body of the book. It might add more information or give resources for more information.
Author Notes	This is sometimes why the author wrote the book or other information the author wants you to know about the book and its topic.
Bibliography	This is a list at the end of the book that cites the books, magazines, or websites that the author refers to within the book.
Boldface Print	This is the darker type used for titles and headings. Some vocabulary words can also be in boldface type. This calls the reader's attention to the word and shows them that it is important.
Bullets	Bullets delineate important facts in a list form.
Captions	Captions are one or two sentences that explain the photograph.
Copyright date	This is found on the back of the title page and tells when the book was published. There is a little sign that looks like this before the date: ©
Dedication	This is the page that the author puts near the beginning if they want the book to be dedicated to one person who is special to them.
Diagrams	This is a picture that shows how something happens. It could be about a volcano showing how it erupts.
Glossary	This is an alphabetic list of important terms that explains tough or unusual words found in the text. It comes near the end of the book. It may show you how to pronounce the word.
Headings	These divide key facts and topics within the book. Headings are usually in bold print and help in finding information that you want easily.
Index	An alphabetic list of key words, topics, and names of people in the text that comes at the end of the book. Next to each item is a page number referring to where this information is found.
Introduction	This part of the text can explain how the author conceived the idea as well as recognizes others who helped the author gather information.
Maps	These help visualize a place the author discusses. They also allow you to follow the path of an explorer, or someone else.

Photographs	These supply an image of an object or person and give extra information about the topic.
Question Format	The author will pose a question with the answer underneath, helping the reader to find the information quickly.
Quotes	This feature can be in a sidebar or in a section of the page outside the story. Quotes give the exact words of a person.
Sidebars	Boxes containing information on a page of a book or magazine article that didn't quite fit into the text. Sidebars can contain a list of fascinating facts, quotes, part of an interview, a newspaper clipping, or a letter.
Table of Contents	Providing chapter titles and pages numbers; it is a quick overview of what you will find in the text.
Timeline	This feature can include key dates in a person's life or other events that relate to the topic covered. It could cover dates of key events in a historical period. It may have illustrations or pictures included with it.
Title Page	This has the name of the book, author, and illustrator with the Library of Congress formatting and copyright date on the back of it.
Copyright Page	The reverse side of the title page. This is where the copyright date, ISBN number, and cataloging information is located.

Figure 10.4 Nonfiction Feature Search

Name _____

Feature	
About the Author	
Appendices	
Author Notes	
Bibliography	
Boldface Print	
Bullets	
Captions	
Copyright Date	
Dedication	
Diagrams	
Glossary	
Headings	
Index	
Introduction	
Maps	
Photographs	
Question Format	
Quotes	
Sidebars	

Table of Contents	
Timeline	
Title Page	
Copyright Page	

GRADE LEVEL: FOURTH GRADE

Lesson Topic/Theme: Research: Famous Scientists

Standards

Common Core: RL.4.1, RL.4.3, RI.4.1, RI.4.3, RI.4.10, L.4.1, W.4.2c, W.4.2d, W.4.2e, W.4.4, W.4.5, W.4.6, W.4.7, SL.4.4, SL.4.5

AASL: 1.3., 1.3.3., 1.3.5, 1.4.1, 1.4 2, 1.4.3, 1.4.4, 3.1.3

Resources

- World Book Online Encyclopedia
- Grolier Online Encyclopedia
- Imagequest (Britannica picture source which is a subscription-based product (http://quest.eb.com/)
- Biography books about famous scientists
- Websites on scientists (http://www.nndb.com/)
- Inventor of the week (http://web.mit.edu/invent/i-search.html)
- S9.com Biographical Dictionary (http://www.s9.com/)
- Timeline program (Timeliner XE, Scholastic, Tom Snyder Production)

Instructional Roles

Librarian's Role

- Assign scientists
- Model note-taking
- Instruct students on using online encyclopedias
- Instruct students on timeline programs
- Instruct students on making a bibliography

Teacher's Role

- Introduce topic in classroom
- Explain about a wax museum
- Give time for students to read books about their scientist
- Teach topic sentences
- Teach concluding sentences
- Instruct how to write in first person
- Practice presentation

Project Description

This project was designed with the collaboration of classroom teachers, a school librarian, and a dedicated science teacher. The conclusion of this project is a parent night at school where the students dress as their scientist with props and become wax figures in a wax museum. Each student will give a short speech about their scientist. Each student will be dressed as their scientist with props and have a small button that says "Press here." Upon pressing the button, the wax figure (student) will present their speech.

Lesson 1

Scientists are chosen from a list by the students. Students can preview books about the scientists to find one that interests them. This can be done randomly or students can be assigned specific people. Students will check out a book about their particular scientist. The list is composed by the librarian and science teacher with the resources that they can find in the school library. Notecards are passed out to students and broad topic headings are written on top of each notecard after brainstorming what kinds of information is needed (i.e., jobs, awards, family, inventions/discoveries, etc.) after discussion with the students on what kinds of information needs to be located. On the first card the students determine that they will find the birthplace and date and the date of death and place. World Book Online Encyclopedia is used first and instruction is given to the students about where to find the dates that they need. On this same card the students determine why this scientist is important so they have a starting point. It also is an important component as this information can be found in the first sentence of the paragraph demonstrating to students how important it is to read closely.

Lesson 2

Additional headings are added to the cards for students to find more information about the person (i.e., jobs, education, awards, inventions/discoveries). The students are reminded that good researchers are like detectives. They never give up. Several sources need to be read and examined for information. Grolier Online Encyclopedia is examined to find information. Note-taking is reviewed and students are shown how to use bullets and short answers for their notes.

Lesson 3

A short review discussion about taking notes is presented so students are reminded about how to take notes and where to look for information. Students are then given time to search additional sources for information for their cards. Teacher and librarian check on students as they are working and help those that need additional assistance.

Lesson 4

Students will have read their books by now. The books are examined for relevant information by using the index. Many times these books will have timelines. More information is added to the note cards. Students are encouraged to locate material about the childhood of their scientist. showing the importance of establishing goals early in life.

Lesson 5

The librarian discusses what a bibliography is and models making one. Since online encyclopedias and a book have been used, students compose a bibliography together.

Lesson 6

Students are shown how to create a timeline. Making a timeline of the person's life helps to demonstrate sequencing and other happenings events in the world at the time.

Lesson 7
Teacher starts instruction on how to write in first person. Several examples are shown to give the students ideas. Students begin writing. The report will consist of five paragraphs. Teacher goes over how to write with details. Students are given time to write. Students that are behind in note-taking are taken by one or the other instructors to find the information that they need during these lessons. With two instructors, it is much easier to work with the students that need additional help.

Lesson 8
After the reports are initially written students will be expected to work in pairs to read each other's writing. Peer editing will take place. Corrections will be given.

The teacher and the librarian will discuss with students about what kinds of props, dress, etc. they might need for the night of presentation. Students will practice their presentations for the classroom teacher. Presentations will be given in the classroom for assessment by the teacher.

Assessment
A rubric was created to assess the timeline that students produced and then graded by the school librarian. The writing will be assessed via a rubric by the teacher. See figures 10.5 and 10.6. The teacher will assess the oral presentation in the classroom.

As the students are working throughout the note-taking process, the librarian and teacher will assess the students via observation. The two educators will confer on what they think might need to be changed, retaught, or taught differently for further understanding by the students.

Another short research project done not too far after this one is the best assessment of what the students have learned during the process. During this project, the students are left more on their own to see if they can recall the steps that they went through.

Note about this project:
This project can be changed very easily. Scientists do not have to be the focus of this lesson. General biographies can be covered in a similar manner. Grouping of biographies such as presidents, scientists/inventors, explorers, the arts (music, art), sports, and people who changed the world (i.e., Martin Luther King Jr., Rosa Parks, Nelson Mandela) can be divided among classrooms. On the night of the wax museum, each classroom can be decorated for the topic of the classroom. For example, for the president's room, "Hail to the Chief" could be playing and it could have a sign that reads, "Welcome to the Oval Office."

Figure 10.5   Assessment Tool for Scientist Reports

Name _____

Category	4	3	2	1
Organization	Information is very organized with well-constructed paragraphs.	Information is organized with well-constructed paragraphs.	Information is organized, but paragraphs are not well-constructed.	The information appears to be disorganized.
Amount of Information	All topics are addressed with at least 4 sentences about each. There are 5 paragraphs.	All topics are addressed with at least 3 sentences about each. There are 5 paragraphs.	All topics are addressed with 2 sentences about each. There are 5 paragraphs.	One or more topics were not addressed and/or only 1 sentence was included.
Mechanics	No grammatical, spelling, or punctuation errors.	Almost no grammatical, spelling, or punctuation errors.	A few grammatical, spelling, or punctuation errors.	Many grammatical, spelling, or punctuation errors.
Notes	Notes are recorded and organized in an extremely neat and orderly fashion.	Notes are recorded legibly and are somewhat organized.	Notes are recorded.	Notes are messy and/or not enough.
Interesting Facts	You have found at least 3 or more unusual facts about your person that I did not ask for.	You have found 2 unusual facts about your person that I did not ask for.	You have found at least 1 unusual fact that I did not ask for.	You have found no unusual facts about your person.

Figure 10.6 Assessment Tool for Scientist Timeline

Name _____

Category	4	3	2	1
Spelling and Capitalization	Spelling and capitalization were checked and are correct throughout.	Spelling and capitalization were checked and were mostly correct.	There were many spelling and capitalization errors.	Spelling and capitalization errors were on most of the facts
Graphics	There is a picture of the scientist on the timeline.		The picture is blurry or too small.	There is no picture of a scientist included.
Content/Facts	Facts were accurate for all events reported on the timeline.	Facts were accurate for almost all events reported on the timeline.	Facts were accurate for most (~75%) of the events reported on the timeline.	Facts were often inaccurate for events reported on the timeline.
Title	The timeline has a creative title and is capitalized correctly. The student's name is also there.	The timeline has a title and is capitalized correctly. The student's name is also there.	The timeline has a title, but is not capitalized correctly. The student's name is there.	The timeline has only the scientist's name and the student's name.
Preparation	The student had notes about all the events and dates s/he wished to include on the timeline before beginning to design the timeline. The student had more than 10 dates.	The student had notes about almost all the events and dates s/he wished to include on the timeline before beginning to design the timeline. The student had 10 dates.	The student had notes about most of the events and dates s/he wished to include on the timeline. The timeline had between 5 and 10 dates.	The student had not prepared adequate notes before beginning to design the timeline. The student had less than 5 dates.

GRADE LEVEL: Fourth Grade

Lesson Topic/Theme: Wander Indiana (or whatever state)

Standards

Common Core: W.1, W.5, W.7, W.8 Math—4.MD.A.2

AASL: 1.1.1, 1.1.3, 1.1.4, 1.1.5, 1.1.6, 1.1.8, 1.2.2, 1.3.1, 1.3.5, 2.1.2, 2.1.3, 2.1.5, 2.1.6, 3.1.3, 3.1.4, 3.1.6

Resources

- State Department of Tourism
- County Chambers of Commerce
- Local Government Offices

Instructional Roles

Librarian's Role

- Lead the research instruction
- Assist with the project creation

Teacher's Role

- Assist with the research instruction
- Lead the project creation

Project Description

This inquiry project scenario is presented to students:

You are about to get ready for a vacation from school. You have the choice to visit one of the counties in Indiana as part of a family vacation. Your task is to determine what you are going to see and how much this family vacation will cost. You will need to factor in things like mileage, lodging, and food for all members of your family. Your final project will be to create a presentation to convince your family on why they would want to visit this Indiana county on their vacation.

Determine the best way for students to select a county.

This project will require mostly online research. Prior to beginning, a lesson on Internet research including terms, strategies, and some recommended resources is needed.

Students may need help organizing their information. Use the research journal in appendix E to help keep their questions and information organized.

Determining the travel cost could vary greatly depending on the price of gas and the miles per gallon of different types of cars. To simplify this part, use the Federal Mileage reimbursement rate (http://www.irs.gov/Tax-Professionals/Standard-Mileage-Rates).

To determine the cost of food, students could visit a few restaurants online and come up with an average cost per person, or you can use the per diem rates the U.S. government uses for reimbursement of expenses (http://www.gsa.gov/portal/content/101518).

Students can use a variety of options for sharing their research information to convince their parents:

- PowerPoint
- Video
- Podcast

Assessment

Figure 10.7   Trip Plan Rubric

	2	1	0
Math	Students successfully budgeted for the trip.	Students set up most of the budget correctly.	The student's budget was not accurate.
Presentation	The student successfully convinced the group to visit the county.	The student almost convinced the group to visit the county.	The student did not convince the group to visit.

11

Sample Lesson Plans—Fifth Grade

GRADE LEVEL: Fifth Grade

Lesson Topic/Theme: United States

Standards

Common Core: W.1, W.5, W.7, W.8

AASL: 1.1.1, 1.1.3, 1.1.4, 1.1.5, 1.1.6, 1.1.8, 1.2.2, 1.3.1, 1.3.5, 2.1.2, 2.1.3, 2.1.5, 2.1.6, 3.1.3, 3.1.4, 3.1.6

Resources

- State Department of Tourism
- State Books
- There are various series from all sorts of publishers: Scholastic Library Publishing, ABDO, Rosen Publishing, etc.
- Grolier Online; World Book Online
- Other online websites

Instructional Roles

Librarian's Role

- Lead the research instruction
- Assist the development of the commercials

Teacher's Role

- Assist with the research instruction
- Assist the development of the commercials

Project Description

Share the following scenario with your students:

You have just been invited by the state tourism bureau to design a campaign to encourage people to visit your state. You need to convince tourists to visit the state and highlight those items in your presentation. You'll also need to design a slogan and advertising materials the state could use to get people to visit.

Once a state has been selected, the research will begin. (Students can work in groups or on their own.) Students can brainstorm where to begin looking for the information they need. This is also a great time to talk with them about keeping their information organized as they research, as well as have a conversation about copyright and citing sources. Use a research journal to help keep students organized. You can see a sample in appendix E.

Students could utilize a variety of resources—print, online encyclopedias, websites, etc. to locate the information they need.

Amount of research time can vary from group to group. Once students have located all the information they need, they can begin to develop their campaign. Their campaign should include a slogan and a commercial to play to encourage people to visit their state. The commercial should include the information they found in their research and should be persuasive.

Assessment

Figure 11.1   States Commercial Rubric

	2	1	0
Commercial	The commercial is creative and interesting to watch. It includes research from students.	The commercial is okay to watch. It includes some of the research information.	The commercial is boring. It does not include some of the research.
Research	Students locate sufficient information to make their commercial.	Students locate some information to make their commercial.	Students located no information.
Persuasive	The commercial is persuasive to get people to visit.	The commercial almost makes people want to visit.	The commercial does not make people want to visit.
Slogan	The slogan is catchy and will get people to visit.	The slogan is complete, but will not convince people to visit.	The slogan was not completed.

GRADE LEVEL: FIFTH GRADE

Lesson Topic/Theme: Reading: Biographies

Standards

CCSS: RL.5.1, RL.5.1, RI.5.4, RI.4.7, RI.4.8, L.5.1, L.5.2, W.5.2, W.5.4, W.5.7, SL.5.4, SL.5.5

AASL: 1.4.1, 1.4.2, 1.4.3, 1.4.4

Resources

- A variety of picture book biographies
- PowerPoint
- Presentation system to project finished project
- Online encyclopedias

Instructional Roles

Librarian's Role

- Introduction of unit
- Read the book *What to Do About Alice?* by Barbara Kerley, Scholastic, 2008.
- Discuss biographies
- Instruction on researching a famous person
- Review of note-taking
- Instruction on producing a two-slide PowerPoint
- Assessing project when finished

Teacher's Role

- Give students time in class to read their biography book
- Assisting students in filling out their preliminary sheet of information after reading their book
- Assessing project when completed including oral presentation

Project Description

Lesson 1

Read a picture book biography of your choice to the students. A good one to use is *What to Do About Alice* by Barbara Kerley (Scholastic, 2008). Short synopsis of book: Teddy Roosevelt has a problem with his daughter, Alice. Alice wants to "eat up the world." She wants to go places, do things that girls didn't usually do. The book takes Alice from when she was born through her childhood, living and growing up in the White House to her own marriage and beyond.

After reading the book to the students, discuss why Alice was famous, and what kind of characteristics she had. Discuss with the students how to figure out when she was born, when she died, and other important happenings in her life from reading the

Clinton, Catherine. *Phillis's Big Test*. Boston: Houghton Mifflin, 2008.

Collins, Tom. *Steven Spielberg, Creator of E.T.* Minneapolis, MN: Dillon Press, 1983.

Collier, James Lincoln. *The Louis Armstrong You Never Knew*. New York: Children's Press, 2004.

Conway, W. Fred. *The Incredible Adventures of Daniel Boone's Kid Brother*. New Albany, IN: FBH Publishers, 1992.

Cooney, Barbara. *Eleanor*. New York: Puffin, 1999.

Cooper, Floyd. *Jump!*. New York: Philomel Books, 2004.

Corey, Shana. *Mermaid Queen*. New York: Scholastic, 2009.

Corey, Shana. *You Forgot Your Skirt, Amelia Bloomer*. New York: Scholastic, 2000.

Coury, Tina Nichols. *Hanging off Jefferson's Nose*. New York: Dial, 2012.

Crowe, Ellie. *Surfer of the Century*. New York: Lee & Low Books, 2007.

Davies, Jacqueline. *The Boy Who Drew Birds*. Boston: Houghton Mifflin, 2004.

Denenberg, Barry. *Nelson Mandela*. New York: Scholastic, 1991.

Dunlap, Julie. *John Muir and Stickeen*. Chanhassen, MN: NorthWord Press, 2004.

Dray, Philip. *Yours for justice, Ida B. Wells*. Atlanta: Peachtree, 2008.

Edwards, Pamela Duncan. *The Bus Ride That Changed History*. Boston: Houghton Mifflin, 2005.

Everett, Gwen. *Li'l Sis and Uncle Willie*. Washington, DC: National Museum of American Art, Smithsonian Institution, 1991.

Farris, Christine King. *March on!*. New York: Scholastic, 2008.

Farris, Christine King, and Chris K. Soentpiet. *My Brother Martin: A Sister Remembers Growing up with the Rev. Dr. Martin Luther King, Jr.* New York: Simon & Schuster, 2003.

Ferris, Jeri. *Noah Webster & His Words*. Boston: Houghton Mifflin, 2012.

Giblin, James. *George Washington*. New York: Scholastic, 1992.

Giblin, James. *Thomas Jefferson*. New York: Scholastic, 1994.

Gilliland, Judith Heide. *Steamboat!*. New York: DK Publishing, 2000.

Giovanni, Nikki. *Rosa*. New York: Henry Holt, 2005.

Golenbock, Peter. *Hank Aaron*. Orlando, FL: Harcourt, 2005.

Golio, Gary. *When Bob Met Woody*. Boston: Little, Brown, 2011.

Goodman, Joan E. *Beyond the Sea of Ice*. A Great Explorers Book series; 1. New York: Mikaya Press, 1999.

Goodman, Joan E. *Despite All Obstacles*. A Great Explorers Book series. New York: Mikaya Press, 2001.

Goodman, Joan E. *A Long and Uncertain Journey*. A Great Explorers Book series. New York: Mikaya Press, 2001.

Green, Michelle Y. *A Strong Right Arm*. New York: Puffin Books, 2004.

Greenberg, Jan. *Action Jackson*. New York: Square Fish, 2007.

Harness, Cheryl. *George Washington*. Washington, DC: National Geographic Society, 2000.

Harness, Cheryl. *The Groundbreaking, Chance-Taking Life of George Washington Carver and Science & Invention in America*. Washington, DC: National Geographic Society, 2008.

Harness, Cheryl. *Young Abe Lincoln*. Washington, DC: National Geographic Society, 1996.

Hartland, Jessie. *Bon Appetit!*. New York: Schwartz & Wade Books, 2012.

Haskins, James. *Delivering Justice*. Cambridge, MA: Candlewick Press, 2005.

Hopkinson, Deborah. *Keep on!*. Atlanta: Peachtree, 2009.

Hopkinson, Deborah. *Sweet Land of Liberty*. Atlanta: Peachtree, 2007.

Huynh, Quang Nhuong. *The Land I Lost*. New York: Harper & Row, 1986.

Jurmain, Suzanne. *George Did It*. New York: Dutton, 2006.

Jones, Carrie. *Sarah Emma Edmonds Was a Great Pretender*. Minneapolis, MN: Carolrhoda Books, 2011.

Keating, Francis Anthony. *George*. New York: Simon & Schuster, 2012.

Kerley, Barbara, and Ed Fotheringham. *What to Do about Alice?: How Alice Roosevelt Broke the Rules, Charmed the World, and Drove Her Father Teddy Crazy!* New York: Scholastic, 2008.

King, Martin Luther. *I Have a Dream*. New York: Schwartz & Wade Books, 2012.

King, Martin Luther. *My Daddy, Dr. Martin Luther King, Jr*. New York: Amistad, 2013.

Klise, Kate. *Stand Straight, Ella Kate*. New York: Dial, 2010.

Knight, Amelia Stewart, adapted by Lillian Schlissel. *The Way West—Journal of a Pioneer Woman*. New York: Simon & Schuster, 1993.

Kroll, Steven. *By the Dawn's Early Light—The Story of the Star-Spangled Banner*. New York: Scholastic, 1994. Blue Dot Book.

Krull, Kathleen. *A Boy Named FDR*. New York: Alfred A. Knopf, 2011.

Krull, Kathleen. *The Boy Who Invented TV*. New York: Alfred A. Knopf, 2009.

Krull, Kathleen. *Kubla Khan*. New York: Viking, 2010.

Krull, Kathleen. *Wilma Unlimited*. San Diego: Harcourt Brace, 1996.

Krull, Kathleen. *A Woman for President*. New York: Walker, 2004.

Kunhardt, Edith. *Honest Abe*. New York: Greenwillow Books, 1993. Blue Dot Book.

Kurtz, Jane. *Mister Bones*. Ready-to-Read series. New York: Aladdin Paperbacks, 2004.

Lasky, Kathryn. *The Librarian Who Measured the Earth*. Boston: Little, Brown, 1994.

Lasky, Kathryn. *Vision of Beauty*. Cambridge, MA: Candlewick Press, 2000.

Lorbiecki, Marybeth. *Escaping Titanic*. North Mankato, MN: Picture Window Books, 2012.

Macy, Sue. *Basketball Belles*. New York: Holiday House, 2011.

Malaspina, Ann. *Heart on Fire*. Chicago: Albert Whitman, 2012.

Malaspina, Ann. *Touch the Sky*. Chicago: Albert Whitman, 2012.

Martin, Jacqueline Briggs. *Snowflake Bentley*. Boston: Houghton Mifflin, 1998.

Marzollo, Jean. *The Little Plant Doctor*. New York: Holiday House, 2011.

McCarthy, Meghan. *Strong Man*. New York: Alfred A. Knopf, 2007.

McCann, Michelle Roehm. *Luba*. Berkeley, CA: Tricycle Press, 2003.

McCully, Emily Arnold. *Marvelous Mattie*. New York: Farrar Straus Giroux, 2006.

McCully, Emily Arnold. *Manjiro*. New York: Farrar Straus Giroux, 2008.

McGinty, Alice B. *Darwin*. Boston: Houghton Mifflin, 2009.

McGovern, Ann. *Wanted Dead or Alive*. Scholastic, 1965.

Michelson, Richard. *Lipman Pike*. Ann Arbor, MI: Sleeping Bear Press, 2011.

Mochizuki, Ken. *Passage to Freedom*. New York: Lee & Low Books, 1997.

Moss, Marissa. *Mighty Jackie*. New York: Simon & Schuster, 2004.

Moss, Marissa. *Nurse, Soldier, Spy*. New York: Abrams, 2011.

Nelson, Kadir. *Nelson Mandela*. New York: Katherine Tegen Books, an imprint of HarperCollins, 2013.

Nelson, Vaunda Micheaux. *Bad News for Outlaws*. Minneapolis, MN: Carolrhoda Books, 2009.

Nivola, Claire A. *Life in the Ocean*. New York: Frances Foster Books, 2012.

Nobleman, Marc Tyler. *Boys of Steel*. New York: Dragonfly Books, 2008.

Orgill, Roxane. *If I Only Had a Horn*. New York: Houghton Mifflin, 1997.

Orgill, Roxane. *Skit-Scat Raggedy Cat*. Somerville, MA: Candlewick Press, 2010.

Parker, Robert Andrew. *Piano Starts Here*. New York: Schwartz & Wade Books, 2008.

Perdomo, Willie. *Clemente!*. New York: Henry Holt, 2010.

Pinkney, Andrea Davis. *Alvin Ailey*. New York: Hyperion, 1995.

Pinkney, Andrea Davis. *Bill Pickett, Rodeo Ridin' Cowboy*. San Diego: Harcourt Brace, 1996.

Pinkney, Andrea Davis. *Dear Benjamin Banneker*. San Diego: Harcourt Brace, 1994.

Pinkney, Andrea Davis. *Duke Ellington*. New York: Hyperion, 1998.

Pinkney, Andrea Davis. *Sojourner Truth's Step-Stomp Stride*. New York: Disney/Jump at the Sun Books, 2009.

Rappaport, Doreen. *Helen's Big World*. New York: Disney/Hyperion, 2012.

Rappaport, Doreen. *Martin's Big Words*. New York: Jump at the Sun/Hyperion, 2001.

Rappaport, Doreen. *John's Secret Dreams*. New York: Hyperion, 2004.

Rappaport, Doreen. *Paiute Princess*. New York: Frances Foster Books/Farrar Straus Giroux, 2012.

Raschka, Christopher. *Mysterious Thelonious*. New York: Orchard Books, 1997.

Raschka, Christopher. *Charlie Parker Played Be Bop*. New York: Orchard Books, 1992.

Ray, Deborah Kogan. *Down the Colorado*. New York: Farrar, Straus and Giroux, 2007.

Riddles, Libby. *Storm Run*. Seattle: Sasquatch Books, 2002.

Rockwell, Anne F. *Only Passing Through*. New York: Dell Dragonfly Books, 2002.

Rubin, Susan Goldman. *The Anne Frank Case*. New York: Holiday House, 2009.

Rubin, Susan Goldman. *The Cat with the Yellow Star*. New York: Holiday House, 2006.

Rubin, Susan Goldman. *Fireflies in the Dark*. New York: Holiday House, 2000.

Rubin, Susan Goldman. *Haym Salomon*. New York: Abrams Books, 2007.

Rubin, Susan Goldman. *Irena Sendler and the Children of the Warsaw Ghetto*. New York: Holiday House, 2011.

Rubin, Susan Goldman. *Jean Lafitte*. New York: Abrams Books for Young Readers, 2012.

Rubin, Susan Goldman. *Music Was It*. Watertown, MA: Charlesbridge, 2011.

Russo, Marisabina. *Always Remember Me*. New York: Atheneum, 2005.

Ryan, Pam Muñoz, David Saylor, and Brian Selznick. *When Marian Sang: The True Recital of Marian Anderson: The Voice of a Century*. New York: Scholastic, 2002.

Schanzer, Rosalyn. *How We Crossed the West*. Washington, DC: National Geographic Society, 1997.

Schroeder, Alan. *Minty*. New York: Dial, 1996.

Schroeder, Alan. *Satchmo's Blues*. New York: Bantam Doubleday Dell, 1999.

Schubert, Leda. *Monsieur Marceau*. New York: Roaring Brook Press, 2012.

Shange, Ntozake. *Coretta Scott*. New York: Amistad/Katherine Tegen Books, 2009.

Sheldon, David. *Into the Deep*. Watertown, MA: Charlesbridge, 2009.

Silverman, Erica. *Liberty's Voice*. New York: Dutton, 2011.

Sis, Peter. *Follow the Dream*. New York: Knopf, 1991.

Sis, Peter. *Starry Messenger*. New York: Farrar, Straus and Giroux, 1997.

Sis, Peter. *The Wall*. New York: Frances Foster Books, 2007.

Smith, Charles R. *Black Jack*. New York: Roaring Brook Press, 2010.

St. George, Judith. *Take the Lead, George Washington*. New York: Philomel Books, 2005. Blue Dot Book.

Sweet, Melissa. *Balloons Over Broadway*. Boston: Houghton Mifflin, 2011.

Tate, Don. *It Jes' Happened*. New York: Lee & Low Books, 2012.

Tavares, Matt. *Henry Aaron's Dream*. Somerville, MA: Candlewick Press, 2010.

Thomas, Peggy. *Farmer George Plants a Nation*. Honesdale, PA: Calkins Creek, 2008.

Thomas, Peggy. *For the Birds*. Honesdale, PA: Calkins Creek, 2011.

Turner, Robyn. *Georgia O'Keeffe*. Portraits of Women Artists for Children series. Boston: Little, Brown, 1991.

Vaughan, Marcia K. *Irena's Jars of Secrets*. New York: Lee & Low Books, 2011.

Wallner, Alexandra. *Beatrix Potter*. New York: Holiday House, 1995.

Weatherford, Carole Boston. *Before John Was a Jazz Giant*. New York: Henry Holt, 2008.

Weatherford, Carole Boston. *Moses: When Harriet Tubman Led Her People to Freedom*. New York: Jump at the Sun/Hyperion, 2006.

White, Linda Arms. *I Could Do That*. New York: Farrar, Straus and Giroux, 2005.

Williams, Brian. *Faraday, Pioneer of Electricity*. Hauppauge, NY: Barron's, 2003.

Wing, Natasha. *An Eye for Color*. New York: Henry Holt, 2009.

Winnick, Karen B. *Mr. Lincoln's Whiskers*. Honesdale, Pa: Boyds Mills Press, 1996. Blue Dot Book.

Winter, Jeanette. *My Name Is Georgia*. Orlando, FL: Harcourt, 1998.

Winter, Jonah. *Frida*. New York: Arthur A. Levine Books, 2002.

Winter, Jonah. *Dizzy*. New York: Arthur A. Levine Books, 2006.

Winter, Jonah. *Jazz Age Josephine*. New York: Atheneum, 2012.

Winter, Jonah. *Roberto Clemente*. New York: Atheneum, 2005.

Winter, Jonah. *Sonia Sotomayor*. New York: Atheneum, 2009.

Winter, Jonah. *You Never Heard of Sandy Koufax?!*. New York: Schwartz & Wade Books, 2009.

Wise, Bill. *Louis Sockalexis*. New York: Lee & Low Books, 2007.

Woelfle, Gretchen. *Write on, Mercy!*. Honesdale, PA: Calkins Creek, 2012.

Yaccarino, Dan. *The Fantastic Undersea Life of Jacques Cousteau*. New York: Alfred A. Knopf, 2009.

Yolen, Jane. *All-Star!*. New York: Philomel Books, 2010.

Yolen, Jane. *Lost Boy*. New York: Dutton, 2010.

Yoo, Paula. *Sixteen Years in Sixteen Seconds*. New York: Lee & Low Books, 2005.

Figure 11.2   Biography Report

Your Name _____ Teacher Name _____

Title of Book _____

Author of Book _____

Main Character _____

When was this person born? (month, day, year)	
When did this person die? (month, day, year)	
Why is this person important?	
Name 5 characteristics of this person.	1. _____ 2. _____ 3. _____ 4. _____ 5. _____

Figure 11.3 Biography Assessment Rubric

Student Name _____

Category	4	3	2	1
Mechanics	No misspellings or grammatical errors.	Three or fewer misspellings and/or mechanical errors.	Four misspellings and/or grammatical errors.	More than 4 errors in spelling or grammar.
Content	Had 5 or more characteristics for the person.	Had 4 characteristics for the person.	Had 3 characteristics for the person.	Had 2 or less characteristics for the person.
Description	Had many interesting facts. Told exactly what their person was famous for on first page.	Had a few interesting facts about their person. Told exactly what their person was famous for on first page.	Had a few facts included. Told why the person was famous.	Told one extra fact about the person. Had why they were famous incorrect.
Captions	Used captions where needed under the pictures.	Used some captions under the pictures.	Used 1 caption under a picture.	Did not use captions at all.
Pictures	Used pictures on the page to hold interest and make a point. Had a picture of their book.	Used enough pictures on each page. Pictures sometimes did not fit with words.	Used only a few pictures. No picture of book they read.	One picture or less or too many pictures that were scattered all over the page.
Oral Presentation	Interesting, with smooth delivery that held the audience's attention. Faced audience when speaking.	Relatively interesting, with a fairly smooth delivery that usually held the audience's attention.	Delivery not smooth, but able to hold audience attention most of the time. Spoke too softly.	Delivery not smooth and audience attention was lost. Had back to audience the whole time.
Other	Had their name on each slide.			Had a name on one slide.

GRADE LEVEL: FIFTH GRADE
Lesson Topic/Theme: Explorers

Standards
Common Core: W.1, W.5, W.7, W.8
AASL: 1.1.1, 1.1.3, 1.1.4, 1.1.5, 1.1.6, 1.1.8, 1.2.2, 1.3.1, 1.3.5, 2.1.2, 2.1.3, 2.1.5, 2.1.6, 3.1.3, 3.1.4, 3.1.6

Resources
- Various biography books
- Grolier Online/World Book Online
- http://www.biography.com

Instructional Roles
Librarian's Role
- Leads instruction on research/inquiry process
- Provides support for final project

Teacher's Role
- Provides support for research/inquiry process
- Guides students with final project

Project Description
During the first visit, students are given time to browse a variety of books about explorers. Students take time to explore the books and get an idea of which explorer they want to research. Depending on how you want to handle it (and resources available), students choose their top choice, or you could ask them to provide their top three or four choices and then divide them up so that not everyone is exploring the same person.

Once the explorers are assigned, students can begin to brainstorm what they want to know about the explorers. It is good to give them some time to brainstorm on their own, and then the class can share as often many of the same questions are brought up. It will also allow the librarian and classroom teacher to help guide them in creating their questions.

Often they will come up with some basic fact questions like:

1. When/where was he born?
2. When/where did he die?

But, school librarians want them to be thinking of higher-level questions such as:

3. Why did he become an explorer?

4. What were some of the traits that made him a successful (or not successful) explorer?
5. Did he ever find what he was looking for?
6. How did his discovery impact the world?

Once the list is developed, students can brainstorm where to begin looking for the information they need. This is also a great time to talk with them about keeping their information organized as they are researching, as well as having a conversation about copyright and citing sources. Students can use a research journal to organize their information. A sample is included in appendix E.

Use a manila file folder, and on the inside glue four envelopes for student to organize their research. There is a cover, inside pages, and rubric for the back. There could be many other ways to do this, too.

Students will utilize a variety of resources such as print, online encyclopedias, and websites to locate the information they need.

Students will take their facts and create a timeline. Mapping out the events will help them see any overlap in dates and how various explorers built on others' work (or were competing against them).

Options for timelines could include:
- http://www.readwritethink.org/files/resources/interactives/timeline/
- paper/pencil
- Timeliner (Timeliner XE, Scholastic, Tom Snyder Production)

Students will also write an essay that demonstrates their opinion as to why their explorer was important and how they impacted the world. This writing will be an opinion piece as the students are explaining whether their explorer was important or not important and back it up with concrete reasons.

Assessment
The writing piece will be assessed with a rubric.

Figure 11.4 Timeline Rubric

	2	1	0
Timeline	Timeline is complete with all major events listed.	Timeline has most of the major events listed.	Timeline is missing many of the major events.
Writing: Content	Writing shares why the explorer was important, what their impact on the world was, and the opinion of the student.	Writing is missing one of the major parts—why the explorer was important, what their impact on the world was, and the opinion of the student.	Writing is missing two or more the major parts—why the explorer was important, what their impact on the world was, and the opinion of the student.
Writing: Grammar	Writing is clean and without grammatical errors.	Writing is mostly without grammatical errors.	Writing contains many grammatical errors.

GRADE LEVEL: Fifth Grade
Topic: Jamestown

Standards
Common Core: W.5.2a, W.5.8, W.5.9
AASL: 3.1.1, 2.1.3, 2.1.4, 4.1.1, 4.1.2

Resources
- Library of Congress website (www.loc.gov)
- Primary source analysis tool found on the Library of Congress website (refer to figure 11.5) (http://www.loc.gov/teachers/usingprimarysources/guides.html)
- Magnifying glasses
- *Captain Smith's Big and Beautiful Bay* by Rebecca C Jones, Schiffer Publishing, 2011.
- *JamesTowne: Struggle for Survival* by Marcia Sewell, Atheneum, 2001.
- Map of Jamestowne in 1619 (Library of Congress website)
- *Pocahontas*. Walt Disney Home Entertainment, 2005. DVD
- National Geographic site (http://ngm.nationalgeographic.com/2007/05/jamestown/jamestown-standalone)
- Jamestowne sites (http://www.historicjamestowne.org and http://www.nps.gov/jame/index.htm)

Instructional Roles
Librarian's Role
- Teaches the skills necessary to analyze maps
- Introduces new vocabulary: cartographer, archaeologist
- Introduces Jamestown map
- Teaches primary source analysis tool to students

Teacher's Role
- Introduces explorers of the New World to the students
- Teacher reads *Captain Smith's Big and Beautiful Bay* and *JamesTowne: Struggle for Survival* in classroom

Describe Project
This project is a good beginning project for using primary sources from the Library of Congress. The Common Core Standards, as do many of the individual state standards, emphasize using primary sources at almost all grade levels. The Library of Congress website has a plethora of materials to use and a teacher page to assist in showing various uses. The Library of Congress sponsors a weeklong summer institute for teachers and school librarians to learn how to use the website, primary source documents,

and developing lesson plans around the documents. It is led by the education staff at the library including a teacher in residence. It is an excellent opportunity for further education and assistance on using primary sources. You can find out more about the institute by going to http://www.loc.gov/teachers/professionaldevelopment/teacherinstitute/.

Day 1

Librarian gives each student a map of Jamestown, 1612, created by John Smith. This is a primary source document from the Library of Congress website. Students then are given a copy of the Primary Source Analysis Tool. This tool is found on the Library of Congress website and can be accessed at http://www.loc.gov/teachers/usingprimarysources/guides.html. Refer to figure 11.5. Students are given five minutes to write down everything they notice on the map in the first column without talking. Students are then given another five minutes without talking to record in the third column any questions about the map they might have. They may use the magnifying glass to look at the map in more detail. Then the students are given another five minutes to fill out the middle column. After this is done, put students in groups of two or three to discuss what they have written.

Explain to them this map was used for 300 years and was accurate except for one point. See if they can figure out what was different after giving them a modern-day map of the area.

Day 2

Jamestown was recorded lost for a period of many years. People believed the original site was in the James River. Bill Kelso, an archaeologist from Iowa, believed differently. He has since proved that Jamestown is on the bank of the river and is excavating the area. He has discovered the post holes of the original fort. It is fascinating to watch the excavation work. The website will tell you more about what is happening presently. Have students explore the following two websites to see what information they can glean about the area: http://www.nps.gov/jame/index.htm and http://www.historicjamestowne.org. Discuss how an archaeologist works.

Day 3

Compare and contrast John Smith, explorer, to John Smith, Disney character. First have students write down facts they think they know about John Smith. Discuss how they know these things. Bring up the Pocahontas movie and the Walt Disney version of John Smith. Students will work in pairs to write down what they know about John Smith, and to categorize it by Disney facts or real facts. Show excerpts of the Disney movie for discussion. Show two pictures of John Smith. One will be from the primary documents on the Library of Congress website and the other will be a Disney version of John Smith. Discuss what movies do to historical characters.

Day 4

Compare and contrast the 1612 Jamestowne map to a present map of Jamestown. Then examine the 1612 map and a real map of the area to compare and contrast. Read an excerpt of John Smith's diary for students to discuss.

Discuss why the early settlers located their towns where they did. What were their needs? What would be needed if people were going to settle on the moon or a different planet? What must it have been like to be an early explorer? Have students work in pairs to discuss these questions and determine answers.

Assessment

Exit cards will be used to have students answer the following two questions:

Where is Jamestowne located?

Why was Jamestowne located in this particular spot?

Figure 11.5

PRIMARY SOURCE ANALYSIS TOOL

OBSERVE REFLECT QUESTION

FURTHER INVESTIGATION

LIBRARY OF CONGRESS | LOC.gov/teachers

Additional Information about Using Primary Source Materials

This lesson plan was based around two picture books using primary source materials from the Library of Congress. Additional units can be planned in the same type of way by using a picture book as a starting point and developing a lesson plan around the topic that it covers. The list below will assist in finding picture books and the source materials that accompany the topic.

Using Primary Sources with Picture Books

Start with a book, find articles, photographs, letters, diaries, etc. to accompany them and to help students delve deeper into the topic. This covers many of the Common Core Standards as it is using informational material and books to expand reading.

Suggested Topics to Use with Corresponding Picture Books

Titanic
- Titanic newspaper articles (http://www.loc.gov/rr/news/topics/titanic-sinking.html)
- Book: *All Stations! Distress* (Don Brown, Viking, 2011)
- Book: *Titanic Sinks!* (Barry Denenberg, Viking, 2011)
- Book: *Titanic: Voices from the Disaster* (Deborah Hopkinson, Abrams, 2012)
- Book: *Pig on the Titanic* (Gary Crew, HarperCollins, 2005)
- Book: *Titanicat* (Marty Crisp, Sleeping Bear Press, 2008)

Niagara Falls
- Book: *Queen of the Falls* (Chris Van Allsburg, Houghton Mifflin, 2011)
- http://www.loc.gov/pictures/item/det1994006563/PP/

Native Americans
- Book: *Black Elk's Vision: A Lakota Story* (S.D. Nelson, Abrams, 2010)
- http://www.loc.gov/search/?q=black+elk

Abraham Lincoln
- Book: *Climbing Lincoln's Steps the African American Journey* (Suzanne Slade, Whitman, 2010)
- Book: *Mr. Lincoln's Whiskers* (Karen B. Winnick, Boyds Mill Press, 1996)
- Book: *Mr. Lincoln's Boys* (Staton Rabin, Viking, 2008)
- Book: *Abraham Lincoln Comes Home* (Robert Burleigh, Holt, 2008)
- http://www.loc.gov/pictures/item/npc2008010778/

Child Labor
- Book: *Counting on Grace* (Elizabeth Winthrop, Yearling, 2006)
- Book: *Kid Blink Bets the World* (Don Brown, Roaring Book Press, 2004)
- http://www.loc.gov/search/?q=child+labor+in+united+states

Christopher Columbus
- Book: *Follow the Dream* (Peter Sis, Knopf, 1991)
- Book: *Encounter* (Jane Yolen, Harcourt, 1996)
- http://www.loc.gov/rr/print/list/080_columbus.html
- http://lcweb2.loc.gov/ammem/today/oct12.html

Declaration of Independence
- Book: *The Declaration from A to Z* (Catherine L. Osornio, Pelican, 2010)
- Book: *The Journey of the One and Only Declaration of Independence* (Judith St. George, Philomel, 2005)
- Book: *The Declaration of Independence* (Scholastic, 2002)
- http://www.loc.gov/search/?q=declaration+of+independence

American Revolution
- Book: *John, Paul, George and Ben* (Lane Smith, Hyperion, 2006)

Lewis and Clark
- Book: *My Name is York* (Elizabeth Van Steenwhey, Rising Moon Press, 1999)
- Book: *How We Crossed the Mountains* (National Geographic, 1997)
- http://www.loc.gov/search/?q=lewis+and+clark&st=gallery

Civil War
- Book: *Drummer Boy* (Anne Turner, HarperCollins, 1998)
- Book: *Pink and Say* (Patricia Polacco, Philomel, 1994)
- Book: *The Last Brother* (Trinka Noble, Sleeping Bear Press, 2006)
- Book: *Off the Map* (Peter and Connie Roop, Walker, 1993)
- Book: *Bold Journey* (Charles H Bohner, Houghton, 1985)
- http://www.loc.gov/search/?q=civil+war&st=gallery

Frontier Life
- Book: *Sarah, Plain and Tall* (Patricia MacLachlan, Harper & Row, 1985)
- Book: *Dandelions* (Eve Bunting, Perfection Learning, 2001)
- http://www.loc.gov/search/?q=frontier+life+in+u.s.&st=gallery

Statue of Liberty
- Book: *Lady Liberty* (Doreen Rappaport, Candlewick, 2008)
- Book: *Naming Liberty* (Jane Yolen, Philomel, 2008)
- http://www.loc.gov/search/?q=statue+of+liberty

Immigration to America
- Book: *When Jessie Came across the Sea* (Amy Hest, Candlewick Press, 1997)
- Book: *How Many Days to America* (Eve Bunting, Clarion, 1988)
- http://www.loc.gov/search/?q=immigration+to+the+united+states&st=-gallery

Suffrage
- Book: *The Ballot Box Battle* (Emily Arnold McCully, Knopf, 1998)
- Book: *A Woman for President* (Kathleen Krull, Knopf, 2004)
- http://www.loc.gov/search/?q=womens+suffrage

Japanese Internment during World War II
- Book: *So Far from the Sea* (Eve Bunting, Clarion, 1998)
- Book: *Baseball Saved Us* (Scholastic, 1993)
- Book: *Music for Alice* (Allen Say, Houghton, 2004)
- Book: *The Bracelet* (Yoshiko Uchida, Putnam, 1996)
- http://www.loc.gov/search/?q=japanese+internment

Martin Luther King Jr.
- Book: *Martin's Big Words* (Doreen Rappaport, Hyperion, 2001)
- Book: *My Brother Martin; A Sister Remembers* (Christine King Farris, Simon and Schuster, 2003)
- Book: *My Uncle Martin's Big Heart* (Angela Farris Watkins, Abrams, 2010)
- Book: *March On* (Christine Farris, Scholastic, 2008)
- http://www.loc.gov/search/?q=martin+luther+king

September 11
- Book: *14 Cows for America* (Carmen Agra Deedy, Peachtree, 2009)
- Book: *The Man Who Walked between the Towers* (Mordicai Gerstein, Roaring Brook Press, 2003)
- Book: *Fireboat; The Heroic Adventures of the John J. Harvey* (Maira Kalman, Putnam, 2002)
- Book: *America Is Under Attack* (Don Brown, Roaring Book Press, 2011)
- http://www.loc.gov/search/?q=september+11

Slavery
- Book: *Barefoot: Escape on the Underground Railroad* (Pamela Duncan Edwards, HarperCollins, 1997)
- Book: *Place Called Freedom* (Scott Sanders, Atheneum, 1997)
- Book: *Sweet Clara and the Freedom Quilt* (Sonia Levitin, Knopf, 1993)
- Book: *Nettie's Trip South* (Ann Turner, Aladdin, 1995)
- Book: *Letters from a Slave Girl* (Mary Lyons, Aladdin, 1996
- http://www.loc.gov/search/?q=underground+railroad&st=gallery
- http://www.loc.gov/search/?q=slavery&st=gallery

Vietnam War
- Book: *The Wall* (Eve Bunting, Clarion, 1990)
- http://www.loc.gov/search/?q=vietnam+war&fa=site%3Apictures&st=gallery

Lighthouses
- Book: *Abbie against the Storm* (Marcia Vaughn, Beyond Words Publishing, 1999)
- http://www.loc.gov/search/?q=lighthouses&st=gallery

Early American History
- Book: *Molly Bannaky* (Alice McGill, Houghton, 1999)

GRADE LEVEL: Fifth Grade

Lesson Topic/Theme: Primary Sources: September 11

Standards

Common Core: W.5.2a, W.5.2d, SL.5.1a, SL.5.2, W.5.8, W.5.9, SL.5.4, SL.5.5
AASL: 3.1.2, 3.1.3, 3.2.1, 3.2.3

Resources

- Materials from the Library of Congress website (www.loc.gov)
- Scholastic Timeline of September 11 (http://www.scholastic.com/browse/article.jsp?id=5237)
- PBS (http://www.pbs.org/newshour/extra/features/july-dec01/bombing_background)
- Library of Congress website (http://www.loc.gov/teachers/)
- Primary source analysis tool sheet from the Library of Congress website (http://www.loc.gov/teachers/usingprimarysources/guides.html)
- Timeliner (Timeliner XP, Tom Snyder Productions)

Instructional Roles

Librarian's Role

- Introduces websites
- Introduces timeline
- Introduces primary source documents

Teacher's Role

- Introduces topic of 9/11 to class
- Shares and reads books on topic
- Creates pairs of students
- Discusses symbolism

Project Description

Lesson 1
The teacher has already introduced the topic of September 11 in the classroom through books and other resources before the first meeting. The teacher also has had a discussion of symbolism with the class. Students will come to the library to examine websites bookmarked on the library website concerning September 11. The librarian will discuss timelines. After taking notes from the website, students will then create a timeline of the events of September 11 to better understand the time frame and the varied happenings on that day.

Lesson 2

Students will work in pairs determined by the teacher. Each group will have a picture from the Library of Congress website concerning September 11. These pictures are superimposed pictures and combine some of the happenings on that day. Refer to the Library of Congress website to see an example of these pictures in the resource section. Give each group a copy of the Primary Source Analysis Tool from the Library of Congress website. Instruct the students to write down under the observation column the first thing they notice in the picture. Then tell them to take five minutes to examine the picture, writing down everything they observe in the picture, without talking to their partner. After they have done this, have them take five minutes to write down any questions or what they might want to know about the picture in the question column still with no discussion. The last column is reflection. Have them write any additional comments they may have about the picture. After this time has elapsed, have them turn to their partner and compare and discuss their picture and what they observed with their partner.

Lesson 3

After giving each group about ten minutes to decide what they want to share with the group have each group show their picture via computer projection to the class. Have them explain what they observed and the conclusions that they came to with the pictures. Make sure they are discussing the symbolism of what they are seeing. Symbolism has been discussed in the classroom already under teacher direction. At this point the class may ask questions of the presenters.

Assessment

Teacher and librarian observation of students work on the Primary Source Analysis tool.

Assessment will be done on the student's presentation to the class in terms of a short rubric.

Figure 11.6

PRIMARY SOURCE ANALYSIS TOOL

OBSERVE REFLECT QUESTION

OBSERVE | REFLECT | QUESTION

FURTHER INVESTIGATION

LIBRARY OF CONGRESS | LOC.gov/teachers

Figure 11.7 September 11 Assessment

Name _____

Category	3	2	1	0
Source Analysis Tool	Filled out completely. Had many deep thoughts about the picture especially in the column labeled reflect.	Filled out completely. Had the observe and question columns filled out, but very little written in the reflect column.	Filled out partially. Had nothing written in the reflection column.	Not filled out at all.
Group Dynamics	Lots of discussion within the group about what they saw in the pictures. Each member talked and discussed.	Some discussion within the group. Some members talked more than others.	Discussion in the group was only by one or two people. Sat quietly most of the time or argued with each other.	No discussion at all from any of the members of the group.
Symbolism	Discussed symbolism at some length. Had discussion among members of the group.	Discussed at least one symbol in the picture.	Mentioned symbolism briefly when asked by the class.	Did not mention symbolism at all.
Presentation	Spoke loudly and clearly for all of the class to hear. Faced audience when talking. Very poised. All members of the group spoke on a different facet of the picture.	Spoke quietly but faced the audience. Answered most questions when asked. All members spoke about the picture.	Spoke quietly and were unsure at times what to say. Went back and forth looking at audience and looking at screen. Only one member of the group spoke.	Could not hear student at all when speaking. Had their back to the audience as they looked at their picture on the screen.
Questions	Answered questions from the class completely. The group would take turns answering the questions.	Answered most of the questions from the class. Were very quiet when answering.	Tried to answer the questions from the audience. Many times were unsure of what the question was or how to answer it.	Could not answer questions from the class at all.

Figure 11.8 September 11 Worksheet

Name _____

After reading the information on the websites, certain information needs to be remembered. This sheet will help you recall these facts as you work on your timeline.

How many hijackers were there altogether?	
How many people were dead or missing from the World Trade Center?	
How may people were dead or missing from the Pentagon?	
What is the Pentagon?	
What were some of the things that the United States did after the attacks on September 11?	
How many people worked in the World Trade Center?	
How many stories high was the World Trade Center?	
How many stories high was Building 7?	

How many people were on each flight? What was the number on each flight?

Flight	
Flight	
Flight	
Flight	

Appendix A: Children's Literature Bibliography

Alliteration
Barretta, Gene. *Dear Deer*. New York: Holt, 2007.
Basher, Simon. *ABC Kids*. New York: Kingfisher, 2011.
Edwards, Pamela Duncan. *Some Smug Slug*. New York: HarperCollins, 1996.
Fleming, Denise. *Beetle Bop*. Orlando, FL: Harcourt, 2007.
Fleming, Denise. *In the Small, Small Pond*. New York: Scholastic, 1993.
Kellogg, Steven. *Aster Aardvark's Alphabet Adventures*. New York: Mulberry Books, 1992.
Sayre, April Pulley. *Vulture View*. New York: Henry Holt, 2007.
Wood, Audrey. *Silly Sally*. San Diego: Harcourt Brace Jovanovich, 1992.

Alphabet and Counting Books
Allen, Susan. *Read Anything Good Lately*. Minneapolis: Millbrook Press, 2003.
April, Bubbles, Chocolate. Compiled by Lee Bennett Hopkins; illustrated by Barrett Root. New York: Simon & Schuster, 1993.
Baker, Keith. *LMNO Peas*. New York: Beach Lane Books, 2010.
Basher, Simon. *ABC Kids*. New York: Kingfisher, 2011.
Bingham, Kelly L. *Z Is for Moose*. New York: Greenwillow Books, 2012.
Boldt, Mike. *123 Versus ABC*. New York: HarperCollins, 2013.
Brennan-Nelson, Denise. *J Is for Jack-O'-Lantern*. Chelsea, MI: Sleeping Bear Press, 2009.
Cabatingan, Erin. *A Is for Musk Ox*. New York: Roaring Brook Press, 2012.
Chapman, Todd. *D Is for Dinosaur*. Chelsea, MI: Sleeping Bear Press, 2008.
Charlip, Remy. *Handtalk*. New York: Aladdin Books, 1986.
Domeniconi, David. *M Is for Majestic; A National Parks Alphabet*. Chelsea, MI: Sleeping Bear Press, 2003.
Edwards, Pamela Duncan. *The Wacky Wedding*. New York: Hyperion, 1999.
Edwards, Pamela Duncan. *Warthogs in the Kitchen*. New York: Hyperion, 1998.

Ehlert, Lois. *Eating the Alphabet*. San Diego: Harcourt Brace Jovanovich, 1989. Blue Dot Book.
Elting, Mary, 1909. *Q Is for Duck*. New York: Houghton Mifflin/Clarion Books, 1980.
Entrekin, Allison Weiss. *For the Love of Dogs*. Chicago: Triumph Books, 2011.
Ernst, Lisa Campbell. *The Turn-Around Upside-Down Alphabet Book*. New York: Simon & Schuster, 2004.
Fredericks, Anthony D. *A Is for Anaconda*. Chelsea, MI: Sleeping Bear Press, 2009.
Gagliano, Eugene M. *V Is for Venus Flytrap*. Chelsea, MI: Sleeping Bear Press, 2009.
Geisert, Arthur. *Pigs from A to Z*. Boston: Houghton Mifflin, 1986.
Geisert, Arthur. *Pigs from 1 to 10*. Boston: Houghton Mifflin, 1992.
Gowan, Barbara. *D Is for Desert*. Ann Arbor, MI: Sleeping Bear Press, 2012.
Grodin, Elissa. *D Is for Democracy*. Series in Alphabet Books. Chelsea, MI: Sleeping Bear Press, 2004.
Grossman, Bill. *My Little Sister Ate One Hare*. New York: Crown, 1996.
Helman, Andrea. *O Is for Orca*. Seattle: Sasquatch Books, 1995.
Hepworth, Catherine. *Antics!*. New York: Putnam, 1992. Blue Dot Book.
Hoena, B. A. *A Desert ABC*. A+ Alphabet Books series. Mankato, MN: Capstone Press, 2005.
Hoena, B. A. *Weather ABC*. A+ Alphabet Books series. Mankato, MN: Capstone Press, 2005.
Johnson, Stephen, 1964. *Alphabet City*. New York: Viking, 1995.
Jonas, Ann. *Splash!*. New York: Mulberry Books, 1997.
Kellogg, Steven. *Aster Aardvark's Alphabet Adventures*. New York: Mulberry Books, 1992.
Knox, Barbara. *A B C Under the Sea*. Alphabet Books series. Mankato, MN: Capstone Press, 2003.
Lobel, Anita. *Alison's Zinnia*. New York: Greenwillow Books, 1990.
Martin, Steve. *The Alphabet from A to Y with Bonus Letter, Z!*. New York: Doubleday/Flying Dolphin Press, 2007.
Merriam, Eve. *Twelve Ways to Get to Eleven*. New York: Simon & Schuster, 1992.
Obligado, Lilian. *Faint Frogs Feeling Feverish*. New York: Puffin Books, 1986.
Osornio, Catherine L. *The Declaration of Independence from A to Z*. Gretna, LA: Pelican Publishing, 2010.
Pallotta, Jerry. *The Beetle Alphabet Book*. Watertown, MA: Charlesbridge, 2004.
Pallotta, Jerry. *The Icky Bug Alphabet Book*. Watertown, MA: Charlesbridge, 1986.
Pallotta, Jerry. *The Yucky Reptile Alphabet Book*. Watertown, MA: Charlesbridge, 1989.
Pelletier, David. *The Graphic Alphabet*. New York: Orchard, 1996.
Raczka, Bob. *3-D ABC*. Minneapolis: Millbrook Press, 2007.
Schroeder, Alan. *Ben Franklin*. New York: Holiday House, 2011.
Schuette, Sarah L. *African Animals A B C*. Alphabet Books series. Mankato, MN: Capstone Press, 2003.
Schuette, Sarah L. *An Alphabet Salad*. Alphabet Books series. Mankato, MN: Capstone Press, 2003.
Seeger, Laura Vaccaro. *The Hidden Alphabet*. Brookfields, CT: Roaring Brook Press, 2003.
Sierra, Judy. *There's a Zoo in Room 22*. San Diego: Harcourt, 2000.
Schwartz, David M. *G Is for Googol*. Berkeley, CA: Tricycle Press, 1998.
Viorst, Judith. *The Alphabet from Z to A*. New York: Atheneum, 1994.
Werner, Sharon. *Bugs by the Numbers*. Maplewood, NJ: Blue Apple Books, 2011.
Wise, William. *Ten Sly Piranhas*. New York: Dial, 1993.
Wood, Audrey. *Alphabet Mystery*. New York: Blue Sky Press, 2003.
Zschock, Martha Day. *Journey around Washington, D.C. from A to Z*. Alphabet Book series. Beverly, MA: Commonwealth Editions, 2004.

Diary Books

Ada, Alma Flor. *Dear Peter Rabbit*. New York: Atheneum, 1994.
Ada, Alma Flor. *With Love, Little Red Hen*. New York: Atheneum, 2001.
Ada, Alma Flor. *Yours Truly, Goldilocks*. New York: Atheneum, 1998.
Ahlberg, Janet. *The Jolly Postman or, Other People's Letters*. Boston: Little, Brown, 1986.
Brisson, Pat. *Kate Heads West*. New York: Bradbury Press, 1990.
Christelow, Eileen. *Letters from a Desperate Dog*. New York: Clarion Books, 2006.
Cleary, Beverly. *Dear Mr. Henshaw*. New York: Morrow, 1983.
Cleary, Beverly. *Strider*. New York: Morrow, 1991.
Clements, Andrew. *Extra Credit*. New York: Atheneum, 2009.
Cronin, Doreen. *Diary of a Fly*. New York: Joanna Cotler Books, 2007.
Cronin, Doreen. *Diary of a Spider*. New York: Joanna Cotler Books, 2005.
Cronin, Doreen. *Diary of a Worm*. New York: Joanna Cotler Books, 2003.
Day, Lucille. *Chain Letter*. Berkeley, CA: Heyday Books, 2005.
Edwards, Pamela Duncan. *Dear Tooth Fairy*. New York: Katherine Tegen Books, 2003.
French, Jackie. *Diary of a Baby Wombat*. Boston: Clarion Books, 2010.
French, Jackie. *Diary of a Wombat*. New York: Clarion Books, 2003.
George, Jean Craighead, 1919. *Look to the North*. New York: HarperCollins, 1997.
Holmes, Sara. *Letters from Rapunzel*. New York: HarperCollins, 2007.
Hopkinson, Deborah. *Birdie's Lighthouse*. New York: Atheneum, 1997.
Mercati, Cynthia. *Wagons Ho!*. Logan, IO: Perfection Learning, 2000.
Nolen, Jerdine. *Plantzilla*. San Diego, CA: Harcourt, 2002.
Orloff, Karen Kaufman. *I Wanna Iguana*. New York: Putnam, 2004.
Pattison, Darcy. *Searching for Oliver K. Woodman*. Orlando, FL: Harcourt, 2005.
Pulver, Robin. *Silent Letters Loud and Clear*. New York: Holiday House, 2008.
Salas, Laura Purdie. *Bookspeak!*. Boston: Houghton Mifflin Harcourt, 2011.
Schlissel, Lillian. *The Way West*. New York: Simon & Schuster, 1993.
Spurr, Elizabeth. *The Long, Long Letter*. New York: Hyperion Books, 1996.
Talbott, Hudson. *Amazon Diary*. New York: Putnam & Grosset, 1998.
Teague, Mark. *Dear Mrs. LaRue*. New York: Scholastic, 2002.
Teague, Mark. *Detective LaRue*. New York: Scholastic, 2004.
Teague, Mark. *LaRue for Mayor*. New York: The Blue Sky Press, 2008.
Whiteley, Opal. *Only Opal*. New York: PaperStar, 1994.

Language Arts

Barrett, Judi. *Things That Are Most in the World*. New York: Atheneum, 1998.
Cleary, Brian P. *The Action of Subtraction*. Minneapolis: Millbrook Press, 2006.
Cleary, Brian P. *The Bug in the Jug Wants a Hug*. Minneapolis: Millbrook Press, 2011.
Cleary, Brian P. *Cool! Whoa! Ah and Oh! What Is an Interjection?*. Minneapolis: Millbrook Press, 2009.
Cleary, Brian P. *Dearly, Nearly, Insincerely*. Series in Words Are Categorical. Minneapolis: Carolrhoda Books, 2003.
Cleary, Brian P. *Hairy, Scary, Ordinary*. Words Are Categorical Series. Minneapolis: Carolrhoda Books, 2000.
Cleary, Brian P. *How Long or How Wide?*. Minneapolis: Millbrook Press, 2007.
Cleary, Brian P. *How Much Can a Bare Bear Bear?*. Words Are Categorical Series. Minneapolis: Millbrook Press, 2005.

Cleary, Brian P. *I and You and Don't Forget Who*. Minneapolis, Minnesota: Carolrhoda Books, 2004.
Cleary, Brian P. *Lazily, Crazily, Just a Bit Nasally: More about Adverbs* Minneapolis: Millbrook Press, 2008.
Cleary, Brian P. *A Lime, a Mime, a Pool of Slime*. Minneapolis: Millbrook Press, 2006.
Cleary, Brian P. *A Mink, a Fink, a Skating Rink*. Words Are Categorical Series. Minneapolis: Carolrhoda Books, 1999.
Cleary, Brian P. *The Mission of Addition*. Minneapolis: Millbrook Press, 2005.
Cleary, Brian P. *Mrs. Riley Bought Five Itchy Aardvarks*. Minneapolis: Millbrook Press, 2008.
Cleary, Brian P. *On the Scale*. Minneapolis: Millbrook Press, 2008.
Cleary, Brian P. *Pitch and Throw, Grasp and Know*. Minneapolis: Carolrhoda Books, 2005.
Cleary, Brian P. *Punctuation Station*. Minneapolis: Millbrook Press, 2010.
Cleary, Brian P. *Quirky, Jerky, Extra Perky*. Words Are Categorical Series. Minneapolis: Millbrook Press, 2007.
Cleary, Brian P. *Rhyme & Punishment Adventures in Wordplay*. Minneapolis: Millbrook Press, 2006.
Cleary, Brian P. *Six Sheep Sip Thick Shakes*. Minneapolis: Millbrook Press, 2011.
Cleary, Brian P. *Skin Like Milk, Hair of Silk*. Minneapolis: Millbrook Press, 2009.
Cleary, Brian P. *Slide and Slurp, Scratch and Burp*. Minneapolis: Millbrook Press, 2007.
Cleary, Brian P. *Stop and Go, Yes and No What Is an Antonym?*. Minneapolis: Millbrook Press, 2006.
Cleary, Brian P. *Straight and Curvy, Meek and Nervy*. Minneapolis: Millbrook Press, 2009.
Cleary, Brian P. *Stroll and Walk, Babble and Talk*. Minneapolis: Millbrook Press, 2008.
Cleary, Brian P. *Super-Hungry Mice Eat Onions*. Minneapolis: Millbrook Press, 2010.
Cleary, Brian P. *To Root, to Toot, to Parachute*. Words Are Categorical Series. Minneapolis: Carolrhoda Books, 2001.
Cleary, Brian P. *Under, Over, by the Clover*. Minneapolis: Carolrhoda Books, 2002.
Cleary, Brian P. *Windows, Rings, and Grapes*. Minneapolis: Millbrook Press, 2009.
Gwynne, Fred. *The Sixteen Hand Horse*. New York: Simon & Schuster, 1992.
Gwynne, Fred. *The King Who Rained*. New York: Prentice Hall, 1980.
Heller, Ruth. *Behind the Mask*. New York: Grosset & Dunlap, 1995.
Heller, Ruth. *A Cache of Jewels and Other Collective Nouns*. New York: Grosset & Dunlap, 1992.
Heller, Ruth. *Fantastic! Wow! And Unreal!*. A Book about Interjections and Conjunctions Series. Scholastic.
Heller, Ruth. *Kites Sail High*. New York: Grosset & Dunlap, 1988.
Heller, Ruth. *Many Luscious Lollipops*. New York: Grosset & Dunlap, 1989.
Heller, Ruth. *Merry-Go-Round (14)*. A Book about Nouns series. Scholastic.
Heller, Ruth. *Mine, All Mine*. New York: Grosset & Dunlap, 1997.
Heller, Ruth. *Up, Up and Away*. New York: Grosset & Dunlap, 1991.
Higgins, Nadia. *Super Apostrophe Saves the Day!*. North Mankato, MN: Child's World, 2012.
Hills, Tad. *Rocket Writes a Story*. Schwartz-Wade Books, 2012.
Jones, Charlotte Foltz. *Eat Your Words*. New York: Delacorte Press, 1999.
Juster, Norton. *As Silly as Knees, as Busy as Bees*. New York: Beech Tree, 1998 [1929].
Martin, Bill. *The Maestro Plays*. New York: Henry Holt, 1994.
Peterson, Mary. *Piggies in the Pumpkin Patch*. Watertown, MA: Charlesbridge, 2010.
Pulver, Robin. *Nouns and Verbs Have a Field Day*. New York: Holiday House, 2006.
Pulver, Robin. *Punctuation Takes a Vacation*. New York: Holiday House, 2003.
Rosenthal, Amy. *Exclamation Mark*. New York: Scholastic, 2013.
Terban, Marvin. *Guppies in Tuxedos*. New York: Clarion Books, 1988.

Terban, Marvin. *I Think I Thought, and Other Tricky Verbs*. New York: Clarion, 1984.
Terban, Marvin. *In a Pickle, and Other Funny Idioms*. New York: Clarion Books, 1983.
Terban, Marvin. *Mad as a Wet Hen! And Other Funny Idioms*. New York: Clarion Books, 1987.
Terban, Marvin. *Your Foot's on My Feet*. New York: Clarion Books, 1986.
Truss, Lynne. *The Girl's Like Spaghetti*. New York: Putnam, 2007.
Viorst, Judith. *The Alphabet from Z to A*. New York: Atheneum, 1994.

Math Books

Adler, David A. *Fraction Fun*. New York: Holiday House, 1996.
Adler, David A. *Money Madness*. New York: Holiday House, 2009.
Adler, David A. *Working with Fractions*. New York: Holiday House, 2007.
Axelrod, Amy. *Pigs Will Be Pigs*. New York: Aladdin Paperbacks, 1997.
Ball, Johnny. *Go Figure!*. London: DK, 2005.
Burns, Marilyn. *The Greedy Triangle*. New York: Scholastic, 1994.
Clements, Andrew. *A Million Dots*. New York: Simon and Schuster, 2006.
Dolphin, Colleen. *Angles to Zeros*. Let's Look A to Z series. Edina, MN: ABDO Publishers, 2009.
Hulme, Joy N. *Sea Squares*. New York: Hyperion, 1993.
Leedy, Loreen. *Follow the Money!*. New York: Holiday House, 2002.
Leedy, Loreen. *Fraction Action*. New York: Holiday House, 1994.
Leedy, Loreen. *The Great Graph Contest*. New York: Holiday House, 2005.
Leedy, Loreen. *Seeing Symmetry*. New York: Holiday House, 2012.
Marvelous Math. Selected by Lee Bennett Hopkins; illustrated by Karen Barbour. New York: Simon & Schuster, 1997.
McMillan, Bruce. *Eating Fractions*. New York: Scholastic, 1991.
Mollol, Tololwa. *My Rows and Piles of Coins*. New York: Clarion Books, 1999.
Murphy, Stuart J. *The Best Bug Parade*. New York: HarperCollins, 1996.
Murphy, Stuart J. *The Best Vacation Ever*. MathStart Series. New York: HarperCollins, 1997.
Murphy, Stuart J. *Betcha*. MathStart Series. New York: HarperCollins, 1997.
Murphy, Stuart J. *Bigger, Better, Best!*. MathStart Series. New York: HarperCollins, 2002.
Murphy, Stuart J. *Bug Dance*. MathStart Series. New York: HarperCollins, 2002.
Murphy, Stuart J. *Captain Invincible and the Space Shapes*. MathStart Series. New York: HarperCollins, 2001.
Murphy, Stuart J. *Coyotes All Around*. New York: HarperCollins, 2003.
Murphy, Stuart J. *Circus Shapes*. MathStart Series. New York: HarperCollins, 1998.
Murphy, Stuart J. *Dave's Down-to-Earth Rock Shop*. MathStart Series. New York: HarperCollins, 2000.
Murphy, Stuart J. *Dinosaur Deals*. MathStart Series. New York: HarperCollins, 2001.
Murphy, Stuart J. *Divide and Ride*. MathStart Series. New York: HarperCollins, 1997.
Murphy, Stuart J. *Earth Day-Hooray!*. MathStart Series. New York: HarperCollins, 2004.
Murphy, Stuart J. *Elevator Magic*. MathStart Series. New York: HarperCollins, 1997.
Murphy, Stuart J. *Emma's Friendwich*. Watertown, MA: Charlesbridge, 2010.
Murphy, Stuart J. *Every Buddy Counts*. New York: HarperCollins, 1997.
Murphy, Stuart J. *Game Time*. MathStart Series. New York: HarperCollins, 2000.
Murphy, Stuart J. *Get up and Go!*. MathStart Series. New York: HarperCollins, 1996.
Murphy, Stuart J. *The Greatest Gymnast of All*. MathStart Series. New York: HarperCollins, 1998.
Murphy, Stuart J. *Hamster Champs*. MathStart Series. New York: HarperCollins, 2005.
Murphy, Stuart J. *Henry the Fourth*. MathStart Series. New York: HarperCollins, 1999.
Murphy, Stuart J. *A House for Birdie*. MathStart Series. New York: HarperCollins, 2004.
Murphy, Stuart J. *It's about Time!*. MathStart Series. New York: HarperCollins, 2005.

Murphy, Stuart J. *Jump, Kangaroo, Jump*. MathStart Series. New York: HarperCollins, 1999.
Murphy, Stuart J. *Just Enough Carrots*. MathStart Series. New York, NY: HarperCollins, 1997.
Murphy, Stuart J. *Leaping Lizards*. MathStart Series. New York: HarperCollins, 2005.
Murphy, Stuart J. *Lemonade for Sale*. MathStart Series. New York: HarperCollins, 1998.
Murphy, Stuart J. *Less than Zero*. MathStart Series. New York: HarperCollins, 2003.
Murphy, Stuart J. *Let's Fly a Kite*. MathStart Series. New York: HarperCollins, 2000.
Murphy, Stuart J. *Mall Mania*. MathStart Series. New York: HarperCollins, 2006. Book.
Murphy, Stuart J. *Mighty Maddie*. MathStart Series. New York: HarperCollins, 2004.
Murphy, Stuart J. *Monster Musical Chairs*. MathStart Series. New York: HarperCollins, 2000.
Murphy, Stuart J. *More or L*. MathStart Series. New York: HarperCollins, 2005.
Murphy, Stuart J. *One ... Two ... Three ... Sassafras!*. MathStart Series. New York: HarperCollins, 2002.
Murphy, Stuart J. *Percy Plays It Safe*. Watertown, MA: Charlesbridge, 2010.
Murphy, Stuart J. *Rabbit's Pajama Party*. MathStart Series. New York: HarperCollins, 1999.
Murphy, Stuart J. *Probably Pistachio*. MathStart Series. New York: HarperCollins, 2001.
Murphy, Stuart J. *Racing Around*. MathStart Series. New York: HarperCollins, 2002.
Murphy, Stuart J. *Rodeo Time*. MathStart Series. New York: HarperCollins, 2006.
Murphy, Stuart J. *Room for Ripley*. MathStart Series. New York: HarperCollins, 1999.
Murphy, Stuart J. *Same Old Horse*. MathStart Series. New York: HarperCollins, 2005.
Murphy, Stuart J. *Shark Swimathon*. MathStart Series. New York: HarperCollins, 2001.
Murphy, Stuart J. *Sluggers' Car Wash*. MathStart Series. New York: HarperCollins, 2002.
Murphy, Stuart J. *Spunky Monkeys on Parade*. MathStart Series. New York: HarperCollins, 1999.
Murphy, Stuart J. *The Sundae Scoop*. MathStart Series. New York: HarperCollins, 2003.
Murphy, Stuart J. *Super Sand Castle Saturday*. MathStart Series. New York: HarperCollins, 1999.
Murphy, Stuart J. *Tally O'Malley*. MathStart Series. New York: HarperCollins, 2004.
Murphy, Stuart J. *Too Many Kangaroo Things to Do*. MathStart Series. New York: HarperCollins, 1996.
Murphy, Stuart J. *Treasure Map*. MathStart Series. New York: HarperCollins, 2004.
Nagda, Ann Whitehead. *Tiger Math*. New York: Henry Holt, 2002.
Napoli, Donna Jo. *The Wishing Club*. New York: Henry Holt, 2007.
Neuschwander, Cindy. *Mummy Math*. New York: Henry Holt, 2005.
Neuschwander, Cindy. *Sir Cumference and All the King's Tens*. Watertown, MA: Charlesbridge, 2009.
Neuschwander, Cindy. *Sir Cumference and the Isle of Immeter*. Watertown, MA: Charlesbridge, 2006.
Neuschwander, Cindy. *Sir Cumference and the Sword in the Cone*. Watertown, MA: Charlesbridge, 2003.
Neuschwander, Cindy. *Sir Cumference and the Viking's Map*. Watertown, MA: Charlesbridge, 2012.
Pallotta, Jerry. *The Hershey's Milk Chocolate Bar Fractions* New York: Scholastic, 1999.
Pallotta, Jerry. *Hershey's Milk Chocolate Weights & Measures*. New York: Scholastic, 2002.
Pinczes, Elinor J. *Inchworm and a Half*. New York: Houghton Mifflin, 2001.
Schwartz, David M. *G Is for Googol*. Berkeley, CA: Tricycle Press, 1998.
Schwartz, David M. *How Much Is a Million?*. New York: Scholastic, 1985.
Schwartz, David M. *If You Hopped Like a Frog*. New York: Scholastic, 1999.
Schwartz, David M. *If You Made a Million*. New York: Lothrop, Lee & Shepard Books, 1989.
Schwartz, David M. *Millions to Measure*. New York: HarperCollins, 2002.
Schwartz, David M. *On beyond a Million*. New York: Random House, 1999.

Mythology

Bryant, Megan E. *She's All That!*. New York: Scholastic, 2010.
Curlee, Lynn. *Mythological Creatures*. New York: Atheneum, 2008.
Johnson, Robin. *Understanding Roman Myths*. Myths Understood series. New York: Crabtree, 2012.
Kelly, Sophia. *What a Beast!*. New York: F. Watts, 2010.
Kopp, Megan. *Understanding Native American Myths*. Myths Understood series. New York: Crabtree, 2013.
Mayer, Marianna. *Pegasus*. New York: Morrow, 1998.
Napoli, Donna Jo. *Treasury of Egyptian Mythology*. National Geographic Kids series. Washington, DC: National Geographic, 2013.
Napoli, Donna Jo. *Treasury of Greek Mythology*. National Geographic series. Washington, D.C: National Geographic Society, 2011.
Otfinoski, Steven. *All in the Family*. New York: F. Watts, 2010.
Wilbur, Helen L. *Z Is for Zeus*. Chelsea, MI: Sleeping Bear Press, 2008.
Williams, Brian. *Understanding Norse Myths*. Myths Understood series. New York: Crabtree, 2013.

Onomatopoeia

Beil, Karen Magnuson. *Mooove Over!*. New York: Holiday House, 2004.
Bruss, Deborah. *Book! Book! Book!*. New York: Arthur A. Levine Books, 2001.
Cronin, Doreen. *Click, Clack, Boo!*. New York: Atheneum, 2013.
Cronin, Doreen. *Click, Clack, Moo*. New York: Simon & Schuster, 2000.
Cronin, Doreen. *Click, Clack, Quackity-Quack*. New York: Atheneum, 2005.
Czekaj, Jef. *Oink-a-Doodle-Moo*. New York: Balzer + Bray, 2012.
Edwards, Pamela Duncan. *Slop Goes the Soup*. New York: Hyperion, 2001.
Fleming, Denise. *The Cow Who Clucked*. New York: Henry Holt, 2006.
Gall, Chris. *Dear Fish*. New York: Little, Brown, 2006.
Greene, Rhonda Gowler. *Barnyard Song*. New York: Atheneum, 1997.
Jorgensen, Gail. *Crocodile Beat*. New York: Bradbury Press, 1989.
MacDonald, Ross. *Achoo! Bang! Crash!*. Brookfield, CT: Roaring Brook Press, 2003.
McPhail, David M. *The Day the Dog Said, "Cock-a-Doodle-Doo!"*. Hello Reader! series. New York: Scholastic, 1996.
Palatini, Margie. *Boo-Hoo Moo*. New York: Katherine Tegen Books, 2009.
Rau, Dana Meachen. *So Many Sounds*. Rookie Reader series. New York: Children's Press, 2001.
Root, Phyllis. *Rattletrap Car*. Cambridge, MA: Candlewick Press, 2004.
Shaskan, Trisha Speed. *If You Were Onomatopoeia*. Minneapolis: Picture Window Books, 2008.
Spence, Rob, and Amy Spence. *Clickety Clack*. New York: Viking, 1999.

Persuasive Writing

Anderson, Laurie Halse. *Thank You, Sarah: The Woman Who Saved Thanksgiving*. New York: Simon & Schuster, 2002.
Biegert, Melissa Ann Langley. *Looking for Fingerprints*. Mankato, MN: Capstone Press, 2010.
Cherry, Lynne. *The Great Kapok Tree*. Fairbanks, AK: Gulliver Books, 1990.
Cherry, Lynne. *How We Know What We Know about Our Changing Climate*. Nevada City, CA: Dawn Pub, 2008.
Cherry, Lynne. *A River Ran Wild*. San Diego: Harcourt Brace Jovanovich, 1992.
Child, Lauren. *But Excuse Me That Is My Book*. New York: Penguin, 2006.

Child, Lauren. *I Will Never Not Ever Eat a Tomato*. Cambridge, MA: Candlewick Press, 2000.
Collard, Sneed B. *Creepy Creatures*. Watertown, MA: Charlesbridge, 1997.
Cronin, Doreen. *Click, Clack, Moo*. New York: Simon & Schuster, 2000.
Gordon, Olivia. *Cold Case File*. New York: Bearport Pub, 2008.
Grambling, Lois G. *Can I Have a Stegosaurus, Mom? Can I? Please*. Mahwah, NJ: BridgeWater Books, 1994.
Hoose, Phillip. *Hey, Little Ant*. New York: Scholastic, 1998.
Howard, Amanda. *Robbery File*. New York: Bearport Pub, 2008.
Kellogg, Steven. *Can I Keep Him?*. New York: Dial, 1971.
Mazer, Anne. *The Salamander Room*. New York: Knopf, 1991.
Orloff, Karen Kaufman. *I Wanna New Room*. New York: G. P. Putnam's Sons, 2010.
Palatini, Margie. *The Perfect Pet*. New York: HarperCollins, 2003.
Scieszka, Jon. *The True Story of the 3 Little Pigs*. New York: Viking Kestrel, 1989.
Teague, Mark. *Dear Mrs. LaRue*. New York: Scholastic, 2002.
Viorst, Judith. *Earrings*. New York: Aladdin Books, 1993.
Watt, Melanie. *Have I Got a Book for You!*. Toronto, ON: Kids Can Press, 2009.
Willems, Mo. *Don't Let the Pigeon Drive the Bus!*. New York: Hyperion, 2003.
Willems, Mo. *Don't Let the Pigeon Stay Up Late!*. New York: Hyperion, 2006.
Winters, Kay. *My Teacher for President*. New York: Dutton, 2004.
Yolen, Jane. *The Mary Celeste*. New York: Aladdin Paperbacks, 2002.
Yolen, Jane. *The Salem Witch Trials*. New York: Simon & Schuster, 2004.
Yolen, Jane. *The Wolf Girls*. New York: Simon & Schuster, 2001.

Poetry

The Bill Martin Jr. Big Book of Poetry. New York: Simon & Schuster, 2008.
Burg, Brad. *Outside the Lines*. New York: G.P. Putnam's Sons, 2002.
Poetry from A to Z. New York: Bradbury Press, 1994.
Cassedy, Sylvia. *Zoomrimes*. New York: Crowell, 1993.
Dickinson, Emily. *Emily Dickinson*. Poetry for Young People series. New York: Sterling, 1994.
Frost, Robert, 1874–1963. *Stopping by Woods on a Snowy Evening*. New York: Dutton, 1978.
George, Kristine O'Connell. *Emma Dilemma*. New York: Clarion Books, 2011.
George, Kristine O'Connell. *Old Elm Speaks*. New York: Clarion Books, 1998.
Graham, Joan Bransfield. *Flicker Flash*. Boston: Houghton Mifflin, 1999.
Grandits, John. *Technically, It's Not My Fault*. New York: Clarion Books, 2004.
Harley, Avis. *Fly with Poetry*. Honesdale, PA: Wordsong/Boyds Mills Press, 2000.
Hopkins, Lee Bennett. *Pass the Poetry, Please!*. New York: Harper & Row, 1987.
Hopkins, Lee Bennett, ed. *Hand in Hand*. New York: Simon & Schuster, 1994.
Katz, Alan. *Poems I Wrote When No One Was Looking*. New York: Margaret K. McElderry Books, 2011.
Kennedy, Dorothy M. *I Thought I'd Take My Rat to School*. Boston: Little, Brown, 1993.
Lewis, J. Patrick. *Doodle Dandies*. New York: Atheneum, 1998.
Marvelous Math. New York: Simon & Schuster, 1997.
Mataya, Marybeth. *Luke and Leo Build a Limerick*. Chicago: Norwood House Press, 2011.
National Geographic Book of Animal Poetry. Washington, DC: National Geographic, 2012.
Once upon Ice and Other Frozen Poems. Selected by Jane Yolen; photographs by Jason Stemple. Honesdale, PA: Wordsong/Boyds Mills Press, 1997.
Peterson-Hilleque, Victoria. *Ana and Adam Build an Acrostic*. Chicago: Norwood House Press, 2011.
Poetry from A to Z. New York: Bradbury Press, 1994.

Prelutsky, Jack. *For Laughing Out Louder*. New York: Knopf, 1995.
The Random House Book of Poetry for Children. New York: Random House, 1983.
Rosen, Michael J. *Food Fight*. San Diego: Harcourt Brace, 1996.
Sierra, Judy. *Antarctic Antics*. San Diego: Harcourt Brace, 1998.
Sidman, Joyce. *MEOW RUFF: A Story in Concrete Poetry*. Boston: Houghton Mifflin, 2006.
Viorst, Judith. *If I Were in Charge of the World and Other Worries*. New York: Atheneum, 1981.

Science Books

Aston, Dianna Hutts. *A Butterfly Is Patient*. San Francisco, CA: Chronicle Books, 2011.
Aston, Dianna Hutts. *A Rock Is Lively*. San Francisco, CA: Chronicle Books, 2012.
Aston, Dianna Hutts. *A Seed Is Sleepy*. San Francisco, CA: Chronicle Books, 2007.
Aston, Dianna Hutts. *An Egg Is Quiet*. San Francisco, CA: Chronicle Books, 2006.
Bardoe, Cheryl. *Mammoths and Mastodons*. New York: Abrams, 2010.
Bishop, Nic. *Butterflies and Moths*. New York: Scholastic, 2009.
Bishop, Nic. *Frogs*. New York: Scholastic Nonfiction, 2008.
Bishop, Nic. *Lizards*. New York: Scholastic Nonfiction, 2010.
Bishop, Nic. *Marsupials*. New York: Scholastic Nonfiction, 2009.
Bishop, Nic. *Snakes*. New York: Scholastic Nonfiction, 2012.
Bishop, Nic. *Spiders*. New York: Scholastic, 2007.
Cherry, Lynne. *A River Ran Wild*. San Diego: Harcourt Brace Jovanovich, 1992.
Cherry, Lynne. *The Great Kapok Tree*. Fairbanks, AK: Gulliver Books, 1990.
Cherry, Lynne. *How We Know What We Know about Our Changing Climate*. Nevada City, CA: Dawn Pub, 2008
Collard, Sneed B. *Animal Dads*. Boston: Houghton Mifflin, 1997.
Cowley, Joy. *Red-Eyed Tree Frog*. New York: Scholastic, 1999.
DePalma, Mary Newell. *A Grand Old Tree*. New York: Arthur A. Levine Books, 2005.
George, Jean Craighead. *The Wolves Are Back*. New York: Dutton, 2008.
Jenkins, Steve. *Actual Size*. Boston: Houghton Mifflin, 2004.
Jenkins, Steve. *Almost Gone*. Let's-Read-and-Find-Out Science series. New York: HarperCollins, 2006.
Jenkins, Steve. *Animals in Flight*. Boston: Houghton Mifflin, 2001.
Jenkins, Steve. *The Beetle Book*. Boston: Houghton Mifflin, 2012.
Jenkins, Steve. *Big & Little*. Boston: Houghton Mifflin, 1996.
Jenkins, Steve. *Biggest, Strongest, Fastest*. Boston: Houghton Mifflin, 1995.
Jenkins, Steve. *Bones*. New York: Scholastic, 2010.
Jenkins, Steve. *Down, Down, Down*. Boston: Houghton Mifflin Harcourt, 2009.
Jenkins, Steve. *The Emperor's Egg*. Cambridge, MA: Candlewick, 1999.
Jenkins, Steve. *Hottest, Coldest, Highest, Deepest*. Boston: Houghton Mifflin, 1998.
Jenkins, Steve. *How Many Ways Can You Catch a Fly?*. Boston: Houghton Mifflin, 2008.
Jenkins, Steve. *How to Clean a Hippopotamus*. Boston: Houghton Mifflin, 2010.
Jenkins, Steve. *I See a Kookaburra!*. Boston: Houghton Mifflin, 2005.
Jenkins, Steve. *Just a Second*. Boston: Houghton Mifflin, 2011.
Jenkins, Steve. *Living Color*. Boston: Houghton Mifflin, 2007.
Jenkins, Steve. *Move!*. Boston: Houghton Mifflin, 2006.
Jenkins, Steve. *My First Day*. New York: Houghton Mifflin Harcourt, 2013.
Jenkins, Steve. *Never Smile at a Monkey*. Boston: Houghton Mifflin, 2009.
Jenkins, Steve. *Prehistoric Actual Size*. New York: Houghton Mifflin Harcourt, 2005.
Jenkins, Steve. *Sisters & Brothers*. Boston: Houghton Mifflin, 2008.
Jenkins, Steve. *Slap, Squeak, & Scatter*. Boston: Houghton Mifflin, 2001.

Jenkins, Steve. *Time to Eat*. Boston: Houghton Mifflin, 2011.
Jenkins, Steve. *Time to Sleep*. Boston: Houghton Mifflin, 2011.
Jenkins, Steve. *What Do You Do When Something Wants to Eat You?*. Boston: Houghton Mifflin, 1997.
Jenkins, Steve. *What Do You Do with a Tail Like This?*. Boston: Houghton Mifflin, 2003.
Jenkins, Steve. *Wings, Stings, and Wriggly Things*. SuperSmarts series. Cambridge, MA: Candlewick Press, 1996.
Leedy, Loreen. *The Edible Pyramid*. New York: Holiday House, 1994.
Leedy, Loreen. *The Furry News*. New York: Holiday House, 1990.
Leedy, Loreen. *Postcards from Pluto*. New York: Holiday House, 1993.
Marrin, Albert. *Oh, Rats!*. New York: Dutton Children's Books, 2006.
Murphy, Jim. *Guess Again*. New York: Bradbury Press, 1986.
Rose, Deborah Lee. *Into the A, B, Sea*. New York: Scholastic, 2000.
San Souci, Daniel. *North Country Night*. New York: Doubleday, 1990.
Sayre, April Pulley. *Ant, Ant, Ant!*. Minnetonka, MN: NorthWord, 2005.
Sayre, April Pulley. *Army Ant Parade*. New York: Henry Holt, 2002.
Sayre, April Pulley. *Bird, Bird, Bird*. Minnetonka, MN: NorthWord, 2007.
Sayre, April Pulley. *Dig, Wait, Listen*. New York: HarperCollins, 2001.
Sayre, April Pulley. *Go, Go, Grapes!*. New York: Beach Lane Books, 2012.
Sayre, April Pulley. *Honk, Honk, Goose!*. New York: Henry Holt, 2009.
Sayre, April Pulley. *Meet the Howlers!*. Watertown, MA: Charlesbridge, 2010.
Sayre, April Pulley *Rah, Rah, Radishes!*. New York: Beach Lane Books, 2011.
Sayre, April Pulley. *South America, Surprise!*. Our Amazing Continents series. Brookfield, CT: Millbrook Press, 2003.
Sayre, April Pulley. *Splish! Splash! Animal Baths*. Brookfield, CT: Millbrook Press, 2000.
Sayre, April Pulley. *Stars beneath Your Bed*. New York: Greenwillow Books, 2005.
Sayre, April Pulley. *Trout, Trout, Trout! A Fish Chant*. MN: NorthWord, 2004.
Sayre, April Pulley. *Turtle, Turtle, Watch Out!*. Watertown, MA: Charlesbridge, 2010.
Sayre, April Pulley. *Vulture View*. New York: Henry Holt, 2007.
Simon, Seymour. *The Brain*. New York: Morrow, 1997.
Simon, Seymour. *Comets, Meteors, and Asteroids*. New York: Mulberry Books, 1998.
Simon, Seymour. *Fighting Fires*. New York: Scholastic, 2002.
Simon, Seymour. *Destination*. New York: Morrow, 1998.
Simon, Seymour. *The Heart—Our Circulatory System*. New York: Scholastic, 1996.
Simon, Seymour. *Our Solar System*. New York: Morrow, 1992.
Simon, Seymour. *Tornadoes*. New York: Morrow, 1999.
Simon, Seymour. *Weather*. New York: Morrow, 1993.
Simon, Seymour. *Wolves*. New York: HarperCollins, 1993.
Siy, Alexandra. *Sneeze!*. Watertown, MA: Charlesbridge, 2007.
Worth, Valerie. *Animal Poems*. New York: Farrar, Straus and Giroux, 2007.

Social Studies

Anderson, Laurie Halse. *Independent Dames*. New York: Simon & Schuster, 2008.
Anderson, Laurie Halse, and Matt Faulkner. *Thank You, Sarah: The Woman Who Saved Thanksgiving*. New York: Simon & Schuster, 2002.
Brennan, Linda Crotta. *The Black Regiment of the American Revolution*. Rockport, ME: Moon Mountain Pub, 2004.
Brown, Don. *Henry and the Cannons*. New York: Roaring Brook Press, 2013.

Catrow, David. *We the Kids: The Preamble to the Constitution of the United States*. New York: Dial, 2002.

Cheney, Lynne V., and Robin Preiss-Glasser. *A Is for Abigail: An Almanac of Amazing American Women*. New York: Simon & Schuster, 2003.

Cheney, Lynne V. *We the People*. New York: Simon & Schuster, 2008.

Cheripko, Jan. *Caesar Rodney's Ride*. Honesdale, PA: Boyds Mills Press, 2004.

Cook, Peter. *You Wouldn't Want to Sail on a 19th-Century Whaling Ship!*. New York: Franklin Watts, 2004.

Cook, Peter. *You Wouldn't Want to Sail on the Mayflower!* New York: Franklin Watts, 2005.

Costain, Meredith. *You Wouldn't Want to Be an 18th-Century Convict!*. New York: Franklin Watts, 2007.

Cummins, Julie. *Women Daredevils*. New York: Dutton, 2008.

Cummins, Julie. *Women Explorers*. New York: Dial, 2012.

Deedy, Carmen Agra, Wilson Kimeli Naiyomah, and Thomas Gonzalez. *14 Cows for America*. Atlanta: Peachtree, 2009.

Ford, Michael. *You Wouldn't Want to Be a Greek Athlete!*. New York: Franklin Watts, 2004.

Fradin, Dennis B. *Let It Begin Here!*. New York: Walker & Co, 2005.

Freedman, Russell. *Give Me Liberty*. New York: Holiday House, 2000.

Fritz, Jean. *Can't You Make Them Behave, King George?* New York: Putnam & Grosset, 1996.

Graham, Ian. *You Wouldn't Want to Be a World War II Pilot!*. New York: Franklin Watts, 2010.

Graham, Ian. *You Wouldn't Want to Be in the First Submarine!*. New York: Franklin Watts, 2009.

Graham, Ian. *You Wouldn't Want to Be on Apollo 13!*. New York: Franklin Watts, 2003.

Graham, Ian. *You Wouldn't Want to Be on the Hindenburg!*. New York: Franklin Watts, 2009.

Graham, Ian. *You Wouldn't Want to Climb Mount Everest!*. New York: Franklin Watts, 2010.

Graham, Ian. *You Wouldn't Want to Work on the Hoover Dam!*. New York: Franklin Watts, 2012.

Graham, Ian. *You Wouldn't Want to Work on the Railroad!*. New York: Franklin Watts, 2001.

Green, Jen. *You Wouldn't Want to Be a Polar Explorer!*. New York: Franklin Watts, 2001.

Harness, Cheryl. *The Adventurous Life of Myles Standish and the Amazing-but-True Survival Story of the Plymouth Colony*. Washington, DC: National Geographic Society, 2006.

Harness, Cheryl. *The Amazing Impossible Erie Canal*. Macmillan, 1995.

Harness, Cheryl. *Franklin & Eleanor*. New York: Dutton, 2004.

Harness, Cheryl. *Ghosts of the Civil War*. New York: Aladdin Paperbacks, 2004.

Harness, Cheryl. *Ghosts of the Nile*. New York: Simon & Schuster, 2004.

Harness, Cheryl. *The Groundbreaking, Chance-Taking Life of George Washington Carver and Science & Invention in America*. Washington, DC: National Geographic, 2008.

Harness, Cheryl. *Our Colonial Year*. New York: Simon & Schuster, 2005.

Harness, Cheryl. *Mark Twain and the Queens of the Mississippi*. New York: Aladdin Paperbacks, 2003.

Harness, Cheryl. *Rabble Rousers*. New York: Dutton, 2003.

Harness, Cheryl. *Remember the Ladies*. New York: HarperCollins, 2001.

Harness, Cheryl. *The Revolutionary John Adams*. Washington, DC: National Geographic Society, 2003.

Harness, Cheryl. *Thomas Jefferson*. Washington, DC: National Geographical Society, 2004.

Harness, Cheryl. *The Tragic Tale of Narcissa Whitman and a Faithful History of the Oregon Trail*. Washington, DC: National Geographic Society, 2006.

Hicks, Peter. *You Wouldn't Want to Live in a Wild West Town!*. New York: F. Watts, 2002.

Hiscock, Bruce. *The Big Tree*. New York: Atheneum, 1991.

Hynson, Colin. *You Wouldn't Want to Be an Inca Mummy!*. New York: Franklin Watts, 2008.

Kerley, Barbara. *Those Rebels, John & Tom*. New York: Scholastic, 2012.

Langley, Andrew. *You Wouldn't Want to Be a Viking Explorer!*. New York: Franklin Watts, 2000.

Lewis, J. Patrick. *Blackbeard the Pirate King*. Washington, DC: National Geographic Society, 2006.

Maestro, Betsy. *Liberty or Death*. New York: HarperCollins, 2005.

McCully, Emily Arnold. *The Pirate Queen*. New York: PaperStar, 1995.

Macdonald, Fiona. *You Wouldn't Want to Be a Medieval Knight!*. New York: Franklin Watts, 2004.

Macdonald, Fiona. *You Wouldn't Want to Be a Samurai!*. New York: Franklin Watts, 2010.

Macdonald, Fiona. *You Wouldn't Want to Be a Slave in Ancient Greece!*. New York: Franklin Watts, 2000.

Macdonald, Fiona. *You Wouldn't Want to Be a Suffragist!*. New York: Franklin Watts, 2009.

Macdonald, Fiona. *You Wouldn't Want to Be a Victorian Servant!*. New York: Franklin Watts, 2007.

Macdonald, Fiona. *You Wouldn't Want to Be an Aztec Sacrifice!*. New York: Franklin Watts, 2001.

Macdonald, Fiona. *You Wouldn't Want to Be in a Medieval Dungeon!*. New York: Franklin Watts, 2003.

Macdonald, Fiona. *You Wouldn't Want to Be Joan of Arc!*. New York: Franklin Watts, 2010.

Macdonald, Fiona. *You Wouldn't Want to Be Mary, Queen of Scots!*. New York: Franklin Watts, 2008.

Macdonald, Fiona. *You Wouldn't Want to Meet a Body Snatcher!*. New York: Franklin Watts, 2009.

Matthews, Rupert. *You Wouldn't Want to Be a Chicago Gangster!*. New York: Franklin Watts, 2010.

Matthews, Rupert. *You Wouldn't Want to Be a Mayan Soothsayer!*. New York: Franklin Watts, 2008.

Malam, John. *You Wouldn't Want to Be a Mammoth Hunter!*. New York: Franklin Watts, 2004.

Malam, John. *You Wouldn't Want to Be a 19th-Century Coal Miner in England!*. New York: Franklin Watts, 2007.

Malam, John. *You Wouldn't Want to Be a Ninja Warrior!*. New York: Franklin Watts, 2012.

Malam, John. *You Wouldn't Want to Be a Roman Gladiator!*. New York: Franklin Watts, 2000.

Malam, John. *You Wouldn't Want to Be a Secret Agent during World War II!*. New York: Franklin Watts, 2010.

Malam, John. *You Wouldn't Want to Be a Skyscraper Builder!*. New York: Franklin Watts, 2009.

Malam, John. *You Wouldn't Want to Be a Victorian Mill Worker!*. New York: Franklin Watts, 2008.

Malam, John. *You Wouldn't Want to Be a Worker on the Statue of Liberty!*. New York: Franklin Watts, 2009.

Malam, John. *You Wouldn't Want to Live in Pompeii!*. New York: Franklin Watts, 2008.

Morley, Jacqueline. *You Wouldn't Want to Be a Pyramid Builder! A Hazardous Job You'd Rather Not Have*. New York: Scholastic, 2004.

Morley, Jacqueline. *You Wouldn't Want to Be a Shakespearean Actor!*. New York: Franklin Watts, 2010.

Morley, Jacqueline. *You Wouldn't Want to Be an American Colonist!*. New York: Franklin Watts, 2013.

Morley, Jacqueline. *You Wouldn't Want to Be an American Pioneer!*. New York: Franklin Watts, 2002.

Morley, Jacqueline. *You Wouldn't Want to Be Cursed by King Tut!*. New York: Franklin Watts, 2012.

Morley, Jacqueline. *You Wouldn't Want to Be in the Forbidden City!*. New York: Franklin Watts, 2008.

Morley, Jacqueline. *You Wouldn't Want to Live in a Medieval Castle!*. New York: Franklin Watts, 2009.

Morley, Jacqueline. *You Wouldn't Want to Meet Typhoid Mary!*. New York: Franklin Watts, 2013.

Morley, Jacqueline. *You Wouldn't Want to Work on the Great Wall of China!*. New York: Franklin Watts, 2006.

Murphy, Jim. *Across America on an Emigrant Train*. New York: Scholastic, 1995.
Murphy, Jim. *An American Plague*. New York: Clarion Books, 2003.
Murphy, Jim. *Blizzard*. New York: Scholastic, 2000.
Murphy, Jim. *The Boys' War*. New York: Clarion Books, 1990.
Murphy, Jim. *The Crossing*. New York: Scholastic Press, 2010.
Murphy, Jim. *Desperate Journey*. New York: Scholastic, 2006.
Murphy, Jim. *The Great Fire*. New York: Scholastic, 1995.
Murphy, Jim. *Inside the Alamo*. New York: Delacorte Press, 2003.
Murphy, Jim. *The Long Road to Gettysburg*. New York: Clarion Books, 1992.
Osornio, Catherine L. *The Declaration of Independence from A to Z*. Gretna, LA: Pelican Publishing, 2010.
Pipe, Jim. *You Wouldn't Want to Be a Salem Witch!*. New York: Franklin Watts, 2009.
Pipe, Jim. *You Wouldn't Want to Be an Aristocrat in the French Revolution!*. New York: Franklin Watts, 2008.
Pipe, Jim. *You Wouldn't Want to Sail on an Irish Famine Ship!*. New York: Franklin Watts, 2008.
Ratliff, Thomas. *You Wouldn't Want to Be a Civil War Soldier!*. New York: Franklin Watts, 2004.
Ratliff, Thomas. *You Wouldn't Want to Be a Pony Express Rider!*. New York: Franklin Watts, 2012.
Ratliff, Thomas. *You Wouldn't Want to Work on the Brooklyn Bridge!*. New York: Franklin Watts, 2010.
Senior, Kathryn. *You Wouldn't Want to Be a Nurse during the American Civil War!*. New York: Franklin Watts, 2010.
Senior, Kathryn. *You Wouldn't Want to Be in the 16th Century!*. New York: Franklin Watts, 2002.
Sheinkin, Steve. *King George*. New York: Roaring Brook Press, 2009.
Smith, Jane. *John, Paul, George, & Ben*. New York: Hyperion, 2006.
St. George, Judith. *The Journey of the One and Only Declaration of Independence*. New York: Philomel Books, 2005.
St. George Judith, and David Small. *So You Want to Be an Inventor?* New York: Philomel, 2002.
Stewart, David. *You Wouldn't Want to Be an Egyptian Mummy!*. New York: Franklin Watts, 2000.
Stewart, David. *You Wouldn't Want to Be Tutankhamen!*. New York: Franklin Watts, 2007.
Stewart, David. *You Wouldn't Want to Explore with Sir Francis Drake!*. New York: Franklin Watts, 2005.
Stewart, David. *You Wouldn't Want to Sail on the Titanic!* New York: Franklin Watts, 2013.
Winter, Jeanette. *The Librarian of Basra: A True Story from Iraq*. Orlando, FL: Harcourt, 2005.

Wordless Picture Books

Aruego, Jose. *The Last Laugh*. New York: Dial, 2006.
Baker, Jeannie. *Window*. New York: Greenwillow Books, 1991.
Hoban, Tana. *Colors Everywhere*. New York: Greenwillow Books, 1995.
Kamm, Katja. *Invisible*. New York: North-South Books, 2006.
Lehman, Barbara. *The Red Book*. Boston: Houghton Mifflin, 2004.
Pinkney, Jerry. *The Lion & the Mouse*. New York: Little, Brown, 2009.
Raschka, Christopher. *A Ball for Daisy*. New York: Schwartz & Wade Books, 2011.
Rohmann, Eric. *Time Flies*. New York: Scholastic, 1994.
Thomson, Bill. *Chalk*. Tarrytown, NY: Marshall Cavendish Children, 2010.
Wiesner, David. *Flotsam*. New York: Clarion Books, 2006.

Appendix B:
Blank Budget Justification Sheet

Project	Teacher/Grade Standards	Resources Currently Available	Additional Resources Needed and Cost	Budget Analysis and Comments

Appendix C: Staff/Student Survey Samples

Staff Survey—Originally published in *No School Library Left Behind* by Carl A. Harvey II

_____ Teacher　　　　_____ Support Staff　　　　_____ Other

Scale: 1–4 with 1 being the lowest and 4 being the highest. If the question does not apply to your role in the building, just leave it blank.

Instruction

	1	2	3	4
1. The school librarian is easily available for co-planning, co-teaching, and co-assessment.				
2. I have co-planned with the school librarian this year.				
3. The school librarian is proactive to suggest ideas for activities or lessons.				
4. I am comfortable going and asking the school librarian for help.				
5. Students are free to come and use the school librarian at any time.				
6. The school librarian regularly communicates with the staff about programming and resources using a variety of methods.				
7. The school librarian provides help to me on an individual basis.				
8. The school librarian provides staff development opportunities.				
9. The school librarian is an integral part of the curriculum instruction at our school.				
10. The school librarian provides support for reading motivation.				

	1	2	3	4
11. The annual author visit is a good use of time and resources.				
12. The school librarian supports my work in meeting school improvement goals.				
13. The school librarian provides instruction that support school improvement goals.				

14. What are (if any) stumbling blocks to using the school librarian more to help with instruction of your students?

15. How could the school librarian more effectively help you with instruction?

16. How could the library program support the school improvement goals?

Facilities and Resources

	1	2	3	4
17. The school library facility is welcoming and inviting.				
18. The school library is always available when I need it.				
19. My students come at least once a week to check out new materials.				
20. I use the school library catalog in my classroom.				
21. I use the school library catalog with state standards search.				
22. I use video streaming resources.				
23. I use electronic databases available from the school library.				
24. The school library has sufficient resources to meet the curriculum.				
25. The resources that are available meet my curriculum and academic standards. They are current and up-to-date.				
26. I recommended resources in our parent library to parents.				
27. I use the Leveled Library resources.				

28. In what areas (if any) do you wish the school library could provide more resources?

29. What are stumbling blocks to accessing the available online tools?

30. What additional resources do you need to meet school improvement goals?

General Information

	1	2	3	4
31. The library facility is available for my use when needed.				
32. The library support staff is efficient in responding to your needs.				
33. The library check out/in procedures are efficient and effective.				

34. What is the most useful part of the school library program?

35. What services do you wish the school library program offered that aren't currently available?

204 Appendix C: Staff/Student Survey Samples

36. List the way(s) you think the school library program could be improved to better serve students and staff.

37. What areas would you like more staff development on in the areas of media/technology?

38. Other comments/concerns/or thoughts?

Student Survey—Originally published in *No School Library Left Behind* by Carl A. Harvey II

Elementary Student Survey

	YES	Not Sure	NO
1. Do you like coming to the school library?			
2. When you come to the school library, do you learn new things?			
3. When you come to the school library can you get answers to your questions?			
4. When you come to the school library, do you learn how to find information?			
5. Can you find books you want to read in our school library?			
6. Can you find books to answer your questions in our school library?			
7. Do you use the school library webpage?			

8. What do you like best about the school library?

9. If you could change one thing about our school library, what would it be?

Secondary Study Survey—Answer the questions below. Please give examples to prove your answer.

1. What are the things in our school library that make you want to come here to study, learn, read, use technology, and socialize?

2. When you come to the school library who or what helps you most as you search for answers to your questions?

3. When you come to the school library, which types of technology and software are most helpful as you try to find information?

Appendix C: Staff/Student Survey Samples

4. What types and subjects of books would you like to find more of in our school library?

5. What other technologies would you find helpful as you seek answers to your questions in our school library?

6. What are the most helpful features of the school library webpage? Which do you use most?

7. What do you like best about the school library?

8. If you could change one thing about our school library, what would it be?

Appendix D: Common Core Bibliography

School Library Monthly has a list of articles from their publication related to the Common Core on their website: http://schoollibrarymonthly.com/pdf/SLM-CCSSarticles.pdf.

Calkins, Lucy, Mary Ehrenworth, and Christopher Lehman. *Pathways to the Common Core: Accelerating Achievement*. Portsmouth, NH: Heinemann, 2012.

Hallermann, Sara, John Larmer, and John R. Mergendoller. *PBL in the Elementary Grades: Step-by-Step Guidance, Tools and Tips for Standards-Focused K–5 Projects*. Novato, CA: Buck Institute for Education, 2011.

Harada, Violet H., and Sharon Coatney. *Inquiry and the Common Core: Librarians and Teachers Designing Teaching for Learning*. Santa Barbara, CA: Libraries Unlimited, 2014.

"Implementing the Common Core State Standards: The Role of the School Librarian." Achieve and American Association of School Librarians, n.d. Accessed January 6, 2014, http://www.ala.org/aasl/sites/ala.org.aasl/files/content/externalrelations/CCSSLibrariansBrief_FINAL.pdf.

Marzano, Robert J., David C. Yanoski, Jan K. Hoegh, Julia A. Simms, Tammy Heflebower, and Philip B. Warrick. *Using Common Core Standards to Enhance Classroom Instruction & Assessment*. N.p.: Marzano Research Laboratory, 2013.

Owocki, Gretchen. *The Common Core Lesson Book, K–5: Working with Increasingly Complex Literature, Informational Text, and Foundational Reading Skills*. Portsmouth, NH: Heinemann, 2012.

Owocki, Gretchen. *The Common Core Writing Book: Lessons for a Range of Tasks, Purposes, and Audiences: K–5*. Portsmouth, NH: Heinemann, 2013.

Suen, Anastasia. *Teaching STEM and Common Core with Mentor Texts: Collaborative Lesson Plans, K–5*. Santa Barbara, CA: Libraries Unlimited, 2014.

Appendix E: Research Journal

Research Journal—Directions
1. Use a file folder to put the journal together
2. Steps 1–2 (Glue to the front cover)
3. I Wonder Pages, Citing Sources, and Self-Evaluation (Staple on the Inside)
4. Rubric (Glue to the back cover)
5. Glue four envelopes—two in front and two in back of the inside of the journal.

BRAINSTORMING WHAT I WANT TO FIND OUT.

I Wonder . . .

Topic: _____

Questions	Check when you find the answer.
1.	
2.	
3.	
4.	
5.	
6.	
7.	
8.	
9.	
10.	
11.	
12.	

13.	
14.	
15.	
16.	
17.	
18.	
19.	
20.	
21.	
22.	
23.	
24.	
25.	
26.	
27.	

| Name: | Teacher: |

What is the topic of your project?

➡ Open journal to the I Wonder . . . page

Where can you look for information?	Is it the best source for this project?
	Yes or No
	Yes or No
	Yes or No
	Yes or No
	Yes or No
	Yes or No
	Yes or No
	Yes or No

My information came from: Encyclopedia Title: _____ Copyright Date: _____ Encyclopedia, Volume Number: _____ Page Numbers: _____	Was it a good source of information: YES NO
My information came from: Encyclopedia Title: _____ Copyright Date: _____ Encyclopedia, Volume Number: _____ Page Numbers: _____	Was it a good source of information: YES NO
My information came from: Encyclopedia Title: _____ Copyright Date: _____ Encyclopedia, Volume Number: _____ Page Numbers: _____	Was it a good source of information: YES NO
INTERNET / ONLINE RESOURCES	
My information came from: Website, the address is: http:// _____ What date did you visit the website? _____	Was it a good source of information: YES NO
My information came from: Website, the address is: http:// _____ What date did you visit the website? _____	Was it a good source of information: YES NO
My information came from: Website, the address is: http:// _____ What date did you visit the website? _____	Was it a good source of information: YES NO
My information came from: Website, the address is: http:// _____ What date did you visit the website? _____	Was it a good source of information: YES NO

BOOKS	
My information came from: Book Title: _____ Book Author: _____ Copyright Date: _____	Was it a good source of information: YES NO
My information came from: Book Title: _____ Book Author: _____ Copyright Date: _____	Was it a good source of information: YES NO
My information came from: Book Title: _____ Book Author: _____ Copyright Date: _____	Was it a good source of information: YES NO
My information came from: Book Title: _____ Book Author: _____ Copyright Date: _____	Was it a good source of information: YES NO
ENCYCLOPEDIAS	
My information came from: Encyclopedia Title: _____ Copyright Date: _____ Encyclopedia, Volume Number: _____ Page Numbers: _____	Was it a good source of information: YES NO

My information came from: Encyclopedia Title: _____ Copyright Date: _____ Encyclopedia, Volume Number: _____ Page Numbers: _____	Was it a good source of information: YES NO
My information came from: Encyclopedia Title: _____ Copyright Date: _____ Encyclopedia, Volume Number: _____ Page Numbers: _____	Was it a good source of information: YES NO
My information came from: Encyclopedia Title: _____ Copyright Date: _____ Encyclopedia, Volume Number: _____ Page Numbers: _____	Was it a good source of information: YES NO

INTERNET / ONLINE RESOURCES

My information came from: Website, the address is: http://_____ What date did you visit the website? _____	Was it a good source of information: YES NO
My information came from: Website, the address is: http://_____ What date did you visit the website? _____	Was it a good source of information: YES NO
My information came from: Website, the address is: http://_____ What date did you visit the website? _____	Was it a good source of information: YES NO
My information came from: Website, the address is: http://_____ What date did you visit the website? _____	Was it a good source of information: YES NO

All of your facts / notes should be in the envelopes, but use this as a "scratch paper" area if you need to draw a picture or take additional notes.

Exit Slips

☐ All the resources I used today have been returned to their home. ☐ Next time I need to: ☐ I need help with:	☐ All the resources I used today have been returned to their home. ☐ Next time I need to: ☐ I need help with:
☐ All the resources I used today have been returned to their home. ☐ Next time I need to: ☐ I need help with:	☐ All the resources I used today have been returned to their home. ☐ Next time I need to: ☐ I need help with:

What is your final product? (a display, a skit, a paper, etc.) How are you going to organize your information?

On what part of your project do you think you did a good job?

What did you think you could have done better?

What was the hardest part of this project?

What was the best place you found information? (give a title of a book or the URL of a website)

What did you already know that was proven to be correct?

What did you think you knew that was proven to be wrong?

Assessment Checklist

Checklist	Yes	No
Student wrote out the Task.		
Student created a list of "I Wonder . . ." questions.		
Student listed potential places to find information.		
Student looked in more than one place for information.		
The student recorded all the information (title, author, etc.) about sources.		
The student used reliable and accurate resources for the project.		
The student took notes from sources. Notes were written on index cards.		
The student recorded one fact per card.		
The student used their own words when taking notes.		
The student found the answers to their "I Wonder . . ." questions.		
The student filed notes into category envelopes.		
The student wrote his or her final project in the box.		
The student completely answered all of the evaluation questions.		
The student avoided "I don't know, everything, or nothing" when answering the evaluation questions.		
Total Points Earned		

Comments

Appendix F: Technology on the Net

There are a variety of web programs or apps that can be found. Many are free to use for education. Some applications on this list are apps to use for presentations and others are for organizational purposes.

Appendix F: Technology on the Net

There are a variety of web programs and apps that can be found. Many are free to use for education. Some applications on this list are apps to use for presentations and others are for organizational purposes.

Name of Program	Website	Explanation
BibMe	http://www.bibme.org	Fast and easy citation tool. Copy and paste web addresses into program
Blogger	https://www.blogger.com/home	Google's blogger so students can share their thoughts
Buncee	http://www.edu.buncee.com	Online presentations
Citation Machine	http://www.citationmachine.net	Uses MLA 7 to create citations
Comic Creator		Creates comics
Diigo	https://www.diigo.com	Curation tool
Easel.ly	http://www.easel.ly	Create and share visual ideas online
Edmodo	https://www.edmodo.com	Connect and collaborate by sharing ideas, problems, and helpful tips
eduClipper	http://www.edutecher.net/educlipper/	Curation tool
Evernote	www.evernote.com	Designed for note-taking and archiving; capture webpages, photographs, voice memo, handwritten notes, notes that you write
Glogster	http://edu.glogster.com	Online posters with color, graphics, and links
Google Maps	https://www.google.com/maps/preview?source=newuser-ws	Great place to go for maps
Google.docs	www.google.docs	Great way to create documents, presentations, and share them with others. Documents are accessible from any computer
Haiku Deck	https://www.haikudeck.com	Slide shows
MyHistro	http://www.myhistro.com	Create interactive timelines
Notely	http://note.ly	Includes a scheduler, calendar, note-taker, to do list, homework planner, etc.
Padlet	http://padlet.com	Sticky notes on the wall
Pixton	http://www.pixton.com	Create your own comics
Poll Everywhere	http://www.polleverywhere.com	Ask a question and kids can answer
Prezi	www.prezi.com	Create zooming presentations that are more engaging and memorable

Printing Press	http://www.readwrite think.org/files/resources/ interactives/Printing_Press/	Used for making online newspapers, brochures, flyers, and booklets
Rasterbator	http://rasterbator.net	Enlarge images to huge posters
ReadWriteThink	http://www.readwrite think.org	Great website with all kinds of lesson plans and apps that are very usable; also printouts for all kinds of lessons
Skype	http://www.skype.com/en/	Connect your classroom to the world
Socrative	http://www.socrative.com	Interactive quizzes you create; student response site
StoryJumper	http://www.storyjumper.com	Make your own children's book online
Symbaloo	https://www.symbaloo.com	Curation tool
Tackk	https://tackk.com	Online flyers or newsletters
Timeline	http://www.readwrite think.org/classroom -resources/mobile-apps/ timeline-b-31047.html	Make your own timelines
VoiceThread	http://ed.voicethread.com	Great digital storytelling program; users can upload pictures and documents, record audio commentary, and have others respond back
Wordle	www.wordle.com	Generate "word clouds" from text that you provide. Clouds give greater prominence to words that appear more frequently in the source text. Tweak your clouds with different fonts, layouts, and color schemes.

Index

AAAs/Subaru SB&F Prices for Excellence in Science Books, 50
ability levels, 18
Achieve, 4, 64, 207
administrators, 1, 12, 16, 19, 23, 27, 40, 47, 60–62
advertising, 19, 156
advocacy, 60–66
advocacy and administrators, 61
advocacy with parents, 64
advocacy with state officials, 65
advocacy with students, 65
advocacy with teachers, 62
Alberti, Sandra, 54
alliteration, 44, 185
Alphin, Elaine Marie, 44
American Association for the Advancement of Science, 4, 50
American Association of School Librarians (AASL), 9–13, 55, 58, 62–64, 207
American Council on the Teaching of Foreign Languages, 4
American Library Association (ALA), 20
American Memory website, 45
anchors, 19, 36
Anderson, Laurie Halse, 42
annual report, 62
Applegate, Katherine, 44
Appleseed, 32
Ask, 32
Assessment, 6, 25, 46
association advocacy, 63
Association for Supervision and Curriculum Development (ASCD), 58
Aston, Dianna Hutts, 34
authors, 12, 26, 30, 34, 36, 40–41, 49–52, 59, 62, 64, 78, 92–94

Baker & Taylor Axis 360, 21
Ballard, Susan, 55
Bauer, Marion, 31
Bayliss, Sarah, 28
bibliographies, 35, 47, 60–62, 64, 74, 111
biographies, 18–19, 31, 34, 37, 41, 67, 92, 150, 158–160
biomes, 12, 110
Bishop, Nic, 12, 18, 30, 38–39
blabberize, 70
blogs, 23, 50, 57
Blos, Joan, 18, 34
Book Creator, 80
Booklinks, 49
Booklist, 49
booktalking, 35
Boss, Suzi, 54
Boyles, Nancy, 54
Bragg, Georgia, 39
Bring Your Own Device (BYOD), 20, 22
Britannica, 67, 131, 148
Brown, Don, 34
budgets, 15–16, 20, 22, 64
Bulletin of the Center for Children's Books, 49
Burns, Elizabeth, 28
Burns, Marilyn, 8
Burroughs, Nathan A., 55
Buzzeo, Toni, 54–55

Calkins, Lucy, 3, 8, 55, 207
Calliope, 32
Callison, Daniel, 38, 55
Cherry, Lynn, 34
Chromebook, 20
Cinderella, 126–130
classroom libraries, 35, 40
Click, 32
close reading, 37–38
Cobblestone, 32
collaboration, 9, 19, 25, 48, 51, 53–54, 62
collection development, 16–20

223

collection development policy, 20
collection map, 20
College, Career, and Civic Life (C3) Framework for Social Studies State Standards, 4
collaboration, 53–54
Comic Life, 141
common core and advocacy, 60
Common Core State Standards (CCSS), 1–8
communication, 48, 65, 86, 113
compare and contrast, 19, 25, 36, 110, 112, 126–127, 172–173
complex text, 27, 59
comprehension, 3, 6, 35, 37
Corsaro, Julie, 55
Council of Chief State School Officers (CCSSO), 1–4
Crabtree Publishers, 33, 143
Cricket, 31–32
critical thinking, 4, 29, 48
Cronin, Doreen, 36, 74, 93

DelGuidice, Margaux, 66
diagrams, 30, 33, 38–39, 144, 146
Dig, 32
digital cameras, 22, 76
digital natives, 22
Discussion Groups, 58
Donham, Jean, 53, 55
Doorey, Nancy A., 8
Drummond, Allan, 33
Duke, Nell K., 55

e-mail, 35, 60–63, 65
eBook, 11–12, 17, 20–22, 27–28, 30–31, 68
eBook platform, 21
Edwards, Pamela Duncan, 44
Ehlert, Lois, 52, 76
Ehrenworth, Mary, 3, 8, 55, 207
Empowering Learners: Standards for School Library Programs, 9
Enchanted Learning, 110
EngageNY, 6
English Language Learners (ELL), 3
Enis, Matt, 28
Entrsekt: Where Learning, Technology and Community Meet, 23
evaluation, 27
Excel, 110
explorers, 150, 168–169
expository text, 33

fables, 37
Facebook, 58

Faces, 32
facilities, 23–24
fairy tales, 25, 93, 126–130
famous Americans, 80
famous scientists, 148–152
farm animals, 70–71
federal government, 1–2
fiction, 12, 16, 19, 25, 32, 34–35, 37, 39–41, 43–44, 50, 67, 73
figurative language, 37, 41
fixed schedule, 24–25
Fleming, Candace, 18, 34
flexible schedule, 24–25
Florian, Douglas, 34, 104–105
folktales, 37, 93
Follett Shelf, 21
Fontichiaro, Kristin, 55
force/motion, 140–142
formative assessment, 6
Fox, Mem, 43, 90–94
fractions, 51
Frazee, Marla, 44
French, Jackie, 36
Fritz, Jean, 41
frogs, 72–74

Ganeri, Anita, 30
Garrison, Kasey L., 28
Gerstein, Mordicai, 39
Glogster, 133
good beginnings, 138–139
Google, 22
Google Images, 133
GoogleDocs, 77, 86–87
graphics, 32, 38
graphing, 12, 51, 110, 112
graphs, 33, 38, 53
Grolier Online, 17, 67, 96, 148–149, 156, 168
Guernsey, Lisa, 28
guest speakers, 26

Haiku Deck, 82–83, 220
Hallermann, Sara, 55
HarperCollins, 20
Harris, Christopher, 28
Harris, Elizabeth Snoke, 32
Harvey, Carl A., II, 28, 66, 201, 204
Hatkoff, Isabella, 31, 101
healthy eating, 75
Hiebert, Elfrieda H., 55
Highlights, 31
Hopkinson, Deborah, 34
Horn Book Magazine, The, 49

Iguana, 32
illustrations, 32, 38, 68, 76, 92–94, 112, 145
Image Quest, 67
information literacy, 29, 54
information/experiences pieces, 40
informational text, 2, 10–12, 21, 27, 29–31, 34–35, 37–39, 43–45, 51, 54, 59, 61, 65
inquire, 10
Inquiry, 45–47
insects, 42, 44, 82–83
instruction, 3, 6, 7, 15–16, 22, 24, 27, 29, 33, 35, 37, 40–41, 46–47, 50–51, 53–54, 62–63, 67
interim assessment, 6
interlibrary loaned (ILL), 16
International Society of Technology Educators (ISTE), 23, 58
iPad, 20, 76, 106
iPod, 76

Jack and Jill, 31
Jaegar, Paige, 58
Jamestown, 171–173
Jenkins, Steve, 12, 30, 34, 93
Johnson, Doug, 28
Judge, Lita, 44

Kaaland, Christine, 55
Kalman, Bobbie, 33
Kellogg, Steven, 49, 93, 96
Kimmel, Sue, 28
Krashen, Steven, 3, 8

Ladybug, 32
Lamb, Annette, 38, 55
landmarks of the United States, 131–133
laptop, 20, 102
Larmer, John, 55, 207

Learning Commons, 24
Leedy, Loreen, 43, 53
legends, 30, 37
legislators, 7, 65–66
Lehman, Christopher, 3, 8, 55, 207
Levitov, Deborah, 66
Library Media Connection, 49
Library of Congress, 19, 45, 145, 171–172, 175, 179–180
Library Sparks, 49
literacy circles, 42
Literary nonfiction, 32, 34
literary text, 10
Loertscher, David, 24
London, Jonathon, 37, 43, 72

long ago and today, 86–87
Luna, Rosa, 66

Mackin Via, 21
magazines, 31–32, 49, 57, 144–145
maps, 32, 38, 68
Math Standards, 2, 3, 51–52
measurement and data, 88–89
Mergendoller, John R., 55, 207
metaphors, 37, 43
Miller, Donalyn, 55
mini lesson, 47
mobile labs, 22
money, 12, 51
Moreillon, Judi, 55
Morris, Betty J., 28
multiuser licensee, 20
Murphy, Jim, 42
Murphy, Stuart, 52, 53
Murvosh, Marta, 66
Muse, 32
myON Reader, 21
myths, 37

Nakano, Dokuohtei, 33
narrative writing, 40
National Coalition for Core Art Standards, 4
National Council of Social Studies, 4, 50
National Governors Association (NGA), 1, 4
National Research Council, 4
National Science Teachers Association, 4, 50
NCTE Orbis Pictus Award for Outstanding Nonfiction for Children, 50
Nerdy Book Club, 50
Neuschwander, Cindy, 52
Next Generation Science Standards, 4
non-summative assessment, 6
nonfiction, 12, 16, 19, 25, 27, 29–32, 34, 39–46, 49–50, 67
Nonfiction Detective, 50
Nonfiction feature search, 143–147
Nonfiction Monday, 50
Norman, Rebecca R., 55
Nortable Social Studies Trade Books for Young People, 50

O'Conner, Jane, 43
Odyssey, 32
online resources, 16–17, 19, 22, 57
1:1 initiative, 17, 20–22
onomatopoeia, 44
opinion pieces, 10, 34, 40–41
Osornio, Catherine, 34

Outstanding Science Trade Books for Students K–12, 50
Overdrive, 21
Owen and Mzee, 101–103

Pallotta, Jerry, 34
Partnership for Assessment of Readiness for College and Careers (PARCC), 5–6
Pearson, P. David, 55
PebbleGo Database, 67, 70–71, 80, 82, 86, 96
Peck, Richard, 42, 138
performance-based assessments (PBA), 6
Personal Learning Network (PLN), 45, 57, 59
personification, 37, 93
persuasion text, 33
persuasive writing, 49
photographs, 18, 30, 32, 38–39, 145–146
picture books, 18–19, 29, 31, 34, 36, 43, 50, 51
Pintrest, 58
Pivan, Hanoch, 43
plays, 37
podcast, 23, 154
poetry, 19, 26–27, 32, 34, 37, 41, 104–105
policy and procedure, 20, 26, 64
PowerPoint, 23, 74, 110, 112, 122, 158–159
presentation skills, 48
Prezi, 23, 133, 220
Primary sources, 18–19, 22, 32, 37, 44–45, 68, 175
procedural texts, 32–33
procedures, 15, 25–26, 47–48, 76, 78
professional development, 21, 45, 57–60, 62, 63
programming, 26–27
project-based learning, 47–48
PTO/PTA, 22, 24, 64
public library, 16
public service announcement, 11
publishers, 12, 18, 20, 21, 59

Race to the Top, 2
Rappaport, Doreen, 34
ratios, 51–52
Ravitch, Diane, 3, 57
Read Write Think, 141
reader advisory, 11
reading aloud, 35, 39
Reading Anchors, 36–37
reading level, 11, 18
Reading Randts, 50
Reading Stamina, 39–40
Reading Standards, 36–37
Reading Standards for Informational Text, 2, 10
Reading Standards for Literature, 10
Reading Standards: Craft and Structure, 36
Reading Standards: Integration of Knowledge and Ideas, 36
Reading Standards: Key Ideas and Details, 36
Reading Standards: Range of Reading, 37
reflection, 27, 48, 180, 182
research skills, 29
Reynolds, Catherine Furlong, 34
Robb, Laura, 143
Robert F. Seibert Informational Book Medal, 50
Roberts, Kathryn L., 55
Rockwell, Anne, 36
Root, Phyllis, 44
Rosen Science Database, 67

Sayre, April Pulley, 44, 98–100
scheduling, 34–35
Schmidt, William H., 55
School Library Journal, 22, 49
School Library Monthly, 49, 207
school library programs, 9, 15, 27, 46, 61
Schwartz, David, 51
September 11th, 179–184
Sewall, Marcia, 19
Seymour, Simon, 12, 30, 33–34, 42–43
shapes, 52, 76
silent reading, 40, 111
similies, 29, 37, 43
Skype, 23, 93, 221
Sleeping Bear Press, 18
Smarter Balanced Assessment Consortium, 5–6
snowflakes, 77–78
speaking skills, 48
Spider, 32
spreadsheet, 16
St. George, Judith, 34
staffing, 23–24
Standards for Mathematical Concept. *See* Math Standards
Standards for Mathematical Practice. *See* Math Standards
Standards for the 21st Century Learners, 9
Standards for the 21st Century Learners in Action, 9
statistics, 51
student choice, 16, 48
students with disabilities, 3
summative assessment, 6
Symbaloo, 23, 221

TeachingBooks.net, 41, 50, 67, 90–93
Teague, Mark, 36
technology, 11, 22–23, 32, 45, 58–61, 67–68
telling time, 106–108
text complexity, 35, 37

The Crosswalk of the Common Core Standards and the Standards for the 21st Century Learner, 9–10
Thomas, Peggy, 36
tone, 37
TPS Journal, 45
True Book series, 31
TrueFLIX, 31
21st Century Skills, 48
Twitter, 58

U.S. Presidents, 135–136
United States, 156–157

Valenza, Joyce, 28
vendors, 17, 19–21, 23
visual aids, 48
visual literacy, 38
vivid language, 29
vocabulary, 18, 39, 40, 43

Voices of Youth Advocates (VOYA), 49
volume, 51

Wander Indiana (state project), 153–154
Ward, Barbara A., 55
webinars, 57–58, 61
websites, 12, 17, 31, 38, 45, 50, 63, 64
Willems, Mo, 42
Winter, Jeannette, 31
Woolls, Blanche, 28
word choice, 37
word problem, 53
World Book Online, 68, 131
writing style, 41–44
writing/animals, 96–97

YALSA Award for Excellence in Nonfiction, 50
Yolen, Jane, 37, 43
Young, Terrell, 55
Young, Terrence, Jr., 28

About the Authors

CARL A. HARVEY II is the school librarian at North Elementary School in Noblesville, Indiana. He was the 2011–2012 president of the American Association of School Librarians (AASL). He was a member of the Association for Library Services to Children (ALSC) 2014 Caldecott Medal Committee. He is also a past president of the Association for Indiana Media Educators (AIME) and the Indiana Library Federation (ILF). He has published several articles in various professional journals including *School Library Journal*, *Library Media Connection*, *School Library Monthly*, and *Teacher-Librarian*. He has written four other books in addition to this title: *The Library Media Specialist in the Writing Process* (coauthored with Marge Cox and Susan Page; 2007); *No School Library Left Behind: Leadership, School Improvement, and the Media Specialist* (2008); *The 21st Century Elementary Library Media Program* (2010); and *Adult Learners: School Librarians and Professional Development* (2012). Carl has also presented at numerous state and national conferences and several online webinars on edWeb.net.

Some of his awards include Outstanding New Library Media Specialist (1999), Outstanding Media Specialist (2007), and the Peggy L. Pfeiffer Service Award (2007)—all from the Association for Indiana Media Educators/Indiana Library Federation. The library program at North Elementary School has been recognized with the Blue Ribbon for Exemplary School Media Programs by the Association for Indiana Media Educators (2005) and the prestigious National School Library Media Program of the Year Award (2007) from the American Association of School Librarians.

He has served on advisory boards for several different companies as well as part of the committee that revised the Library Media Standards for the National Board for Professional Teaching Standards in 2010. Carl is also a part-time consultant for C.L.A.S.S. (Connected Learning Assures Successful Students) in Indianapolis, Indiana.

LINDA L. MILLS is the school librarian at Greensburg Elementary school in Greensburg, Indiana, a school of 1,000 students, K–5. She also worked at Sunman Elementary in Sunman, Indiana, for fourteen years. She has taught a graduate librarian course at Indiana University and IUPUI Indianapolis, Indiana, as an adjunct lecturer since 1994. She is a member of the American Association of School Librarians (AASL), the American Library Association (ALA), the Indiana Library Federation, and the Association of Indiana Media Educators, where she served as president, secretary, and on various chairs of committees including the Young Hoosier Book Award committee. She is also a member of the National Education Association, the International Reading Association, and the Association of School and Curriculum Development. She has published articles in *School Library Monthly*.

Linda has presented at Indiana state library and computer conferences along with national conferences such as the American Association of School Librarians (AASL) and the International Society of Technology Educators (ISTE). She attended a one-week-long seminar in 2012 at the Library of Congress to be trained to instruct using primary sources.

She has won the Peggy L. Pfeiffer Service Award from the Association for Indiana Media Educators/Indiana Library Federation. She serves on the education board for the Indiana State Museum and is active in the Indiana Historical Society.